BAR

# SUSTAIN ME

## A HANDBOOK OF
## NATURAL REMEDIES

*THE 9 FOUNDATIONAL*
*PILLARS FOR HEALTH*

BALDWIN, WISCONSIN
UNITED STATES OF AMERICA

*This book is dedicated to the
Creator of this amazing body with
its fine and detailed system of
healing and restoration.*

# BARBARA O'NEILL

# SUSTAiN ME

## A HANDBOOK OF NATURAL REMEDIES

### THE 9 FOUNDATIONAL PILLARS FOR HEALTH

Barbara O'Neill,
PO Box 156, Baldwin WI 54002

www.barbaraoneill.com
www.facebook.com/realbarbaraoneill
www.instagram.com/realbarbaraoneill

Copyright © 2024 US edition, Barbara O'Neill

ISBN: 978-0-6486118-6-8

Ebook ISBN: 978-0-6486118-7-5

Library of Congress Control Number: 2024909545

**This book**

Proofread by Silvia Mogorovich

Designed by Shane Winfield/Advent Design

Cover illustrations by iStockphoto and Shane Winfield

Images used under licence from

iStockPhoto.com—pages, 11–29, 34–41, 50–54, 62–92, 106–116, 118–141, 145, 146, 152–197, 206–235, 246–256, 291, 299, 304–308, 310, 315, 318, 320–323, 324–331.

Henry Stober—page 8

Dreamstime.com—pages, 31, 50, 51, 56, 204, 243, 248, 309, 319, 323.

Peopleimages.com—pages, 46, 331.

Shane Winfield—pages, 96, 117, 142, 147, 149, 199, 240–241, 292–297, 300, 302, 312, 314, 317.

littlehomeinthemaking.com—pages 49.

Sharri Keller/Terra Sura Photography—page 336, 342, back cover.

Typeset 10/12 Rosales

Special thanks to Emma Loberg and Jessica Russ.

Printed by Modern Press, New Brighton, MN
United States of America

# CoNTENTS

# PREFACE

On contemplating writing this book, my aim was to provide a handbook for every home of some simple tools to help with common ailments.

I first became interested in natural and alternative treatments after my first daughter was given four courses of antibiotics over six weeks for an earache. I remember keenly my frustration of not wanting to give my daughter more antibiotics, but not wanting to put her at risk and not knowing what else to do. This experience was the catalyst for investigating alternatives. My search was richly rewarded and the answers came in many forms. Old books of herbs, the Bible, natural treatments from the ladies who are long past now, all came together to form the book you now hold in your hands.

My journey has spanned over 45 years and I have had the privilege of being able to testify that these methods work, no one has ever been hurt or harmed by them, and many have experienced relief and healing through them.

As I pass into my 70th year, I realize the importance of putting this information, and some of my experiences, into a volume for the benefit of many.

This book in no way claims to have the cure for disease, but rather offers some simple solutions to relieve and often resolve the many discomforts that assail humankind today.

For the reader looking for medical counsel: although the information, ideas, and suggested procedures contained within this book are based on years of personal experience and study—many backed up with scientific findings—no part of this book is intended to be used as a medical diagnosis or treatment tool, because every medical condition is unique to the individual.

I thank God for His guidance and confirmation through this journey for He made this body and these natural health laws and can guide each one of us personally on our own private journey.

Barbara O'Neill

# CHAPTER 1

# NATURE'S DOCTORS SUSTAIN ME?

## NINE FOUNDATIONAL PILLARS FOR HEALING

Do you ever feel drained of energy, as if your body is breaking down or not working to its full potential? Is your life feeling overwhelmed with problems? How do you SUSTAIN ME to be strengthened or supported physically or mentally?

Let us begin by establishing this undeniable fact: the human body has been designed to heal itself.[1] Our living organism is self-healing, self-running, and self-regulating.

Let's work with that!

The purpose of this book is to show how we can work with our inherent healing forces to maintain equilibrium and prevent disease and how to boost these forces into action if disease occurs.

The blood is correctly called the river of life or the *life of the flesh*.[2] It is the carrier of oxygen, water, nutrients, white blood cells, and also takes away waste.

Constantly, the river of life pulsates through the body at an astonishing rate,

---

1.  See my book *Self Heal By Design*, available from www.barbaraoneill.com or in Australia at https://shop.mmh.com.au/collections/books-and-dvds or Amazon.com.
2.  Leviticus 17:11

bathing every cell with its life-giving cargo. It takes one minute for one drop of blood to complete this marvelous circuit.

Supplying the river of life with adequate water, vital oxygen, and top-quality nutrients allows it to be the life of the flesh, whereas depriving the blood of these elements can cause it to be the death of the flesh.

No drug can heal. No herb or food can heal. The body, and the body only, has the power to heal, and it will, if given the right conditions.

Obtaining vibrant health is not difficult to understand, nor is it a mystery. True health lies in the knowledge and practice of nine simple foundational pillars.

SLEEP    ABSTAINING    NUTRITION

USE OF WATER    (from anything harmful)    MODERATION

TRUST IN    INHALE

SUNSHINE    DIVINE POWER    (fresh air)    EXERCISE

## This is how we SUSTAIN ME.

Florence Nightingale called them the *Laws of Nursing*. Dr Jackson from New York, who owned and ran a health retreat in the late 1800s, called them the *Laws of Life*. Pioneering nineteenth-century health reformer Ellen G. White, in her book, *The Ministry of Healing*, called them the *Laws of Health*. Some refer to them as the *natural doctors*.

They are the basic formula for health and healing, and the conditions that the body requires for optimum performance. We will touch on each of them now, and throughout this book show how they can be applied to various ailments and diseases.

This book is the result of my own personal discoveries over many years of studying and working with patients seeking better health outcomes. Where possible I've quoted scientific studies that have also discovered the healing power of these free and natural principles.

# SUNSHINE

The sun is the doctor in the sky, not the enemy, but you can over-visit your doctor! Six to seven sunburns in your life can double the risk of skin cancer.

Most sunscreens contain many toxic chemicals and also completely block the ultraviolet (UV) rays. A suntan that is developed by short, daily sun exposure is the best protection from sun damage.

Our brain also needs sun and this comes from the healing rays entering through the eyes. The sun's rays go through the eyes into neurochemical pathways that stimulate different parts of the brain. In his book, *Better Eyesight Without Glasses*, Dr William Bates shows the importance of eyes having sun exposure for better eyesight.

A vitamin D deficiency can also increase your risk of skin cancer. Vitamin D is formed under the skin when the UV rays from the sun (specifically UVB rays) hit the skin. This steroid/vitamin is essential in the assimilation and utilization of calcium in the body. Every cell in the body requires vitamin D to function effectively.

Vitamin D helps the pituitary gland regulate hormones. This vitamin helps the pineal gland so you can sleep better at night and can even boost your mood. For 300 years, children suffered and died from rickets, a bone disease that, in the 1920s, was finally acknowledged to be a vitamin D deficiency.

> **Every cell in the body requires vitamin D to function effectively.**

The amount of sun needed depends on the colour of your skin and time of year and day. People with dark skin need far more exposure than those with light skin.

3. Webb AR, et al (2018) Colour Counts: Sunlight and Skin Type as Drivers of Vitamin D Deficiency at UK Latitudes. Nutrients. 2018 Apr 7;10(4):457. <https://www.mdpi.com/2072-6643/10/4/457>.

## USE OF WATER

The body is made up of 50-75% water. Water lubricates and cushions the joints, forms the basis of blood, digestive juices, urine, and perspiration, and is contained in muscle, fat, and bones.

It is water, and water alone, that can cleanse every tissue in the body. Disease thrives in a body with filthy corners in it. Just as our external body needs a daily wash to cleanse us from the waste that is thrown off via our skin, the inside of our body also needs a cleanse.

Your body is constantly losing water through breathing, sweating, urinating, and bowel movements. On average, two and a half liters are lost every 24 hours. Two liters of pure water must be replaced, and the other half a litre can be supplied by herbal teas, fruits, and vegetables.

Our body can better utilize the water if it is taken in little by little over the day. A crystal of Celtic salt—with its 82 minerals—can be placed under the tongue before every glass of water to ensure that the water is taken inside the cells.

### WHERE IS WATER USED?

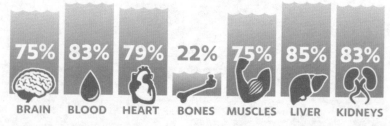

| 75% | 83% | 79% | 22% | 75% | 85% | 83% |
|-----|-----|-----|-----|-----|-----|-----|
| BRAIN | BLOOD | HEART | BONES | MUSCLES | LIVER | KIDNEYS |

# SLEEP

Our daily performance of mental, emotional, spiritual, and physical activities is largely dependent on our nightly sleep.

Light and dark signals are sent through the eyes along the optic nerve to the suprachiasmatic nucleus, also known as our body clock, which communicates with the pineal gland, causing hormones to be released while we sleep.

This explains why sunshine in the day and sleeping in the dark are so important. The most intense release of rest and rejuvenation hormones are between the hours of 9pm and 2am (or 10pm and 3am daylight saving time).

Two things can totally shut the nightly hormones down and prevent sleep. Being worried or annoyed is one, and the other is the blue light from the screens of various electronic devices when viewed in the evening and early morning hours.

Eating breakfast like a king, lunch like a queen, and dinner like a pauper allows you a more restful sleep, as the stomach can join in the rest time.

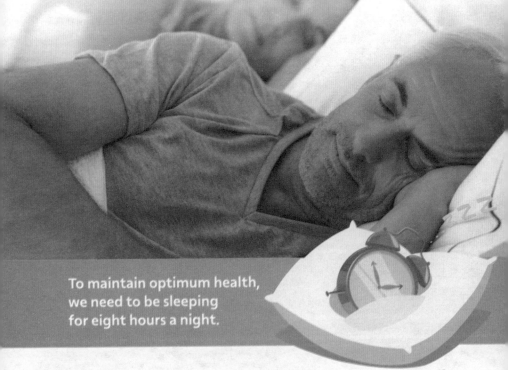

To maintain optimum health, we need to be sleeping for eight hours a night.

# TRUST IN DIVINE POWER

This law covers the spiritual, emotional, and mental aspects of health and sickness.

*"A merry heart does good, like a medicine, but a broken spirit dries the bones"*—Proverbs 17:22

We need to laugh more. It is a major help in the trials and tribulations we face on a daily basis.

*"In everything give thanks; for this is the will of God in Christ Jesus for you"*—1 Thessalonians 5:18

This is also called the attitude of gratitude. Being thankful for everything that happens to us changes our mindset, frees up the positive emotions, and shuts out the negative and damaging emotions.

A beautiful invitation from the great God of Heaven is:

*"Come to Me, all you who labor and are heavy laden, and I will give you rest. Take My yoke upon you and learn from Me, for I am gentle and lowly in heart, and you will find rest for your souls. For My yoke is easy and My burden is light."*—Matthew 11:28–30

*"Give your burdens to the Lord, and he will take care of you. He will not permit the godly to slip and fall."*—Psalm 55:22 NLT

## ABSTAIN

While recommended dietary guidelines have changed over the years, the strongest evidence has always proven that for optimum body performance, there are some articles that should not enter the body. They are:

### ❯ Refined Sugar

Refined sugar is a pure acid and is toxic to the body. John Yutkin, in his acclaimed book, *Pure, White and Deadly*, claims that it is so toxic, it should be banned!

There is nothing wrong with sugarcane; it is the pure acid that is extracted from it that is harmful.

The brain suffers, as it can only hold a two-minute supply of glucose, and the body's responding highs and lows (to try to adjust to this fuel disrupter) has a disastrous effect on brain function. The pancreas also suffers, as it constantly attempts to maintain a steady fuel supply to the cells despite the drastic highs and lows that sugar causes.

## › Caffeine

Caffeine is loved by so many and yet causes a multitude of problems. The Italians have mastered the art of making coffee in such a way as to bring the caffeine content to a bare minimum whilst also removing the bitterness. Unfortunately, it is a rare find in Australia today.

Not only does caffeine cause a rise in blood pressure, it also has a devastating effect on the neurotransmitters in the brain, resulting in a chemical imbalance.

In his book, *Caffeine Blues*, the author Stephen Cherniske compares having a cup of coffee to meeting a tiger on the path: crisis! The resulting brain spark and energy boost is used as an excuse by many as to why they need it. Eventually, it takes its toll and can contribute to several forms of mental illness.

## › Alcohol

The facts are well documented. This neurotoxin effectively kills brain cells, those invaluable little gray cells that we depend on for clarity of mind and effective decision making. The nerve cells in the brain cannot regrow. Once they are gone, they are gone.

**Chemicals are one of the most common environmental poisons that we are exposed to today.**

## › Tobacco

The pictures on cigarette packets say it all. The 4,000 chemicals in cigarettes not only make them the number one cause of lung cancer, but also contribute to damage in the endothelial cells that line our arteries.

Heart disease is the number one killer in developed countries today, and even the medical industry acknowledges that cigarette smoking is a contributing factor.

## › Chemicals

Chemicals are one of the most common environmental poisons that we are exposed to today. They are in our food, toothpaste, shampoos, and laundry detergents. In fact, they are everywhere. It is wise to become knowledgeable of the ingredients in these articles and take steps to reduce our exposure.

*The Lancet*, a well-respected medical journal and leading platform of peer-reviewed scholarly literature, classified fluoride as a neurotoxin.[4]

---

4.  *The Lancet*, "Neurobehavioural Effects of Developmental Toxicity", by Dr Philippe Grandjean, MD and Philip J Landrigan, MD. https://www.thelancet.com/journals/laneur/article/PIIS1474-4422(13)70278-3 Published: March 2014, accessed July 2023.

The herbicide glyphosate, found in Roundup, kills plants by inhibiting the pathway that the plant uses for the biosynthesis or breakdown of amino acids. Human gut bacteria has this same pathway. By killing off the beneficial bacteria in our gut through the suppression of this pathway, not only can pathogens multiply, but the synthesis of amino acids is also compromised.

## 〉 Electromagnetic Field (EMF) Excess

We are in a technological age. We love it, but we need to be mindful of the dangers and limit our exposure.

We spend a third of our lives in bed, and we sleep best in a technology-free area. Unfortunately, many use their iPhones for their alarm—80% of Americans sleep with their phones. Australians aren't far behind. Ensuring your device is at least two feet away from you as you sleep will reduce your exposure by two thirds. Use a speaker or ear pieces when using the phone. Endeavor to have the phone away from your person when not in use.

The worst place to put your laptop is on your lap. Protect your reproductive organs by putting it on a desk or the arm of your chair. We are electrical people, and the EMF coming off these devices interferes with our own electrical energy, causing disruptions. These are particularly manifested in neurological problems.

## 〉 Drugs

Drugs never cure disease. They change the form and location, and they can hide the symptoms of disease. A drug may save a life in a crisis, but continued use can end up causing even more problems. It is the body, and the body alone, that can heal, and that happens when it is given the right conditions.

## 〉 Mercury

Mercury is a neurotoxin, and there is no safe dose. There are three main things that can expose us to mercury. Eating fish is one of the three, and the larger the fish, the higher the dose, as mercury is bioaccumulative, meaning it builds up in the body's tissues.

The other two areas are mercury amalgam fillings in the teeth and some vaccines, which contain mercury in the form of thimerosal (ethylmercury).[5]

5. Clarkson TW, Magos L, Myers GJ. (2003) "The toxicology of mercury—current exposures and clinical manifestations." *New England Journal of Medicine*. 2003; 349:1731–1737, DOI: 10.1056/NEJMra022471.

# INHALE (FRESH AIR)

Oxygen is the most vital element needed for life. Most living things need oxygen to survive.

Cancer cannot live in the presence of oxygen.

- The energy cycles in our cells give us 18 times more energy when they have the required oxygen.
- The leaves of trees purify the air and give us this valuable element.
- Country air is higher in oxygen than city air. Car exhaust fumes, factory waste through chimneys, mold waste, cigarette smoke, and thousands of people in a small space all contribute to the air in major cities being considerably lower in oxygen.
- To ensure that we have access to this most valuable commodity, it is important to carefully analyze the air we breathe at home, work, and when sleeping.

We spend a third of our lives in bed, so that is a good place to begin the investigation. Assess your pillows, bedding, and mattress, and also the availability of fresh air while sleeping.

How we breathe is also vitally important. We are designed to breathe through our noses. Mouth breathing is an oral habit associated with a cascade of events leading to chronic health problems.

# NUTRITION

Many theories abound on the correct diet. History shows us that a diet high in plant foods contains all the nutrients necessary for the body to perform its necessary functions, and this is confirmed by science. The three essential food groups are fibre, protein, and fats.

Your gut needs help to move and remove the waste in your digestive system, and that's where fibre plays a role. The highest-fibre foods are plants, with vegetables and fruit being the highest.

Half of the membrane around every cell is protein. The cleanest burning fuel regarding protein is plant protein. This includes whole grains, legumes (well prepared), nuts, and seeds.

The other half of the membrane around every cell is fat. The best fats are those found in nuts and seeds. Fats from the two oils extracted from the flesh of plants are coconut and olive, and these oils have been used for centuries.

**Vegetables and fruits contain plant chemicals, vitamins, and minerals that are vital for life.**

# MODERATION

Moderation in all things beneficial, is vital for health. Even good things can turn to poison, if overdone. Not many people over eat lettuce, but overeating honey can negate the positive health benefits due to honey's high fructose content.

Eating is essential to supply the body with the nutrients it requires to function. If too much food is eaten, the stomach is overloaded and unable to effectively extract the necessary components needed by every cell. We explore this more in the chapter The Gastrointestinal Tract on page 77.

Moderation can include anything from scaling back portion size, limiting sweets, adding more nutritional variety to your meals and activities, avoiding certain foods for a time to allow your body to rest and heal, or any combination of these options.

# EXERCISE

The body was designed to do daily activity, which contains its preserving power. Exercise is the single most powerful way to oxygenate the body.

Strength comes from exercise. There is no other way to achieve strength, so it is simply a matter of finding out which activity works for you. High Intensity Interval Training (HIIT) has been shown to be the most effective exercise for increasing muscle strength and endurance. As the name implies, this involves intervals of high-intensity (HI) exercise and recovery, the ideal being 30 seconds of high-intensity exercise with 90 seconds of recovery for a cycle of six.

High-intensity exercise is anything that increases the heart rate and respiration. Most related research has been conducted on exercise bikes, which are helpful for those who have a balance problem or issues with the knees or ankles. The rebounder is another effective way to get the body moving.

An easy way to remember these simple yet powerful nine foundational pillars is in the acronym **SUSTAIN ME.** These health principles will lead to your optimal health and the opportunity to enjoy life.

Life should be great!

In the following chapters we will explore how to apply SUSTAIN ME to various diseases or health problems, and the role they play in aiding the body to heal itself. These principles will often overlap as they are the foundational structure for all healing.

# CHAPTER 2

# BEGiNNiNG AT THE TOP
# THE HEAD

## PART 1 MIGRAINES AND HEADACHES

Aching heads is common for many people. In case of any sickness, the first step is to ascertain the cause, and migraines can have several causes, which can be different in every case.

## COMMON CAUSES

### Hormones

Often, migraines begin at puberty. This indicates a hormone imbalance. Not everyone with a hormone imbalance will have migraines, but it is one of the symptoms.

The remedy is to balance the hormones. There are several herbs that can aid the body in the process of restoring the balance. Tre Lune Wild Yam Cream contains extracts from wild yam and the chaste tree, this is known to help balance hormones. Other herbs include dong quai, maca, evening primrose, and black cohosh.

### Allergies

Allergies to food and chemicals are common triggers for migraines. Some of the more likely culprits include aged cheese, milk, peanuts, eggs, alcohol, red wine, and the plant chemical theobromine. Theobromine is found in various pharmaceutical products, cocoa, chocolate-based foods, caffeine, and tea.

Others have found that their migraines subsided when they ceased consuming products from the nightshade family. This includes tomatoes, capsicum (bell peppers), eggplant, and white potatoes.

## Dehydration

The brain uses water for many functions.

Each nerve cell is bathed in water, and it is required for effective neuronal activity and the firing of messages from cell to cell. The brain is a hydroelectric system: no hydration means no electricity.

Water keeps the cell membrane soft and pliable.

Water also surrounds the brain, acting as a shock absorber and protector.

In a state of dehydration, the brain suffers first. The nerve cells can shrink, which causes pain. Some of the most common dehydrators are drug medication, caffeine, alcohol, cigarettes, refined sugar, and not drinking enough water.

### Spine and Skull Misalignment—Injury

A spinal misalignment can sometimes be the cause of migraines.

A chiropractor, osteopath, or physiotherapist can help, as they are experts in spinal alignment.

The misalignment may have been caused by a difficult birth or previous injury to the head or spine. Even poor posture, including the very unnatural pose of looking at a computer all day, can cause migraines.

A blow to the head or spine, whatever the reason, can cause damage not only to the skull or spine but also to the way the bones that make up the skull and spine sit and align with each other.

## Malnutrition

Every cell in the body requires a generous supply of quality proteins, fats, minerals, and vitamins to function, repair, and heal effectively. Often, past injuries don't repair themselves—as the body is designed to do—because of a lack of available nutrients.

When someone suffers from migraines, these causes need to be considered and lifestyle adjusted to ensure that the best conditions are given to the brain to prevent migraines.

# THE SOLUTIONS

## STEP ONE: BRING RELIEF

> **Hydrotherapy**

Relief can be brought to someone suffering from a migraine by having a hot water foot bath. The water should be as hot as the person can bear. The water is kept hot for at least half an hour. A cold compress, such as a wet washcloth, can be applied to the forehead and base of the neck if the person desires.

Often, the blood pooling in the brain (caused by any or all of the points discussed) is what causes the pain. When the feet are placed in hot water, excess blood is drawn to them, and any areas of congestion in the body will be relieved by the blood being directed to the feet.

When the treatment has ended, cold water is poured over the feet to equalize the circulation. The feet are then thoroughly dried. A foot massage at this point may also be beneficial.

The only time the hot water foot bath is unwise is if the person suffers from chronic cold feet or has lost feeling in their feet. If this is the case, only lukewarm water should be used and slowly brought to a mild heat. It is often found that a person with a migraine has cold feet.

> **Herbs**

**Feverfew** is a very bitter herb that has been known to bring relief to migraine sufferers. A plant can be grown near the house and the fresh leaves chewed on at the first indication of pain. The bitterness in the mouth appears to help dilate the blood vessels to the brain. Feverfew is also available in capsule or tablet form, as a tincture or a tea.

There are a few herbs that have an analgesic effect on the body:

**Willow bark,** which is what aspirin was originally made from, and **cayenne pepper** are two herbs that have an analgesic effect and can help relieve pain.

**Frankincense** can be used as an essential oil. This herb has been used for centuries to bring relief from pain. One drop is placed on the thumb and pressed to the roof of the mouth.

### ⟩ Still Point Inducer

This device can be purchased or made easily at home. To make it, all you need is a sock of 25-30 cm (ten inches) in length and two tennis balls.

The balls are placed side by side, in the toe of the sock. The remainder of the sock is twisted several times and then drawn back over the balls, twisted and drawn again, and then secured. This will use the whole sock. What is produced is a tight, compact formation that will nestle at the back of the head.

To use it, lay down flat on your back on the floor and place a small, rolled hand towel at the base of the head behind the neck. The Still Point Inducer (the balls in the sock) is placed at the back of the skull behind the ears, so there is a ball sitting behind each ear. The balls sit between the occipital protuberance (the bone lump at the top of the back of the skull) and the base of the skull.

It is called the Still Point Inducer because the pressure it applies to this area causes the fluid that moves around the brain to be induced into a momentary still point. As the fluid resumes its flow, it moves in a more balanced ratio around the brain, which can result in reducing pain in the head.

Ideally, the Still Point Inducer is used for at least ten minutes. This can be repeated every hour or two if needed.

For some, the pain reduction is mild and for others quite significant. Much depends on the cause of the migraine.

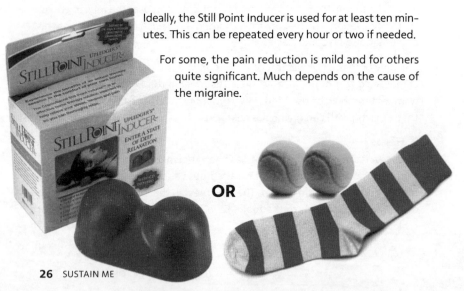

**OR**

## STEP TWO:
### MANAGEMENT THROUGH 'SUSTAIN ME'

**SUNSHINE:** Daily sunshine to maintain vitamin D levels to ensure strong bones and spine. For some, sunshine can trigger headaches or full-blown migraine attacks but this is often simply due to dehydration.

**USE OF WATER:** Keeping well hydrated prevents brain cells shrinking, as this causes pain. Pure water is best.

**SLEEP:** Eight hours of sleep nightly guarantees the reduction of pressure build up in the brain cells

**TRUST IN DIVINE POWER:** Headaches can be the result of stress and worry, 1 Peter 5:7 says *"Give all your worries and cares to God, for he cares about you"* (NLT).

**ABSTAIN:** Refrain from all known substances that may induce headaches, the most common being alcohol, chocolate, and caffeine.

**INHALE:** Breathing through the nose causes a rise in nitric oxide and carbon dioxide. Both of these gases have a vasodilation effect, meaning an opening of the blood vessels in and out of the brain.

**NUTRITION:** Brain cells need nourishment to function efficiently, especially in times of stress. High-fibre, generous proteins, and healthy fats will supply this.

**MODERATION:** An overloaded stomach can cause headaches—an indication as to how the whole body is affected when a person eats to excess.

**EXERCISE:** Exercise will encourage efficient blood flow through the whole body, preventing pressure build-up in the brain.

# TESTIMONY
## JUNE'S HEADACHE

Two months before her visit to our retreat, June was hurrying to a meeting and walking through a parking lot with her arms full of folders.

Not realizing her surroundings, she walked under an automatic gate, which came down hard on the top of her head, causing her to fall to the ground. The pain was extreme, and a couple of men working nearby came to her aid.

Not a woman to be distracted from her work, June rested for 15 minutes and then resumed her walk to the meeting. The pain had reduced by half, but she pushed on, finished the conference, then drove to the airport, sat in an airplane for an hour, and drove another hour home. She told me later that she thinks she was still in shock.

After a restless night, her husband insisted she be assessed by the doctor. Her head pain was increasing as the shock wore off. X-rays didn't reveal any damage, although there was some bruising on the skin. She was offered painkillers and told to rest. A visit to a chiropractor seemed to help a little.

June is a principal at quite a large school and is in charge of 200 teachers. She felt a great responsibility to perform her duties, though the pain in her head was becoming quite debilitating.

School holidays enabled June to attend the health retreat. She told me her pain levels averaged eight to nine out of ten most days. Although she had learned to live with this pain, she desperately desired to be free from it. Within an hour of being at the retreat, we helped June to lie on the Still Point Inducer. June was encouraged to lie for at least ten minutes.

After 15 minutes, she came running out of the room with a big smile, declaring that her pain had gone down from an eight to a five out of ten. Nothing, not even painkillers, had brought the pain down like that.

Twice a day, June lay on the Still Point Inducer. By Wednesday, June's pain was a three out of ten. This is something she had not known for the two months since the accident.

When June left the retreat after her stay, her pain levels were at a one or two. A different woman arrived home that day. June's family and staff were overjoyed to see the 'old' June return. The transformation was astounding, as pain can be so debilitating. June now takes her tennis balls in a sock everywhere she goes.

Not everyone has experienced results as dramatic as June's. Much depends on the source of the pain, but the Still Point Inducer has helped many to manage, and sometimes conquer, their headaches.

**PART 2**
# EYE HEALTH MADE EASY

Eye health is often taken for granted, until it begins to deteriorate. In his book, *Better Eyesight Without Glasses*, Dr William Bates shows how eyes can be strengthened and even improved under the right conditions.

## COMMON CAUSES

### Technology

Equal long and short distance viewing is necessary for efficient eyesight. Unfortunately, in this technological age, our short range eye muscles are getting overworked, and our long range muscles are being used less and less.

Not only is eye muscle development being impaired, but also screens are being viewed on various devices when eyes should be resting.

The eyes are an extension of the brain. Light and dark signals are fed through the optic nerve to a control center in the brain where the body clock is located, and that communicates with the pineal gland. The pineal gland releases hormones between the hours of 9pm and 2am. These hormones are responsible for rest and rejuvenation during sleep, as well as housekeeping and filing all the day's messages.

The brain and eyes suffer when they are denied these vital processes, and this happens by not sleeping in the hours mentioned.

> **Other factors that can cause eye problems**

1. Devitalized food causes devitalized eye cells—the cells do not have the basic nutrients required for eye function.

2. Injury, this could be a blow to the eyes or foreign objects entering the eye.

3. Dehydration—the eye is constantly bathed in water and the very structure of the eye contains significant amounts of water.

4. Lack of sunshine—there are receptor sites on the retina designed to take the sun's rays through to the brain, as the brain is an extension of the eyes. Both brain and eye function is comprised when there is a lack of exposure to sunshine.

5. Stress causes eye strain and eye strain weakens the eyes.

6. Lack of sleep—in the night hours the eyes rest and rejuvenate. Tiredness strains the eyes, especially in the hours we should be sleeping, that is 9pm to 5am, straining the eyes in these hours weakens them.

Doctor William Bates lists the health doctors, or foundational pillars, mentioned in the first chapter of this book, as basic requirements for better eyesight.

# THE SOLUTIONS
## STEP ONE: BRING RELIEF

> **Conjunctivitis or Red, Bloodshot, or Infected Eyes**

A grated potato poultice over the eye can not only bring relief but also reduce inflammation and help the eye to heal.

Potato is very cooling if the eye is inflamed and can also draw out pus. The poultice can be worn overnight or for a few hours. Repeat as often as necessary until healed. See my chapter on Healthy Healers on page 305, for more information on how to make and apply poultices.

Charcoal and psyllium husks can also be mixed together in equal amounts and applied to the eyes. Try alternating them nightly.

### ❯ Dry Eyes

The herb eyebright helps all eye problems.

Goldenseal is a herb with strong antimicrobial activity, and its nickname is 'king of tonics to all mucous membranes'.

A tea can be made with these two herbs by pouring a cup of boiling water on half a teaspoon of each herb. This is then covered and allowed to cool. Then, the liquid can be strained and refrigerated. Using an eye bath, the eyes can be washed with this tea two to three times a day.

After the eyewash, a drop of castor oil can be wiped over the eyelid and lashes. This is very safe and is an old remedy that has been used for centuries. It may be sticky at first but will soak through to the eye within half an hour.

### ❯ Glaucoma

The treatments used for dry eyes can also help glaucoma, with the addition of cayenne pepper. When making the eyebright and goldenseal tea, add 1/8 of a teaspoon of cayenne pepper. Strain well when cool. This may smart a little but will not damage the eye, and the discomfort will be brief.

### ❯ Cataracts

The treatments for dry eyes will also help eliminate cataracts, especially the castor oil. This oil penetrates deep and can gradually break up unnatural formations, such as cataracts.

## STEP TWO:
## MANAGEMENT THROUGH 'SUSTAIN ME'

 **SUNSHINE:** Eyes need sun, as does the brain, and the eyes are how the brain receives its sunlight.

We should never look directly at the sun, except for early morning and late afternoon. This gentle sun gives messages to the brain, which benefits our sleep at night.

It is this light that resets our circadian rhythm, essential for proper brain function. As the brain receives these light signals, it releases serotonin, the mood hormone.

If a person wears glasses or contact lenses, they can spend a portion of the day outside with no lenses, which inhibit the sunlight going into the eyes.

Dr William Bates, in his previously mentioned book, states that the eyes need daily sun. The sun's rays increase blood supply to the eyes, which brings nutrients, oxygen, and water to every eye cell.

**USE OF WATER:** It is essential for the blood to deliver adequate water to each eye cell; therefore, it is important to the eyes that we take in an abundant supply of pure water. At least two liters of water each day is required. Water and water alone will supply the eyes' need for fluid.

**SLEEP:** Light and dark signals are fed through the optic nerve to a control center in the brain where our body clock, the suprachiasmatic nucleus, is located. This communicates with the pineal gland and releases hormones between the hours of 9pm and 2am while we sleep. Ensuring that our eyes are closed and sleeping in these hours allows the eyes to rest and recover from the day's activity.

**TRUST IN DIVINE POWER:** This includes mental, spiritual, and emotional health. Anything that reduces stress reduces eye strain.

How we perceive a situation also affects our stress levels, sleep, and overall health. In Matthew 6:22 Jesus said, *"The lamp of the body is the eye. If therefore your eye is good, your whole body will be full of light."* Here the eye is used as a metaphor of a lamp which lights the entire body. Our eyes are the entrance to our hearts and minds and, as such, they provide a doorway to our very souls. In other words, how you see reality (good or bad eyes) determines how your body responds to your environment.

**ABSTAIN:** This law considers anything that may impair eyesight. Straining eyes that are already tired weakens the eyes. Exposure to bright lights, especially screens, when the eyes should be sleeping between the hours of 9pm and 5am weakens the eyes by robbing them of rest and revival. The short range muscles in the eye can be overused with excessive short range viewing and the long range muscles under used. This causes an imbalance in the eye, which can affect vision.

Abstain from stimulants, such as alcohol, tobacco, refined sugar, caffeine, and drugs, all contain dehydrating agents that can impact the eyes.

**INHALE:** Each eye cell requires oxygen to produce adequate energy in order to function efficiently. Breathing fresh air through the nose, especially while sleeping, is vital for seeing well.

**NUTRITION:** For the blood to carry adequate nutrition, we must supply the body with sufficient nutrients, including vitamins, minerals, protein, and fats. A plant-based food program, as previously discussed, will ensure this.

**MODERATION:** We need to spend more time gazing at objects at a distance compared to short range viewing. Read a printed book over reading a screen, walk in nature instead of watching a documentary about nature. Eyes react differently to physical activity compared with mental activity, maintain the balance.

High levels of screen time on smart devices (such as looking at a smart phones) is associated with around a 30% higher risk of myopia (nearsightedness) and, when combined with excessive computer use, that risk rose to around 80%.[1]

**EXERCISE:** This is the most powerful way to oxygenate every cell. Exercise also increases blood supply to the eyes, which means not only is there more oxygen but also more nutrition, water, and waste removal.

High Intensity Interval Training (HIIT) is a form of exercise that promotes quick and effective movement of blood while in the HI phase.

In addition, eye exercises can strengthen eyesight. Rebounding can be achieved by changing the focus on an object every ten jumps from long to short range objects. Continually alternating this long and short focus challenges and thus strengthens the long and short muscles in the eye, therefore improving eyesight. See *Rebound to Better Health: The Physiology of Rebound Exercise* by Albert Earl Carter.

Unfortunately, these days, our eyes spend too much time viewing objects in a short range and not enough time viewing them long range.

# TESTIMONy

We have had many testimonies from people who have used these treatments and testified that their cataracts have reduced, to the astonishment of their eye doctors.

Much depends on the severity of the eye complaint and how diligent the person is at applying the treatments.

---

1. American Optometric Association, "Myopia (nearsightedness)" <https://www.aoa.org/healthy-eyes/eye-and-vision-conditions/myopia?sso=y> accessed July 2023.

# PART 3
# EASY ON THE EARS

While there are many ailments that can affect the ears, tinnitus, and vertigo are often the most common of these ailments.

Tinnitus is the perception of sound when there is no corresponding external sound present. It is often described as ringing or buzzing in the ear. The damage is often sustained by very loud noises that the ears were exposed to in the past for a prolonged period of time.

Vertigo is a condition where a person has the sensation of movement or surrounding objects moving when they are not. This affects their balance.

Even though these conditions are different, they can both respond to similar treatments and have similar causes.

## COMMON CAUSES

1.  **DAMAGE** to the fine mechanisms in the ear is the most common cause in both cases. This includes very loud music; musicians in rock bands often experience tinnitus. This is also experienced by soldiers manning heavy artillery, such as machine guns, missile launchers, and cannons, as well as miners who have used jackhammers and explosives.

    It is the prolonged exposure to these extremely loud noises that damages the delicate and sensitive mechanisms in the inner ear.

2.  **INJURIES** to the head, neck, or ear may lead to tinnitus and vertigo.

3.  **SIDE EFFECTS OF MEDICATIONS** can be a causative factor. Tinnitus is recognized as one of the possible side effects of some vaccines.[2]

4.  **ALLERGIES** is another factor that can contribute to tinnitus and vertigo, the most common allergens being chemicals, mold, and food. Items such as wheat, peanuts, dairy, oats, red wine, caffeine, and refined sugar top the list.

    Allergies can affect the mucous membranes in the nasal, sinus, and trachea areas, causing an increase in mucus secretion. This excess mucus tends to build up in the Eustachian tubes and can inhibit air flow and disrupt balance. The Eustachian tubes are like small canals that link the ears, nose, eyes, and mouth. These partial blockages in the Eustachian tubes can contribute to tinnitus and vertigo.

---

2. Australian Therapeutic Goods Administration "COVID-19 vaccine safety report - 28-07-2022" <www.tga.gov.au/news/covid-19-vaccine-safety-reports/covid-19-vaccine-safety-report-28-07-2022>

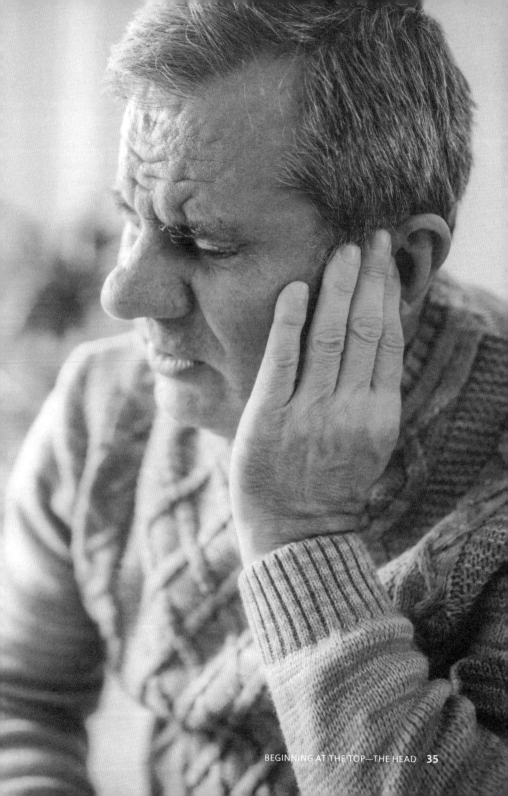

# THE SOLUTIONS

## STEP ONE: BRING RELIEF

There is no quick fix for these ailments which is why prevention is far better. Damage to the fine mechanisms in the ear cannot be totally reversed, but we can strengthen what remains. This is where the natural doctors play a role.

## STEP TWO:
## MANAGEMENT THROUGH 'SUSTAIN ME'

**SUNSHINE:** Vitamin D is essential for optimal health as it strengthens bones as well as reduces inflammation, modulates cell growth, and controls the nerves, muscles, and immune system. Recent studies[3] have also revealed a correlation between vitamin D deficiency and inner ear diseases, including Menière's, tinnitus, and vertigo. Exposing our skin to sunlight is the best and most natural way to improve vitamin D levels.

**USE OF WATER:** Keeping well hydrated, with eight glasses of water a day, helps ear health.

**SLEEP:** The ears heal best when we sleep, with studies revealing the suppression of tinnitus during intense NREM sleep.[4]

**TRUST IN DIVINE POWER:** God has promised His grace is sufficient for us (1 Corinthians 12:9), many cope by learning to live with the buzz. We can choose to listen to the buzz or ignore it. This can be likened to people who live near train lines and no longer hear each train. Our brain is an amazing piece of machinery that can be trained to pick and choose what it hears.

**ABSTAIN:** Eliminating all known contaminants and stimulants is vital. Ceasing all food allergens can help to clear the Eustachian tubes. Once these foods are out of the diet, it can take at least two months to experience a difference.

**INHALE:** Ensure the air is as clean and free from contaminants as possible.

3. Nowaczewska M, et al (2021), "The role of vitamin D in subjective tinnitus" PLoS One, *The National Library of Medicine*, <https://www.ncbi.nlm.nih.gov/pmc/articles/PMC8372974> accessed July 2023.
4. Linus Milinski et al (2022), "Tinnitus: at a crossroad between phantom perception and sleep", *Brain Communications*, Vol 4, Issue 3. <https://doi.org/10.1093/braincomms/fcac089>

**NUTRITION:** Eating a well prepared organic plant-based diet, will supply all the nutrients the ears need to function and heal.

**MODERATION:** When exposed to consistent noises you can use ear protection. It is not the occasional loud noise that does the damage but prolonged exposure.

**EXERCISE:** Exercise every day. Rebounding helps with vertigo, as our balance is set by the bottom of our feet and the inner ear. Bouncing on the rebounder stimulates both.

Vertigo can be managed using the Brandt-Daroff exercise routine, a group of moves and positions that have been found to successfully ease vertigo.

# TESTIMONY
## GEOFF FINDS PEACE

Geoff came to work at Misty Mountain Lifestyle Retreat 20 years ago, when he was in his mid 50's. He initially came to build some fences, however we soon discovered he was a man of varied talents and could be depended upon to fix most problems that arise in country living.

Geoff had worked in the mines for many years, handling heavy equipment, including a hard rock drill, which is like a jackhammer. As a result, tinnitus plagued him, and he told us he often had interrupted sleep because of it.

As time went on, Geoff became interested in our lifestyle and very much enjoyed the food, as he often joined us for the main meal at 1:30pm. Eventually, Geoff became a Christian; ceased all alcohol, caffeine, and meat; and began to implement the Misty Mountain lifestyle and dietary principles.

Today, Geoff shares his story with all who are interested as to how this changed his life. The aches and pains in his joints have ceased, and his tinnitus no longer interrupts his sleep—in fact, he states that he never hears it unless he chooses to hear it!

# PART 4
# HANDLING HAIR LOSS

There is always a cause with any condition, and hair loss is no exception. Every case is different, and though there may be multiple reasons, we will cover the main contributing factors.

## COMMON CAUSES

1. **GENETICS** can be a factor, but remember that although genetics loads the gun, it is lifestyle that pulls the trigger.

2. **CHEMICALS** are the most common cause of past damage to the hair follicles. Hair dyes and perming solutions can weaken the follicles gradually over many years and eventually create damage. The hair follicle is the root, so to speak, of the hair. Hair grows from the follicle. Many shampoos contain sodium lauryl sulphate, which has been shown to damage hair follicles.

3. **HORMONE IMBALANCE** can affect the proper functioning of the body in different ways, especially in women. For some, it results in hair loss.

4. **MINERAL DEFICIENCY** is common in hair loss. Hair, fingernails, and toenails are made of hard keratin. Skin is soft keratin. Keratin is manufactured in the body from minerals. A lack or imbalance of minerals affects nails and hair.

5. **SUDDEN SHOCK** or distress can cause hair loss in some people.

6. **MEDICATIONS** or side effects of medical treatments may cause hair loss.

# THE SOLUTIONS
## STEP ONE: BRING RELIEF

In case of sickness, the first step is to eliminate the cause, then aid the body in its healing process as follows.

You cannot change the genes, but you can change the way they are expressed.

Coconut and castor oils are both very nourishing to the scalp. Rosemary essential oil directly affects the scalp and can stimulate hair follicles.

The scalp can be massaged with a mix of half a cup of coconut or castor oil and ten drops of rosemary essential oil. This can be left for several hours before being washed out. Massaging also stimulates blood flow to the hair follicles. Ensure that you use a chemical-free shampoo.

## STEP TWO:
## MANAGEMENT THROUGH 'SUSTAIN ME'

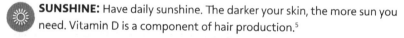 **SUNSHINE:** Have daily sunshine. The darker your skin, the more sun you need. Vitamin D is a component of hair production.[5]

**USE OF WATER:** Keep the scalp well hydrated. Drinking eight to ten glasses of pure water daily will help the strength of your hair, increasing growth. Dehydration immediately halts hair growth.

**SLEEP:** The hormone melatonin regulates the sleep cycle as well as increases hair growth. Sleep has a direct impact on the human body's natural hormones, which means that poor sleep reduces the amount of melatonin, potentially causing hair loss. Sleeping from 9pm to 5am every night, will greatly enhance hair production.

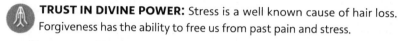 **TRUST IN DIVINE POWER:** Stress is a well known cause of hair loss. Forgiveness has the ability to free us from past pain and stress.

God gives us one day at a time, thank Him for each day. The body's process of healing is gradual, and to the impatient, it may seem slow, given time and the right conditions, it will improve. Being thankful for even slight improvements paves the way for greater improvements.

---

5.  Demay MB, et al (2007). "Role of the vitamin D receptor in hair follicle biology." *The Journal of Steroid Biochemistry and Molecular Biology*. Vol 103, Issues 3, pages 344-346. <https://doi.org/10.1016/j.jsbmb.2006.12.036> National Library of Medicine adapted.

In Luke 12:7 Jesus assures his followers not to fear or be worried about the future because *"the very hairs of your head are all numbered. Do not fear therefore; you are of more value than many sparrows"*.

**ABSTAIN:** Eliminate anything that will interfere with the mineral balance or disrupt the hormones in your body. Many stimulants particularly refined sugar, caffeine, alcohol, cigarettes, and drugs, leach minerals from your body.

Free your house of all environmental poisons and do your best to avoid chemicals. Enjoy and make the most of your hair in its natural state. If considering using a hair dye, try a dye made from herbs, such as henna.

Choose a shampoo that is biodegradable and contains no harmful chemicals.

**INHALE:** Hair growth has four phases: growth, regression, rest, and shedding. In a high oxygen environment there is increased hair fibre growth during the growth phase and a delayed onset of the shedding phase.[6] Breathing pure air through your nose will ensure you are taking in more oxygen.

**NUTRITION:** Eat food that is high in minerals and fibre, with generous amounts of protein and healthy fats. Minerals make a difference, as that is what feeds the hair follicles. A supplement of super greens can be taken twice daily. Greens are the highest source of minerals.

In his book, *The Calcium Lie*, Dr Robert Thompson shows how our soil today has 50% less nutrients compared to the 1950s. This equates to mineral-deficient food. The remedy is to eat organically grown plant foods and cease all the stimulants that are depleting our mineral stores.

**MODERATION:** The structure of the hair follicle is highly affected by various hormones, and hair loss can occur when there is an imbalance. Bring back the balance! Become aware of what can cause an imbalance in the hormones. Applying wild yam cream can restore the balance.

**EXERCISE:** One of the most common forms of hair loss can be triggered by chronic or intense stress. This is where regular exercise can be beneficial. Not only does exercise help our bodies stay physically healthy, but cardio exercises such as jogging, a brisk walk, or a bike ride, will get your blood pumping and drop your stress levels, which can help prevent hair loss.

---

6. Kato H, et al (2020). "The Effects of Ischemia and Hyperoxygenation on Hair Growth and Cycle." *Organogenesis*, Vol 16, 2020 Issue 3, pages 83-94.

## PART 5
# TOUGHEN TEETH & GUARDING GUMS

Contrary to popular opinion, teeth are alive! As living organisms, teeth are able to maintain their integrity and strength, heal and regenerate, just like every other part of the human organism.

We don't doubt that a scratch, graze, cut, or broken bone will heal. So too, can teeth heal. No different to any other part of the body, teeth can and will heal, if given the right conditions. It is no surprise that the conditions are basically the same as those for any other part of our anatomy.

## COMMON CAUSES

1.  **NUTRITIONAL**: Most tooth decay and infected gums are due to poor nutrition. This begins even before conception. The health status of the parents greatly affects the genetic code passed on to the baby. The correct conditions (enter again nature's doctors) throughout pregnancy ensure the developing fetus forms with good health.

2.  **MEDICAL INTERVENTION**: Teeth problems often develop in childhood and can be a result of medical intervention at birth or bottle feeding. Natural birth and breastfeeding are essential for strong bone and teeth development in a baby.

    Breastfed babies work much harder at extracting the milk compared to bottle-fed babies. This action not only strengthens and widens the jaw but also the roof of the mouth. Traditionally, babies were breast-fed for several years. This not only met their emotional, bonding, and nutritional needs but also affected the development of the tongue, and upper and lower jaws in preparation for well-positioned teeth.[7]

3. **REFINED FOODS** are probably the biggest contributing factor to tooth decay.

4. **ENVIRONMENTAL POISONS,** including chemicals and heavy metals, also have a damaging effect on the living tissue of the teeth.

5. **ROOT CANAL FILLINGS** are one of the most dangerous dental practices, as the process kills the tooth. Teeth are similar to other organ systems in your body in that they require an active blood supply, nerves, and connection to the lymphatic system.

6. The inside of a tooth is full of a soft tissue called pulp, that contains blood vessels, nerves, and connective tissue that extends into the root of the tooth. Root canal therapy removes this pulp and fills the hollowed out area with a rubber-like material called *gutta-percha*. Once the nerve is removed, the tooth is no longer living.

The very structure of the tooth, which is like honeycomb, creates a perfect breeding ground for pathogenic bacteria once this natural pulp is removed. This explains why many root canal fillings develop abscesses behind the filling, with these dead teeth typically becoming one of, if not the worst, sources of chronic bacterial toxicity in your body.[8]

7. **MOUTH BREATHING** is one of the most common damaging oral habits in children. It is often a result of a blocked nose (see 'Repairing and Restoring the Respiratory Organs' on page 47). When we mouth breathe we bypass our natural filters in the nose and take dirty air into the mouth. Mouths are for eating, drinking, singing, talking, and laughing, but it is the nose that was made for breathing.

8. **DENTAL HYGIENE:** Leaving food trapped between teeth can lead to a build-up of bacteria which can contribute to decay.

Our teeth are fed from within; our saliva is formed from within. To understand why teeth are deteriorating, we need to look within.

---

7.  Anyanechi CE, Ekabua KJ, Ekpenyong AB, Ekabua JE. Parturients' "Awareness and Perception of Benefits of Breast Feeding in the Prevention of Infant and Childhood Oral and Dental Diseases". *Ghana Medical Journal*, June 2017, page 83–87.

8.  See *Root Canal Cover Up*, by George E. Meinig and *Nutrition and Physical Degeneration* by Weston A. Price

# THE SOLUTIONS
## STEP ONE: BRING RELIEF

1. **Removal of all mercury based fillings as well as root canals before problems arise.** A biological dentist who is aware of the dangers is the best choice when considering replacing amalgam fillings.

2. **Restore your correct pH balance.** In her book, *Holistic Dental Care*, Nadine Artemis refers to 'super saliva' and explains how saliva can mineralize or demineralize teeth. Nadine shows how the enamel on the teeth can dissolve if the saliva is too acidic, as well as create calculus build up if the saliva is too alkaline. I cover this more in the chapter Arresting Arthritis and Gout on page 271.

3. **Floss and brush your teeth after meals.** Calculus can develop from food being trapped between teeth. In the warm, moist environment of the mouth, these remnants can begin to decay and feed bacteria, which leaves a waste product that can form plaque, leading to tartar, and eventually, calculus.

## STEP TWO:
## MANAGEMENT THROUGH 'SUSTAIN ME'

**SUNSHINE:** Sunlight and vitamin D are essential for the access and assimilation of calcium, which is called the 'trucker' of other minerals, as it increases their ability to enter the cells. Bones/teeth need the whole array of minerals for good health.

**USE OF WATER:** Drinking adequate water throughout the day ensures liberal supply for correct viscosity of the saliva, which is constantly bathing and cleansing teeth and helping to maintain their integrity.

Our vital internal fluids are dependent on an adequate water supply. At least eight glasses of water a day are required for optimum health.

**SLEEP:** The teeth need to sleep eight hours a night to allow regeneration. Give the teeth a rest between meals.

**TRUST IN DIVINE POWER:** *"Confidence in an unfaithful man in time of trouble is like a bad tooth and a foot out of joint."* Proverbs 25:19, the one you want to trust is one who has proven himself faithful—and who has done it over the long haul of life. God has proven himself trustworthy through acts of faithfulness over time, putting your trust in Him ensures a great reduction in stress levels. We have been given an incredible body with teeth that will serve us well if treated correctly. Faith in God and the regenerating power that God put into the body will aid in maintaining teeth health.

**ABSTAIN:** Eliminating all known tooth weakeners/destroyers allows the teeth to heal. Refined foods, especially carbohydrates and refined sugars, not only feed bacteria in the mouth (which can damage teeth) but also leach the minerals that make up the basic structure of our teeth.

Don't use mercury fillings. Mercury is a known neurotoxin and should never be used for teeth fillings.

Stimulants, including caffeine, alcohol, and drugs, contribute to leaching the very minerals that compose the structure of the teeth.

**INHALE:** Breathe through the nose because it reduces the amount of bacteria that can cause dental diseases, bad breath, and bacterial infections in the mouth. The function of the nose is to take in air, which is then warmed, moistened, and filtered.

**NUTRITION:** Minerals, minerals, minerals—this is what makes up our teeth. Our bones are made of 12 minerals and 64 trace minerals. There is no limit to the recommended intake of fresh vegetables, especially greens, as these are the highest source of minerals.

Include fruit and vegetables daily and ensure adequate plant proteins with well-prepared legumes, nuts, and seeds. Only organic food contains the optimum levels of the necessary vitamins and minerals.

Celtic salt is another source of the amount and proportion of minerals that our bones and teeth need. A crystal can be taken before each glass of water, as well as generously sprinkled on food.

Nourishing, delicious fats include nuts, seeds, and coconut and olive oils, and these can be included in every meal. These fats help us access the fat-soluble vitamins in our vegetables.

**MODERATION:** Aim for 50% raw and 50% cooked. The chewing of crunchy foods increases gum, teeth, and jaw strength.

**EXERCISE:** The teeth need exercise. Hard crunchy foods such as apples and other raw food give great workouts to teeth. Exercise the whole body daily to guarantee optimum blood and lymph flow to the teeth.

## THE TWO FLUIDS

Two important fluids are considered in teeth maintenance:

1. **Saliva** bathes the outside of the tooth.

2. **Dental fluid** bathes the inside of the tooth. This fluid can be likened to the sap of a tree. As the sap in the tree delivers nutrients for constant rebuilding and maintenance of the tree, so dental fluid provides these for the tooth structure.

These fluids are rendered vital or destructive depending on the dietary and lifestyle practices of the tooth owner.

Teeth can be maintained, protected, and healed through honoring these natural doctors. If adhered to, these nine SUSTAIN ME doctors ensure that these two fluids fulfill the roles that they were designed to do, which is cleaning, nourishing, and healing the teeth.

Then, they can complete the roles of 'super saliva' and 'super dental fluid'.

## FURTHER READING INCLUDES:

- Dr Hal Huggins, *It's All in Your Head; Solving the MS Mystery; Uninformed Consent*
- Dr Bruce Fife, *Oil Pulling Therapy*
- Dr Robert O. Nara, *How to Become Dentally Self-Sufficient*
- Dr Western Price, *Nutritional and Physical Degeneration*
- Dr George Meinig, *Root Canal Coverup*
- Alan Watson, *Cereal Killer*

## MAINTENANCE

In her book, *Holistic Dental Care*, Nadine Artemis gives some excellent advice on simple tools to ensure oral hygiene after meals:

1. Rinse the mouth with a saline mixture after meals. An appropriate rinse is one teaspoon of Celtic salt to 500ml of water. A drop of essential oil can be added, with peppermint often being the oil of choice. Ensure you choose a high quality oil. Swish several times and spit.

   Sodium bicarbonate can also be added to this mix.

2. Scrape the tongue.

3. Gently brush the gum from gum to tooth.

4. Polish teeth with an electric toothbrush. Only brush the teeth you want to keep.

5. Floss. You can swish with a drop of food grade essential oil before flossing.

6. Rinse again.

7. Oil pulling for ten minutes several times a day also strengthens gums and teeth and prohibits bacterial activity.

Nadine's book is well worth the read to explore this subject.

# CHAPTER 3

# REPAIRING AND RESTORING THE RESPIRATORY ORGANS

## COUGHS, COLDS, FLU, SINUS PROBLEMS, LARYNGITIS, ASTHMA, BRONCHITIS, AND BRONCHIECTASIS.

Mucous membrane lines the insides of organs and cavities throughout our body that are exposed to particles from the outside. The body makes mucus all the time, and it plays an important role lubricating and protecting the respiratory organs from abrasive particles, bodily fluids, and invasive pathogens. While this is beneficial to the body, producing too much mucus can cause breathing difficulties and an increased risk of infection. The areas most commonly affected are the throat, tonsils, trachea, sinuses, and lungs. In the lungs, this can result in a variety of respiratory issues.

### COMMON CAUSES

There are three main groups of irritants that can cause too much mucus.

### 1. Chemicals

Breathing in chemicals can result in an allergic response. This includes cigarettes. With over 4,000 known chemicals in cigarette smoke, smokers and passive smokers are both affected.[1]

Every year, millions of tons of manufactured chemicals are released into the environment as emissions, water discharges, and hazardous waste.

---

1. Levels of Toxic Chemicals in Cigarette Smoke, *Association of Schools of Public Health* 2008 https://www.ncbi.nlm.nih.gov/pmc/articles/PMC2099323/ accessed July 2023.

Some of the culprits are cleaning products, including laundry and dishwashing detergents. Others are disinfectants, antiseptics, scented candles and cards, perfumes, crop dusting, and any exposure to any sort of chemical fumes. Heated plastic also releases toxic chemicals.

Even low levels of air pollution harm children's lung function and growth, and increase the incidence of respiratory diseases such as asthma, bronchiolitis, respiratory infections, and bronchitis.

## 2. Mold
Another toxic chemical, though sadly, not often viewed as such, is mold.

Many an asthmatic and sinus sufferer has found their problems began or were exacerbated, after exposure to mold.[2] This includes moldy pillows, mattresses, and quilts. The bed is an easy place for mold to develop, as we exhale about 2–3 cups of water while we sleep. Moisture gathered in ceilings or behind walls, can also be a source of mold exposure while sleeping.

Cleaners who are required to regularly clean moldy bathrooms are at risk, especially when using chemical cleaners such as bleach.

Gardeners are often exposed to moldy mulch and compost, which can put them in danger. A healthy compost usually has mold because it is a warm, humid environment that is perfect for supporting fungal growth.

## 3. Food
In the 1990s, Mayo Clinic researchers found the cause of most chronic sinus infections is not an allergic reaction, but rather an immune system response to fungus. As long as fungi remain, so will the irritation.[3]

Management of yeast and/or fungus reactions requires the elimination of all foods that might contain yeast or mold. Dairy, some cheeses, and the hybridized wheat of today are common food that can harbour fungus and cause a physical reaction that seems similar to an allergy. The body reacts by creating excess mucus in an attempt to protect the body. Refined sugar plays a role, as it feeds the fungus that establishes itself in dark, warm areas, such as the sinuses.

Antibiotics and over-the-counter decongestants are widely used to treat chronic sinusitis. In most cases, antibiotics are not effective for chronic sinusitis because they target bacteria, not fungi.[3]

2.  The Fungal Microbiome and Asthma, *Frontiers in Cellular and Infection Microbiology*, November 2020, https://doi.org/10.3389/fcimb.2020.583418

3.  Mayo Clinic. "Mayo Clinic Study Implicates Fungus As Cause Of Chronic Sinusitis." *ScienceDaily*. 10 September 1999. <www.sciencedaily.com/releases/1999/09/990910080344.htm>

# THE SOLUTIONS
## STEP ONE: BRING RELIEF

Identifying and removing any irritants is the fist step. Depending on the symptoms you are suffering there are several natural remedies that can bring relief.

## CHEST COMPLAINTS

For issues such as flus, asthma, bronchitis, and pneumonia the following can assist in healing:

### The Flu Bomb
The Flu Bomb, which is described in the Healthy Healers chapter on page 305, can be taken three times a day to ease the symptoms of respiratory discomfort, whether it be a sinus infection, cold, or the flu.

### Onion Feet
Split a chopped onion into two plastic bags, one for each foot. Place each foot into the plastic bag so that the soles of the feet are resting on the chopped onion. Twist the bag at the ankle and cover each foot with a sock. Do this overnight. This can greatly reduce coughing at night and bring much relief. It can also contribute to helping the respiratory organs heal.

### Garlic Feet
For babies and small children, a couple pieces of finely sliced garlic can be wrapped onto the bottom of the feet. Make sure there is a piece of cloth between the garlic and the skin to prevent a blister. Put a sock or bootie on the foot to hold it in place.

## ONION COUGH SYRUP

A very effective cough syrup can be made by alternating a layer of chopped onion with a heaped teaspoon of honey in a jar, until the jar is full.

Leave it for 24 hours so the syrup can form. Strain and store in the refrigerator.

A teaspoon can be taken three times a day or whenever needed for all respiratory discomfort.

# HERBS TO BRING RELIEF

Specific herbs can have a cleansing and toning effect on the bronchial system. These be can taken as a tea, swallowed as pills, used for aromatherapy, or bought from a herbalist in high-potency tincture form, making them easy to take. These herbs include:

> **LICORICE.** When taken as a tea, licorice root will stimulate your immune system, coating and calming your cells and mucous membranes with its anti-inflammatory qualities. Licorice root is especially helpful for aiding and preventing respiratory irritation at the first sign of a cold.

LICORICE ROOT

HOPS

> **HOPS.** This is the dried, flowering parts of the hop plant. Using hops essential oil in aromatherapy with helps reduce inflammation and soothe the irritated parts of your respiratory tract. Thus, it effectively reduces coughing and congestion too.

> **ELECAMPANE.** This flowering herb is unique in its ability to clean out the small bronchioles in the lungs. The roots can be used in teas or tinctures as a natural expectorant that thins mucus, promotes sweating, alleviates vomiting, and kills bacteria, making it a great, all purpose cough remedy.

> **THYME.** This common herb has anti microbial, antibacterial, and antifungal properties that help the lungs, digestive system, and skin. It works as an expectorant, designed to bring up 'things', such as phlegm or mucus. Thyme is also a bronchodilator, meaning it makes breathing easier, can help with coughing fits, and calms the respiratory muscles.

ELECAMPANE

THYME

> **PLANTAIN.** This is an expectorant that is high in immune boosting vitamins A and C and rich in mucilage. Mucilage moistens and coats the airways with a protective layer which relieves discomfort and reduces the irritation that causes a dry cough.

PLANTAIN

> **MARSHMALLOW.** This herb contains a natural mucilage which, when drunk as a tea or as an infusion, soothes irritated mucous membranes caused by sore throats, coughs, and indigestion. When applied topically it can also soothe dry, chapped skin.

MARSHMALLOW

PEPPERMINT

> **PEPPERMINT.** When inhaled the menthol in peppermint creates a cooling sensation that can help to relax the muscles of the windpipe and soothe or numb a scratchy throat. Peppermint oil is a natural decongestant and fever-reducer which can ease breathing in people with coughs.

> **LEMONGRASS.**
The powerful antibacterial and antifungal properties of lemongrass can help heal coughs, colds, and the flu. Its high levels of vitamins C and A, and antioxidants triggers the immune system and keeps diseases at bay. Brew a hot cup of lemongrass tea with a dash of turmeric to effectively ease congestion, move mucus from the chest, and soothe a sore throat.

LEMONGRASS

> **ECHINACEA.** Both the plant's upper parts and roots can be used in tablets, tinctures, extracts, and teas for the prevention or treatment of upper respiratory tract infection. Echinacea is commonly combined with mint or other ingredients such as lemongrass to make a more pleasant-tasting tea.

ECHINACEA

> **BONESET.** In virtually every instance where there is inflammation or infection, boneset has proven itself most effective. It contains antiviral properties, stimulates the white blood cells, and strengthens the immune system by enhancing communication between protein cells. This triggers the protective defenses of the immune system to eradicate pathogens and reduce inflammation in the respiratory tract.

BONESET

### Hydrotherapy

A hot water foot bath lasting 20 minutes can ease congestion in the chest.

Hot and cold compresses can be applied to the chest, greatly relieving congestion—three minutes hot and 30 seconds cold, three times. This is explained in more detail in the Hydrotherapy section on page 291.

### Poultices

Charcoal and slippery elm poultices may bring relief when applied to the chest.

Castor oil compresses can be applied to the chest with a hot water bottle over the top to warm the compress. This can be worn for several hours. See my chapter on Healthy Healers, page 305, for instruction on how to assemble and use these health techniques.

# ASTHMA

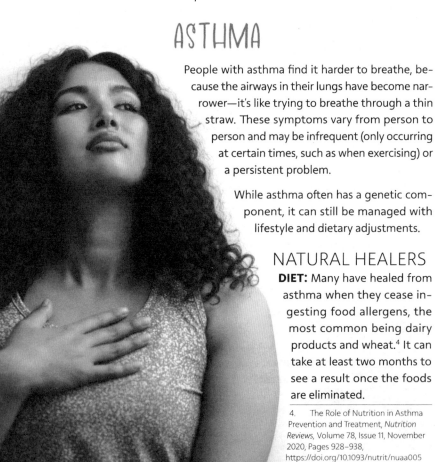

People with asthma find it harder to breathe, because the airways in their lungs have become narrower—it's like trying to breathe through a thin straw. These symptoms vary from person to person and may be infrequent (only occurring at certain times, such as when exercising) or a persistent problem.

While asthma often has a genetic component, it can still be managed with lifestyle and dietary adjustments.

## NATURAL HEALERS

**DIET:** Many have healed from asthma when they cease ingesting food allergens, the most common being dairy products and wheat.[4] It can take at least two months to see a result once the foods are eliminated.

4.    The Role of Nutrition in Asthma Prevention and Treatment, *Nutrition Reviews*, Volume 78, Issue 11, November 2020, Pages 928–938, https://doi.org/10.1093/nutrit/nuaa005

**HERBS:** All the herbs listed to help with chest complaints on the previous page can be beneficial. Two herbs with special bronchodilating properties (to open the airways when taken as a tea or used for aromatherapy) are thyme and lobelia.

**HOT AND COLD COMPRESSES:** Alternation between hot and cold compresses on the chest can help to open the airways. This is discussed more in my chapter on Hydrotherapy, page 291.

**HOW WE BREATHE:** Russian professor, Dr Konstantin Buteyko, created the Buteyko Breathing Technique in the 1950s. This therapeutic breathing method uses breath retention to control the speed and volume of your breath.

Buteyko discovered that when carbon dioxide levels are raised in the blood, the smooth muscle that surrounds the bronchi relaxes, causing these airways to open, which allows the optimum exchange of air in and out of the lungs. The constriction in these airways, characteristic of asthma, is relieved.

The retention of breath is the retention of carbon dioxide. Nose/abdominal breathing are stressed in the Buteyko Breathing Technique, with many hospitals holding classes to teach the technique. Learning the Buteyko breathing technique can assist you to improve the way you breathe and thereby get relief from physical, emotional, and psychological symptoms associated with hyperventilation and other aspects of dysfunctional breathing.[5]

**ESSENTIAL OILS:** Peppermint and eucalyptus oils are well known for their airway-opening effect on the lungs. Being essential oils, they are quite strong, so only a drop is necessary to rub into the hands and inhale.

**SALT:** The Buteyko Breathing Technique encourages taking a crystal of Celtic salt before each glass of water. Celtic salt contains 82 minerals, with three forms of magnesium, which aid in relaxing tight muscles in the chest.

Himalayan salt is almost as good, with 75 minerals.

---

The Himalayan Salt Company sells a salt inhaler to relieve restricted breathing. This device is made of clay and has approximately a quarter cup of salt crystals in its base. The pipe rising from the top is used to inhale, causing the mineral-rich air to infiltrate the lungs and relax and open the airways.

HIMALAYAN
SALT INHALER®
For Health & Wellness

---

5. For more information on the Buteyko Method see https://buteyko.info

# SINUS CONGESTION

Sinusitis is one of the most common reasons for clinical visits, affecting as much as 14% of the United States population.[6] The sinuses consist of a group of four air-filled spaces within the bones of the face that surround the nasal cavity. It is essential for health that air and fluid can pass freely through this area.

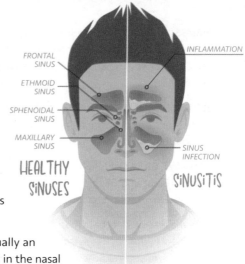

FRONTAL SINUS

ETHMOID SINUS

SPHENOIDAL SINUS

MAXILLARY SINUS

INFLAMMATION

SINUS INFECTION

HEALTHY SINUSES

SINUSITIS

Chronic sinus conditions are usually an immune disorder caused by fungi in the nasal passages causing them to become inflamed or blocked, leading to symptoms such as congestion, facial pain or pressure, nasal discharge, and headaches.

## NATURAL HEALERS FOR THE SINUS

In addition to the remedies for chest complaints, relief for sinus congestion and pain can also be found in the following natural methods:

**HUMMING:** Humming a tune is often associated with cheerfulness and thoughtful absorption. While it is a great way to lift your mood, it is also being recognized as very simple and enormously effective means of increasing sinus ventilation.

When we breathe through our nose, the sinus naturally produce nitric oxide, a gas with antifungal, antiviral, and antibacterial properties.[7] This helps to open up airways, kill the pathogens causing blocked sinus, and maintain a sterile environment for the sinuses. Humming dramatically increases the production of this gas by 15- to 20-fold compared with quiet exhalation.[8] The vibration caused by humming also has a toning and strengthening reaction for all the respiratory organs.

Nitric oxide is a potent bronchodilator, significantly increasing the lungs' oxygen-absorbing capacity,[7] which can also assist in managing asthma.

6.  Battisti AS, Modi P, Pangia J. (2023) "Sinusitis." [Updated 2023 Mar 2]. In: StatPearls [Internet]. StatPearls Publishing; 2024 Jan-. Available from: <https://www.ncbi.nlm.nih.gov/books/NBK470383>.

7.  Ruth A, (2015) "The health benefits of nose breathing." *Nursing in General Practice*, page 42 <http://hdl.handle.net/10147/559021> accessed March 2024.

8.  Weitzberg E and Lundberg J (2002) "Humming Greatly Increases Nasal Nitric Oxide." *American Journal of Respiratory and Critical Care Medicine*. Vol 166, Issue 2, pages 129-246 <doi.org/10.1164/rccm.200202-138BC>

**GOLDENSEAL:** The root of this herb is known as the 'king of tonics to mucous membranes', containing strong antimicrobial actives, including anti-staphylo-coccus, anti-streptococcus, antibiotic, and antifungal properties.

Sniffing goldenseal powder into the sinus through the nostrils can help to clean out the sinus cavity and boost healing. Only a very small amount is used. Sniff lightly and slowly. This can be done three times a day in an acute phase and eased off as the sinus heals.

**STEAM:** One of the most widely used home remedies to soothe and open the nasal passages is steam inhalation. To achieve this, carefully pour boiling water into a bowl containing a few drops of eucalyptus oil. Drape a towel over the back of your head and lean over the hot water creating an enclosed space. Be careful to avoid making direct contact with the water. Inhale slowly and deeply through your nose for at least two to five minutes.

It is vital to finish this treatment with a 20–30 second cold wet wipe over your face to seal the pores, equalize the circulation, and prevent chilling.

# ADENOIDS, TONSILS, AND SORE THROAT

Following the sinuses down we get to the adenoids. Adenoids are glands that sit at the very back of the nasal passage. This is the *rear guard* defense of the nasal system, working as infection fighters for babies and young children. When we breathe through our nose, airborne bacteria and viruses entering the body are filtered and trapped by hairs and mucus in the nose; the remainder are de-stroyed by antibodies and white blood cells made by the adenoids.

As adenoids trap germs that enter the body, they can become overloaded causing inflammation and reduced airflow through the nose. Inflammation is a healthy response to infection and injury, but swollen adenoids can be un-comfortable and the restricted airflow is the most common cause of mouth breathing in children. This can impact their dental and facial development, and is a leading cause of obstructive sleep apnea in children.[9]

If mouth breathing becomes a habit, the tonsils will also suffer.

Tonsils are small, round pieces of tissue located in the back of the mouth on both sides of the throat. Like the adenoids, tonsils are 'sentinels at the gate' ready to sound an alarm bell and fight if something comes into the body that may cause a problem. The tonsil's battalion is made up of a lot of white blood

---

9.   Lizhuo L, et al. (2022) "The impact of mouth breathing on dentofacial development: A concise review." *Frontiers in Public Health*, Vol 10 <https://doi.org/10.3389/fpubh.2022.929165>

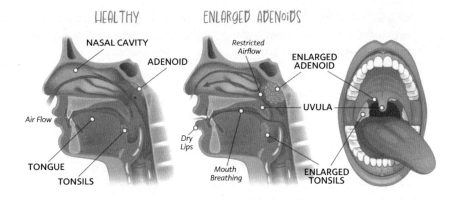

HEALTHY     ENLARGED ADENOIDS

cells used to *catch and kill* germs entering via the mouth or nose. Allergens or an influx of pathogens, can cause the tonsils to become overworked, very inflamed and infected. This is what causes tonsillitis.

Both tonsils and adenoids usually start to shrink after about age 6. By the teenage years, the adenoids are almost completely gone. However, their job is not finished and they can all swell up again with infections.

Tonsillectomy is the most common pediatric elective surgery for children in Australia.[10] It makes no sense to cut out these sentinels. Listen to them and give them the support they need to work efficiently. They are reacting for a reason, the most common being an allergy, as previously discussed.

# NATURAL HEALERS FOR TONSILS AND ADENOIDS

Tonsillitis is a common childhood illness that will usually go away on its own within a few days. There are several natural methods than can relieve pain and assist the tonsils and adenoids to protect the body, and prevent future infections. First, all allergens or irritants that are causing the inflammation need to be identified and eliminated. Follow this with some of the remedies for chest complaints as described previously. More specific treatments include:

**ICE:** Sucking on ice can be highly effective in treating pain, inflammation, and swelling that often comes with inflamed tonsils. The ice produces a local cooling effect on the nerve endings in the throat, thereby reducing the pain signals.

**SOOTHING TEAS:** The herb slippery elm contains a substance called mucilage, which turns into a gel-like matter when mixed with water. Drinking this gel

---

10. Greig SR. (2017). "Current perspectives on the role of tonsillectomy." *Journal of Paediatrics and Child Health.* Vol 53, issue 11, page 1065. doi: 10.1111/jpc.13745. PMID: 29148201.

can help coat your throat, soothing and protecting it when it is sore. Sipping hot ginger tea or lemon tea can also soothe the pain.

**ONION:** Wrapping an onion poultice around your throat overnight can bring great relief to a sore throat. To do this, finely slice an onion and place it in a clean sock; lay the sock over the front of the throat, then wrap a scarf around your neck to keep it warm and hold the sock in place.

**WET CLOTH:** Another old remedy is a wet cloth placed around the neck. Cover the cloth with plastic then wrapped with a scarf or bandage around it. This is good to wear overnight and is called a heating compress. It can greatly relieve a sore throat and instantly reduce coughing.

**SALT:** Gargling salt water is a common home remedy to relieve inflammation, swelling, and pain associated with enlarged adenoids. Another way salt can be used is in a saline (salt water) nasal spray. Researchers have found this is just as effective as an anti-inflammatory steroid nasal spray at easing breathing issues while sleeping, preventing the need to remove tonsils and adenoids.[11]

# STEP TWO:
## MANAGEMENT THROUGH 'SUSTAIN ME'

**SUNSHINE:** Allow the sunshine into your home, especially the bedroom. Sunshine on the skin produces vitamin D, a deficiency of this vitamin is significantly associated with recurrent tonsillitis.[12]

Sunshine purifies the air, and permitting the sun to rest on the face and chest helps the rays penetrate deep under the skin increasing blood circulation to these areas.

**USE OF WATER:** A tiny droplet of water is present in every alveolus, the tiny sacs that fill the lungs, and there are approximately 300 million of them. The alveoli are the site of gaseous exchange in the lungs. The surface tension property of water causes a total collapse of the alveoli, releasing all the carbon dioxide when we exhale. This total release means we can inhale a greater amount of air, so we breathe in more oxygen.

A well-hydrated body means more oxygen.

It is important to drink pure water, which is free from chlorine and fluoride.

11. Baker A, (2023) "Intranasal mometasone furoate for sleep-disordered breathing in children" *JAMA Pediatrics*, Vol 177, issue 3, pages 240–247. doi:10.1001/jamapediatrics.2022.5258.

12. Mirza AA, et al (2020), "The Association Between Vitamin D Deficiency and Recurrent Tonsillitis: A Systematic Review and Meta-analysis." *Otolaryngology—Head and Neck Surgery.* 2020 Nov; 163(5):883-891. doi: 10.1177/0194599820935442.

**SLEEP:** We sleep better when able to breathe fresh air all night, as oxygen soothes the nerves.

The bodies healing and regenerating hormones are most abundantly released in the early parts of the night. Going to sleep from 9pm is the optimal time for these hormones to perform their tasks in the respiratory organs.

 **TRUST IN DIVINE POWER:** Our respiratory organs require us to believe they will heal as we give them the right conditions.

Resist any thoughts that could interfere with this process, and access the power of thanking God daily for these wonderful organs that deliver us life-giving oxygen. *"Let everything that has breath praise the Lord."* Psalm 150:6

 **ABSTAIN:** Eliminate all known causative factors such as ceasing to ingest all known food allergens.

Aim for a chemical-free home, replacing personal care and cleaning products with biodegradable alternatives.

Investigate whether there is any trace of mold in the home, especially the bedroom. This includes mattresses, pillows, quilts, and carpets.

Abstain from mouth breathing.

**INHALE:** Our nose acts as a sort of natural medical device filtering toxins, humidifying and pressurizing the air, and producing the nitric oxide that the lower airways and lungs require to work effectively. Mouth breathing does none of these things. Ensure you breathe through your nose.

Nose breathing maintains adequate amounts of carbon dioxide which relaxes smooth muscle causing a bronchodilation effect. Studies have shown that breathing lightly and only through the nose is the ideal technique for relaxation, optimal health, and decreasing asthma related symptoms.[13]

The abdominal muscles were designed to aid in the breathing process. When the shoulders are back and the spine upright, this allows the diaphragm to fully expand to guarantee a complete gaseous exchange between air and carbon dioxide. This will maintain the correct level of oxygen the body needs.

Usually, nose breathing with long slow breaths is ideal, but when a person is in breathing distress, such as during an asthma attack, the Buteyko method of breathing can bring great relief by relaxing and opening the bronchioles.

---

13. Hassan, E.E.M., et al (2022). "Effect of the Buteyko breathing technique on asthma severity control among school age children." Egypt J Bronchol;. <https://doi.org/10.1186/s43168-022-00149-3>

The steps for the Buteyko Breathing Technique are as follows:[14]

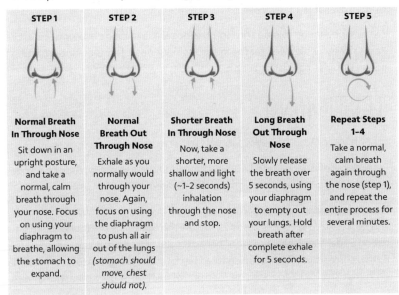

| STEP 1 | STEP 2 | STEP 3 | STEP 4 | STEP 5 |
|---|---|---|---|---|
| **Normal Breath In Through Nose** | **Normal Breath Out Through Nose** | **Shorter Breath In Through Nose** | **Long Breath Out Through Nose** | **Repeat Steps 1-4** |
| Sit down in an upright posture, and take a normal, calm breath through your nose. Focus on using your diaphragm to breathe, allowing the stomach to expand. | Exhale as you normally would through your nose. Again, focus on using the diaphragm to push all air out of the lungs *(stomach should move, chest should not).* | Now, take a shorter, more shallow and light (~1-2 seconds) inhalation through the nose and stop. | Slowly release the breath over 5 seconds, using your diaphragm to empty out your lungs. Hold breath after complete exhale for 5 seconds. | Take a normal, calm breath again through the nose (step 1), and repeat the entire process for several minutes. |

**NUTRITION:** Choose foods that are less likely to be mucus-forming. This includes gluten free grains. Make sure the grains are not hybridized or genetically modified. It is important to prepare grains in an easily digestible way, such as by pressure cooking or culturing the flours to make sour-dough bread.

Ideally, eat legumes daily. Soak, rinse, and pressure cook the dried beans.

Include nuts and seeds with each meal as well as eating organic, tree-ripened fruits and vegetables freely—some raw and some cooked.

Finally, include healthy coconut and olive oils in your diet.

These essential food groups will supply the respiratory organs with the basic building materials for healing.

**MODERATION:** Be appropriately dressed for the weather conditions. Both under and overdressing can cause problems.

**EXERCISE:** High Intensity Interval Training is the most effective type of exercise for the lungs. It gives the bronchioles a major workout, forcing them to open more and more every day.

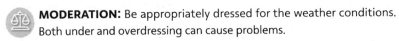

14. Adapted from *A Short Guide to Breathing Right—the Buteyko Breathing Method* by IM Health Team <https://innovativemedicine.com/short-guide-breathing-right-buteyko-breathing-method>

The result is not only an increase in lung capacity but also a higher amount of oxygen available for every cell.

Always inhale and exhale through the nose. Nitric oxide is produced in the nasal airways when we breathe in through our nose, this is an important first line of defense against infection.

# TESTIMONY
## PETER'S ASTHMA JOURNEY

Peter's grandfather suffered from asthma until the age of 50, when he discovered that eliminating dairy from his diet cleared it.

Peter's aunt suffered severely from asthma. The youngest of five children, she was hospitalized several times as a child. At the age of 45, she found that eliminating all dairy and wheat reduced her asthma attacks dramatically. Learning the Buteyko Breathing Technique enabled her to stop taking Ventolin, an asthma drug that she had depended on for most of her life. She is now asthma free.

At the age of ten months, my son Peter had his first asthma attack. It is a frightening experience seeing your child unable to breathe properly. The simple treatments I had used with my four other children seemed almost ineffective when Peter had an asthma attack.

Within 24 hours of getting a cold, Peter would be in severe breathing distress. We rushed him to the hospital where they gave him Ventolin and kept him in for observation for a few days. This gave minor relief. Keeping him calm and holding him seemed to help the most.

Peter was hospitalized at 10, 12, and 13 months.

Upon reading a newspaper article quoting a medical study that found Ventolin reduced lung capacity, I decided to explore alternatives.

The naturopath acknowledged that Peter was not well and explained that every time he was sick, it was an opportunity to use herbs and water treatments to strengthen his lungs. I had not heard this before.

He advised that I feed Peter very lightly when he first developed a cold. Peter was 14 months now and fully breastfed, eating a little.

Hydrotherapy treatments were also suggested to ease his breathing distress, as well as a warm water enema, and hot and cold compresses to the chest.

The herbs the naturopath suggested were slippery elm and licorice mixed with warm water, taken three times daily.

I eliminated the small amount of dairy we were having in our diet, then discovered that the herb plantain, which was growing freely in our yard, is an expectorant. It works on the lungs, to cleanse and strengthen them. At the first sign of a cold, I would make a tea from the herb, add a small amount of honey and lemon, and give at least a litre a day to Peter. I believe this played a part in his healing.

Two weeks after this visit to the naturopath, Peter came down with a cold. The only food I gave him was watermelon. His main sustenance was breast milk. After 24 hours, he was in severe breathing distress. Using the wonderful art of distraction, I was able to give Peter an enema with a cup of warm water.

With a pile of books to read and the children's help, we managed to give him hot and cold compresses on his chest. He also took the herbs.

The severe breathing distress was cut from 24 hours to five hours! I was impressed and thanked God for this advice I had received on how to work with the body to bring relief and healing.

We treated Peter's asthma like this twice more in the following year.

When Peter was two and a half, he got a cold. I was heavily pregnant with my sixth child. Fearing the worst, I asked God to help me trust Him that Peter would be fine as I went into labor. Thankfully William was an easy birth, and Peter did not go into breathing distress. In fact, Peter never again went into breathing distress.

Peter is in his mid-30s now and looks like a bodybuilder. He has a very strong body and has fathered two children, who show no signs of having asthma.

This experience has proved to me two things:

▶ Though genetics may load the gun, it is lifestyle that pulls the trigger.

▶ The human body has been created to heal itself, when given the right conditions.

# CHAPTER 4

# LOVE YOUR HEART WITH ALL YOUR HEART

Heart disease is the number one killer in the world today.[1] King Solomon, the wisest man in world taught *"Knowledge is easy to him that understands"* Proverbs 14:6. As we understand how the heart, blood, and blood vessels function in the body, we will gain the knowledge on how to give them the optimum conditions to prevent and conquer heart disease.

The heart is a muscle; therefore, it can be strengthened or weakened. Its role is to pump blood around the body.

Proverbs 4:23 says, *"Keep your heart with all diligence, for out of it spring the issues of life"*, and Leviticus 17:11 states that *"the life of the flesh is in the blood."* We know blood carries water, nutrients, and oxygen to every cell and carries away waste. Blood also contains white blood cells, which are an important part of our immune system. Therefore, it is the LIFE of the flesh. Without blood, the cells die.

There are three main subjects we will discuss here:

1. The heart
2. The blood
3. The vessels that carry the blood

In this discussion, we will address the causes and cure of high blood pressure, heart arrhythmia, heart disease, and blocked arteries.

---

1. The Top 10 Causes of Death, *World Health Organization*, https://www.who.int/news-room/fact-sheets/detail/the-top-10-causes-of-death December 2020.

# THE SOLUTIONS

## STEP ONE: BRING RELIEF

To bring quick relief to a racing heart, palpitations, heart arrhythmia, or possible stroke and heart failure, these tips may help:

### > Cayenne Pepper

Take a capsule or one teaspoon of cayenne pepper. Cayenne pepper is a vasodilator (opens blood vessels), it thins the blood which causes a more effective flow of blood through the circulatory system.[2]

### > Breath

Inhaling through the nose, slow, low, and deep for a count of five seconds, holding breath for three seconds and exhaling for over five seconds causes an increase of nitric oxide and carbon dioxide. This can be repeated ten times. These two gases have a vasodilator effect in the blood capillaries.

### > Magnesium

Magnesium is the fourth most abundant element in the human body and is central to a healthy heart rhythm.

Most people get all the magnesium they need from food such as leafy green vegetables like spinach, or legumes, nuts, seeds and whole grains. However when suffering health problems such as high blood pressure, magnesium deficiency or irregular heartbeat a 500mg dose of magnesium citrate, (a type of magnesium in salt form that is combined with citric acid) can help.[3] Magnesium citrate is absorbed relatively well by the body and can easily dissolve in water, this can be taken several times a day whilst symptoms persist. As a muscle relaxant, magnesium relaxes the heart at rest, thus helping to reduce high blood pressure, relax palpitations and a racing heart.

This mineral can play an important role in conquering these conditions while waiting for lifestyle changes to take effect.

---

2. McCarty MF, et al. (2015), "Capsaicin may have important potential for promoting vascular and metabolic health." *Open Heart*, doi: <10.1136/openhrt-2015-000262>
3. Houston, M. (2011), "The Role of Magnesium in Hypertension and Cardiovascular Disease." *The Journal of Clinical Hypertension*, abstract Vol 13 Issue 11 <https://doi.org/10.1111/j.1751-7176.2011.00538.x>

# 1. THE HEART

## STEP TWO:
## MANAGEMENT THROUGH 'SUSTAIN ME'

**SUNSHINE:** Exposure to sunshine ensures adequate levels of vitamin D, which is essential for the delivery of calcium and magnesium to the heart muscle. Calcium constricts, and magnesium relaxes. These two minerals are required for the peak efficiency of heart function, namely, the beat!

Studies have shown that getting at least 30 minutes of sunlight exposure a day can reduce blood pressure to a degree great enough to reduce your risk of cardiovascular disease.[4]

**USE OF WATER:** All cells require water to aid in the elimination of waste and every single other function. Dehydration inhibits the heart's ability to effectively perform its tasks.

The average water loss in 24 hours is two and a half liters. Two liters need to be replaced with pure water. The remaining half a litre can be replaced with liquid from fresh fruit and vegetables, herbal teas, and vegetable juice.

It is best to drink between meals to ensure effective digestion.

**SLEEP:** Getting enough quality sleep is an essential component of good heart and brain health. Between the hours of 10pm and 3am in summer and 9pm to 2am in winter, is the best time to sleep. This is when the brain releases hormones that are responsible for rejuvenation, rest, and repair. The heart muscle needs you to be sleeping in these hours for optimum heart

---

4.   Weller, RB (2016). "Sunlight Has Cardiovascular Benefits Independently of Vitamin D." *Blood Purification.* Vol 41 Issue 1–3, pages 130–134.

maintenance and development. Over time, poor sleep patterns can also lead to unhealthy habits that can further hurt your heart, including higher stress levels, less motivation to be physically active, and unhealthy food choices.

**TRUST IN DIVINE POWER:** Holding a grudge affects your cardiovascular and nervous system,[5] it may be someone who has hurt you, or you may be feeling guilty for hurting someone else. When you focus on these events it can increase your heart rate, blood pressure, and muscle tension. You may feel like you don't have control but forgiveness can reverse these effects.

Remember that no matter how much we have wronged God, out of love, He aways forgives us. So too, we need to be willing to forgive others.

*"Make allowance for each other's faults, and forgive anyone who offends you. Remember, the Lord forgave you, so you must forgive others."* Colossians 3:13 NLT

We can prevent many problems in life by ensuring that our body and heart are given the required conditions for optimum performance.

**ABSTAIN:** This is defined as not taking anything into the body that would interfere with heart function. A sure and steady heartbeat is important for proper heart health. There are a few things that commonly cause or aggravate allergies, and thus can disrupt the heartbeat. This can manifest itself as heart arrhythmia. Examples of such disrupters are:

> **Wheat**
> People with heart arrhythmia are best to abstain from having wheat in their diet.[6] The hybridization of wheat in the 1950's created a protein or gluten structure that is very complex. This complex structure is difficult for the gut to digest and can cause partially digested particles to enter the bloodstream. This can cause an allergic response, which may produce heart arrhythmia.

> **Smoking**
> If you smoke, you are four times more likely to die of heart disease.[7] With its 4,000 chemicals, tobacco has the potential to damage the heart muscle. The carbon monoxide that is released by the cigarette competes with oxygen, which effectively robs the heart cell of oxygen.

5.  Chida Y, Steptoe A. (2009). "The association of anger and hostility with future coronary heart disease: a meta-analytic review of prospective evidence." *Journal of the American College of Cardiology.* Vol 53, Issue 11, pages 936-946. doi: 10.1016/j.jacc.2008.11.044.

6.  Dr. William Davis (2014). "Wheat And Atrial Fibrillation? A Look At the Correlation" <https://drdavisinfinitehealth.com/2014/05/wheat-and-atrial-fibrillation/> accessed July 2023."

7.  "Smoking and your heart" National Heart Foundation of Australia < https://www.heartfoundation.org.au/bundles/your-heart/smoking-and-your-heart> accessed July 2023.

> **Alcohol**
Alcohol is a well-known poison and has the ability to interfere with blood pressure and heart rate causing heart palpitations, especially in patients with previous heart problems.

> **Red Meat**
Consuming red (and processed) meat has been associated with increased deaths from cardiovascular disease. Evidence from observational studies indicates a higher intake of red meat is associated with a higher risk of stroke.[8]

> **Other**
Other disrupters include some drugs and vaccines[9] that have side effects which are known to affect heart function. Refined sugar may also have this effect on some people.

**INHALE:** When a cell receives adequate oxygen to allow the energy to move to the Krebs cycle (the cell's energy cycle), it can produce 18 times more energy. The heart is made up of cells, and when every heart cell receives adequate oxygen, the heart will perform with greater efficiency. Inhaling and exhaling through the nose maintains sufficient carbon dioxide in the blood, which is necessary for the cells to receive optimal oxygen.

Be mindful that you breathe the best quality air.

**NUTRITION:** Keeping the heart working efficiently includes ensuring the cells are well nourished. Several nutritional items that can assist in heart health include:

> **Fibre**
A plant-based diet contains all the nutrients needed for optimum performance. High fibre (which a plant-based diet contains in abundance) not only provides a broom to aid bowel movements but also vitamins and minerals vital for an effective heartbeat.

Vegetables, particularly dark, green leafy vegetables, beans, whole and gluten free grains, seeds, and nuts are all high sources of fibre and minerals, and are able to help the body maintain correct blood cholesterol levels.

> **Salt**
Not all salts are the same, Celtic salt contains 82 minerals; devitalized salt (such as common table salt) only contains two minerals, sodium and

---

8.  Chen GC, et al (2013). "Red and processed meat consumption and risk of stroke: a meta-analysis of prospective cohort studies." *European Journal of Clinical Nutrition.* Jan 2013; 67(1):91-5.

9.  Paknahad, MH, Yancheshmeh FB, Soleimani A. (2023) "Cardiovascular complications of COVID-19 vaccines: A review of case-report and case-series studies." *Heart & Lung.* Vol 59 pages 173-180.

chloride. These two minerals are quite harsh and require all the other minerals to buffer them. This also causes an imbalance of minerals in and out of the cell, which can increase blood pressure.

Taking a small crystal of Celtic salt before each glass of water ensures you will receive adequate minerals. See The Relationship between Water and Salt on page 118 for more about the benefits of Celtic salt.

> **Protein**

Generous protein not only allows for function, but also repair. The best quality proteins are found in legumes (always soaked, rinsed, and pressure cooked), nuts, and seeds. Legumes are frequently consumed as an alternative to meat and have been proven to reduce cardiovascular disease.[10]

> **Fats**

Healthy fats such as from nuts, seeds, avocados, and coconut or olive oils contain essential nutrients that are required for heart cell membrane function and repair.

It is often taught that fats cause a build up of cholesterol which leads to heart and blood vessel problems. In his book *The Great Cholesterol Con*, Dr Malcolm Kendrick shows that there is no proof that high cholesterol leads to heart disease and explores in detail the history of the erroneous theory that fat causes heart disease, which has never been proven.

**MODERATION:** Moderation in all things protects the heart. Many studies have been done to see if there's a direct link between caffeine, coffee drinking, and coronary heart disease with some believing that coffee can have a beneficial effect on heart health. The results are conflicting, however it is acknowledged that caffeine has an effect on the body similar to a crisis by activating the noradrenaline neurons,[11] which are part of your body's emergency response system to danger. For those prone to heart issues, caffeine-related palpitations can come from drinks that are high in caffeine.[12] Caffeine robs the body of magnesium and calcium, the two minerals that directly affect the beat of the heart and the relaxation between beats. Try switching highly concentrated caffeinated drinks for natural foods containing lots of nutrients.

10.  Miller V, t al. (2017). "Fruit, vegetable, and legume intake, and cardiovascular disease and deaths in 18 countries (PURE): a prospective cohort study." *The Lancet.* Vol 390, Issue 10107, pages 2037–2049. doi: 10.1016/S0140-6736(17)32253-5. Accessed January 2024.

11.  Nehlig A, Daval JL, Debry G. (1992) "Caffeine and the central nervous system." *Brain Research Reviews.* Vol 17, Issue 2, May–August 1992, Pages 139–170.

12.  Dr Michael Giudici (2016) "Understanding heart palpitations" The University of Iowa Hospitals & Clinics, <https://uihc.org/health-topics/understanding-heart-palpitations> accessed July 2023.

**EXERCISE:** The most effective exercise for heart strength is High Intensity Interval Training (HIIT). As the name implies, these are intervals of High Intensity (HI) and Recovery (RE), usually comprising 30 seconds HI and 90 seconds RE. Ideally, this is done for a cycle of six.

▶ Dr Doug McGuff explains the benefits in his book, *Body by Science*.

▶ See also Dr Michael Mosley's book, *Fast Exercise: The simple secret of high intensity training.*

▶ Dr Al Sears, in his book, *Pace: The 12-Minute Fitness Revolution*, adds to the list of research and clinical practice on the powerful effect of HIIT exercise on the heart.

As the heart is a muscle, the more you use it, the stronger it gets. This requires consistency and diligence.

## HERBS FOR THE HEART

Hawthorn berry is a herb that strengthens the heart. It can even bring the heart rate back to normality in the case of heart arrhythmia.

This berry can be also used to reduce high blood pressure. As all herbs do, it works with the body's systems. The plant's active ingredients have a balancing effect, so they can also raise the blood pressure if it is too low.

If taken as a tea, the recipe is two teaspoons of dried berries to one cup of water. This is gently simmered for ten minutes.

The dose is to drink one litre over the day. The more seriously ill patient may need higher dosages and can take the herb in tablet form at 3,000–4,000mg a day. This is a very safe herb and can be taken in conjunction with medication.[13] As the blood pressure balances, so the amount of hawthorn berry taken can be reduced.

---

13. Tassell MC, et al (2010). "Hawthorn (Crataegus spp.) in the treatment of cardiovascular disease." *Pharmacognosy Reviews*. Vol 4, Issue 7, Jan–Jun, 2010, pages 32–41.

# 2. BLOOD
## MANAGEMENT
## THROUGH 'SUSTAIN ME'

Considering that blood contains nutrients, water and oxygen, ensuring adequate supplies of all three is essential for top quality blood.

Conditions were covered in our previous discussion on the heart, but let us peruse these subjects a little more in relation to blood.

For the heart to pump blood effectively and efficiently, blood must be thin. Thick blood is hard to pump.

**SUNSHINE:** Exposure to the sun has many benefits, even helping thin the blood. Exposure to ultraviolet light, which comes naturally from the sun, dilates blood vessels which significantly lowers blood pressure.[14]

**USE OF WATER:** The most effective blood thinner is water. In dehydration, the blood can become thicker, and this puts an extra load on the heart. Sipping water throughout the day allows the body to use water more effectively and maintain the desired fluidity of the blood. Ideally, no more than half a glass of water should be drunk at a time. The blood benefits more from taking water in smaller amounts regularly than it does from drinking large amounts all at once. Red blood cells carry oxygen, keeping well hydrated to prevent them from clumping together enables hemoglobin to better carry the oxygen.

As blood is salty, mineral rich whole salt is also required. A small crystal of Celtic salt before you begin each glass will replace the minerals lost the day before. Dr Robert Thompson explains this in his book, *The Calcium Lie.*

If a person is not used to salt, start with small doses.

**SLEEP:** As with the heart, so with blood fluidity, the body needs to sleep eight hours at night. A regular lack of sleep may lead to high blood pressure (hypertension) in children and adults. Sleep helps the body control hormones needed to control stress and metabolism. Over time, a lack of sleep could cause

---

14. Feelisch M, et al (2010). "Is sunlight good for our heart?" *European Heart Journal*, Vol 31 Issue 9, May 2010, Pages 1041–1045. <https://academic.oup.com/eurheartj/article/31/9/1041/591567?>

swings in hormones. Hormone changes can lead to high blood pressure and other risk factors for heart disease.[15]

**TRUST IN DIVINE POWER:** Leviticus 17:14 speaks of the importance of blood for life, stating, *"For it [blood] is the life of all flesh. Its blood sustains its life."* Although physical blood sustains physical life, Jesus' lifeblood is the only blood that provides eternal life (Colossians 1:13-14).

Stress has the ability to cause muscle tightening throughout the body which can affect blood flow, but when we consider all that God has done for us through His Son we have reason to rejoice and let Him take away the stress in our life.

*"But let all those rejoice who put their trust in You; Let them ever shout for joy, because You defend them; Let those also who love Your name be joyful in You."* Psalm 5:11.

**ABSTAIN:** This is what we don't want.

Caffeine, alcohol, drugs, refined sugar, and altered or heated fats all have a dehydrating effect on the blood, thus contributing to thick or dense blood where the red blood cells can clump together.

Recent medical procedures (which claim to prevent viral illnesses) that contain spike proteins, have been shown to cause an increased risk of venous thromboembolism, a term referring to blood clots in the veins.[16]

**INHALE:** Breathing in and out through the nostrils, not only purifies, humidifies, and warms the air but also has a stabilizing effect on blood. Evidence has shown that a slow and deep breathing rate, around 10 breaths per minute or less, significantly reduces blood pressure.[17]

**NUTRITION:** Food that strengthens the heart will also contribute to supplying the essential nutrients to make top quality blood. Especially dark green, leafy vegetables which are naturally high in chlorophyll (the pigment that gives plants their green colour) as this makes them most effective blood cleansers.

---

15. Francisco Lopez-Jimenez, M.D. (2022) "Sleep deprivation: A cause of high blood pressure?" Mayo Clinic, 09 Aug 2022 <https://www.mayoclinic.org>.

16. Li X, Burn E, Duarte-Salles T, et al. (2022) "Comparative risk of thrombosis with thrombocytopenia syndrome or thromboembolic events associated with different Covid-19 vaccines: International network cohort study from five European countries and the US." *British Medical Journal*, 26 Oct 2022, <https://www.bmj.com/content/379/bmj-2022-071594>.

17. Russo MA, Santarelli DM, O'Rourke D (2017). "The physiological effects of slow breathing in the healthy human." Breathe. Vol 13 Issue 4, pages 298-309.

**MODERATION:** People taking prescription blood thinners should be careful when using natural remedies without talking with their doctor first. Even though they are natural, some substances and foods may thin the blood too much, especially when people take them in conjunction with medications. This can increase the risk of bleeding. If you are on blood thinning medication this will need to be monitored and your medication adjusted.

**EXERCISE:** Exercise not only ensures an increase of oxygen in the blood by increasing respiration and lung capacity, but also increases blood movement throughout the whole body by increasing and strengthening the heart rate.

## HERBS FOR THE BLOOD

> **Cayenne Pepper**
This herb is not only an effective blood thinner but also dilates the blood vessels and strengthens the arterial walls.

To begin with, a quarter teaspoon can be taken in a third of a cup of water three times daily. This dose can be increased to half a teaspoon as required.

The well-known herb book written in the early 1900s, *Back to Eden* by Jethro Kloss, devotes ten pages to cayenne pepper. Other herbs are given half a page. He shows that this is a very safe herb and cannot be overused. *Curing with Cayenne* by Sam Biser explains in detail the wonders of cayenne pepper.

> **Garlic and Ginger**
Garlic and ginger both contain blood thinning and cholesterol-lowering active ingredients in their chemical structure.

> **OMEGA-3**
Omega-3 is an essential fatty acid found in flaxseed, chia seeds, and walnuts. With three double bonds in its chemical structure, this oil has a blood thinning effect.

Many fish contain Omega-3, but are commonly found to contain high amounts of mercury and dioxins.

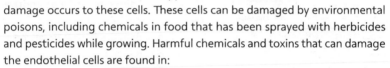

ENDOTHELIAL CELLS

# 3. BLOOD VESSELS
## MANAGEMENT
## THROUGH 'SUSTAIN ME'

As with heart and blood, the same SUSTAIN
ME principles can be applied.

The inner lining of blood vessels are called
endothelial cells. A common and early
event in cardiovascular disease happens when
damage occurs to these cells. These cells can be damaged by environmental
poisons, including chemicals in food that has been sprayed with herbicides
and pesticides while growing. Harmful chemicals and toxins that can damage
the endothelial cells are found in:

▶ Cleaning products, including dish washing, laundry detergents, and soaps
▶ Personal care products such as shampoo, toothpaste, sunscreens, perfumes, and cosmetics
▶ Paints and glues
▶ Cigarettes, which contain an estimated 4,000 chemicals or more
▶ Heavy metals such as mercury, can be found in amalgam tooth fillings, fish, and some vaccines
▶ Mold
▶ Altered and polyunsaturated fats such as canola and vegetable oils. These become especially carcinogenic when heated
▶ Margarine and food deep fried in polyunsaturated fats top the list of toxic fats
▶ Even some fabrics contain chemicals, including polyester, acrylic, and nylon. Brominated fire retardants (used in many consumer products) are known to overstimulate the adrenal gland in a way that may lead to the development of cardiovascular disease.[18]

Doctor Natasha Campbell-McBride describes this process in her book *Put Your Heart in Your Mouth* where she devotes the first few chapters of her book to defining the many environmental poisons that have been shown to damage the endothelial cells.

---

18. Endocrine Society (2016) "Common flame retardant chemical disrupts a hormone that is essential to life." *ScienceDaily*. <https://www.sciencedaily.com/releases/2016/04/160404091227.htm>.

# CHOLESTEROL

As this damage to the endothelial cells occurs, the body has a process of repairing and rebuilding. Low Density Lipoprotein (LDL) is the cholesterol made by the body to heal this damage. LDL literally plugs up the holes that result from the damage sustained by these environmental poisons.

Most are unaware of the damage these articles cause, so the weakening of the blood vessel walls continues along with the corresponding attempt by LDL to repair the problem. This buildup and resulting scar tissue is called atherosclerosis.

LDL is often referred to as the *bad* cholesterol, as it is found to be clogging up the arteries, but as already discussed, it's just doing its job of repair. LDL has another role, which is to deliver cholesterol to the brain. The brain is the fattiest organ in the body, and cholesterol plays an important role, not only in brain function but also in protection against damage.

High Density Lipoprotein (HDL) is considered the *good* cholesterol, as it carries any excess cholesterol from the arteries back to the liver. Blaming cholesterol for heart disease is like blaming fire trucks for fires!

Something else is happening that compounds the problem.

A diet high in sugar and wheat results in excess glucose being present in the blood. The presence of high glucose can result in a connection with protein molecules, and this union creates a sticky substance that sticks to the arterial wall, contributing to the buildup. These sticky molecules often dislodge and move, blocking the artery, and becoming one of the main causes of heart attacks and strokes.

## FURTHER READING

There are several writers and doctors who have blown the whistle on the fact that it is not cholesterol that causes heart disease but damage to the arterial wall. These include:

- *The Great Cholesterol Con*, by Dr Malcolm Kendrick,
- *The Great Cholesterol Deception* by Dr Peter Dingle,
- *The Great Cholesterol Myth* by Johnny Bowden,
- *The Great Cholesterol Lie* by Dr Dwight Lundell,
- *Put Your Heart in Your Mouth* by Dr Natasha Campbell-McBride and
- *Cereal Killer* by Alan Watson.

These books also explain the danger of cholesterol-lowering medication.

The lifestyle and dietary principles outlined previously will do much to keep the blood thin, strengthen the arterial walls, and aid in the cleaning and eliminating of buildup on the artery walls.

# TESTIMONy
## HARRY'S RETREAT

Harry came to our retreat to have a rest. As a retired judge, he had had a hectic life, and was taking six medications. These were to thin his blood and manage high blood pressure, cholesterol, blood sugar, gout and stomach ulcers.

At the age of 68, Harry was carrying 40kg of extra weight and wished to lose this to help him enjoy his retirement.

The lectures and experience at the retreat opened Harry's eyes. He had never realized how much diet and lifestyle can affect our health, and he agreed to try the hawthorn berry.

As Harry left the retreat, he was excited to begin implementing what he had learnt when he went home. As a bachelor, he felt he could easily make some changes. He felt he had nothing to lose.

Four months later, Harry rang to see if he could visit, so we invited him for lunch. I did not recognize Harry when I opened the door. He had lost 20kg.

"I have a few stories for you," he declared, with a big smile. "My doctor has taken me off all my medications. My blood pressure is 125/75, best it's been since my 40s. My blood sugar, cholesterol, and blood viscosity are all in a normal range. I have no more gout or stomach ulcers, and I do not need to have my knee replacement! My doctor is astonished. He has been my attending physician for 25 years."

What I love about Harry's story is that he heard the principles and went home and took action. He proved to his doctor that he was able to manage his health problems. So, his doctor quickly ceased all medication, as the medication would just keep doing its job, and Harry's levels would begin to go too low.

One year later, Harry wrote to state that he had lost an additional 18kg of weight being a total of 38kg since changing his diet and lifestyle.

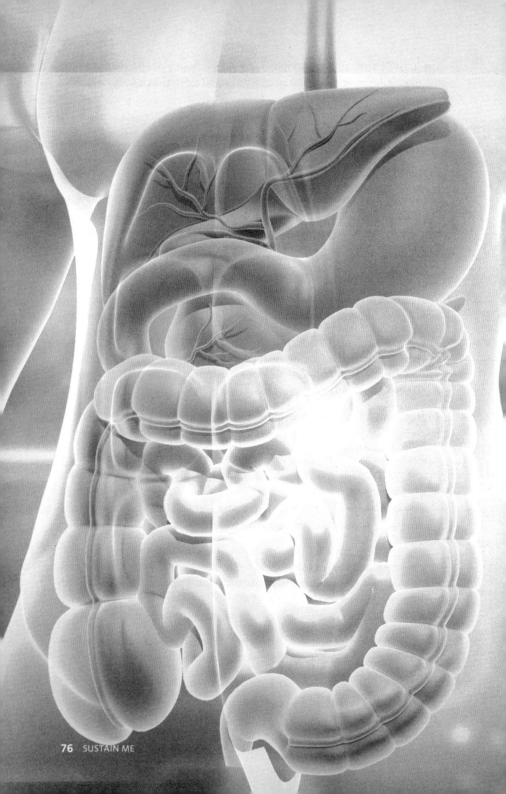

CHAPTER 5

# THE GASTROiNTESTiNAL TRACT

Your digestive system is uniquely designed to do the job of turning the food you eat into the nutrients and energy you need to grow, repair cells, stay healthy, and live. When it's done extracting the things your body needs, it packages the waste into a solid stool for disposal in your next bowel movement.

There are many parts and functions of the gastrointestinal tract; a series of hollow organs joined in a long, twisting tube from the mouth passing through the oesophagus, stomach, small intestine, and large intestine, to the anus. Each of these sections of the tract has a specific purpose. We will consider these purposes to gain an understanding on how they work and ensure optimal performance. *"Knowledge is easy to him who understands"* Proverbs 14:6.

## TO STRENGTHEN THE STOMACH

The poor old stomach is much misunderstood and overworked, and yet, its efficient or inefficient functioning affects digestion all the way down the gastrointestinal tract. As a result, the whole body and absolutely every cell is affected.

To understand the stomach, we need to consider the entry point: the mouth.

# THE MOUTH

The mouth is the only part of the gastrointestinal tract that we have a say over:

1. We decide WHAT goes in

2. We decide HOW MUCH goes in

3. We decide HOW LONG it stays in the mouth

4. We decide HOW OFTEN and WHEN food goes in

5. We decide the ENVIRONMENT we are in as we eat.

## 1) What Goes In

We choose whether we eat nourishing, wholesome food or refined and devitalized foods. The nourishing food helps the body to function efficiently and repair, whereas devitalized foods not only prevents proper function and repair but also causes damage to cells.

The three essential food groups are fibre, protein, and fat.

**FIBRE:** All plant foods contain fibre.

**PROTEIN:** The best protein is from plant seeds, as they contain all the nutrients necessary for growth and life. Legumes, nuts, and seeds are ideally eaten at every meal to access their life giving properties.

**FAT:** The seeds of plants also contain high-quality fats. Coconut and olive oils are two fats extracted from the flesh of the plant. That means high heat and chemical equipment are not required to extract the oils, as in the case of hard seeds. It is best to obtain the oils from the seed by eating the seed or nut.

We also choose whether we drink with our meals. While drinking water is vital for health, large amounts of fluid during a meal can leave you feeling bloated, or affect gastric reflux and slow digestion.

To avoid this, hydrate between meals, ceasing about half hour before the meal. This can help you fend off cravings that are really just dehydration in disguise, and eliminates the desire to drink large amounts at meal times, this includes fruit juices and teas.

## 2) How Much Goes In
The stomach can only hold so much food. Overeating burdens the stomach, causing it to expand beyond its normal size to adjust to the large amount of food. The expanded stomach pushes against other organs, making you un-comfortable. To digest the extra food the stomach produces more hydrochloric acid and this acid may back up into the oesophagus resulting in heartburn.[1]

This burden calls on extra forces from the brain and muscles, and many can testify they feel fatigued and sleepy when they overeat. It is best to stop eating before you feel full.

## 3) How Long in the Mouth
Even though we think our stomach does all the digestion of food the truth is our stomachs don't have teeth! The teeth are designed to masticate, or break down, our food into very fine pieces. This produces a larger surface area for the digestive enzymes to work on, which allows the tongue to message the brain to monitor what food types are in the mouth. These messages are sent to the appropriate organs, giving them time to prepare for different types of food.

When food is not effectively chewed, all these processes are compromised. Chewing your food slowly and thoroughly also helps you eat less naturally and prevent overeating.

---

1.  The University of Texas MD Anderson Cancer Center (2018) "What happens when you overeat?".

## 4) How Often

Your stomach squeezes food and mixes it with acid and enzymes to break it down. This process can take three and a half to four hours to digest a meal. It is important to grant it sufficient time to do this. Giving the stomach a rest of one hour after digestion gives the gastric glands time to replace the stomach juices in preparation for the next meal. This requires a five to six hour break between meals. Studies have also shown that eating only two meals a day, preferably breakfast and lunch with a five to six hour gap between the meals, is an effective strategy for weight control and preventing obesity.[2]

## A STOMACH WITH A WINDOW

Dr William Beaumont proved the need for breaks between meals in his landmark study in the early 1800s. His book, *Experiments and Observation on The Gastric Juice and The Physiology of Digestion*, rocked the nutritional world and immediately received international acclaim. The book was first written in 1833. I have the 1959 edition.

He discoveries occurred in a very unique way. Dr Beaumont was called to an accident in a trading store. An 18-year-old man (Alexis St Martin) had sustained a gunshot wound to his right side, which had injured his stomach and some of his ribs. He eventually healed but was left with a hole in his stomach, somewhat like a mouth. Dr Beaumont saw the opportunity and began experimenting using a silk thread with a piece of food tied to the end.

At intervals of one, two, three, four, and five hours, he would check the stage of digestion of the food. He found that digestion averaged three and a half to four hours. There were exceptions depending on the food eaten, how much of it there was, and whether the patient was stressed when eating.

Beaumont meticulously documented his findings in his book and while his experiments are often criticized from a modern medical ethics standpoint, his discoveries have remained important nearly 200 years later[3] and are still quoted in most anatomy and physiology books today.

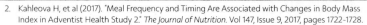

2. Kahleova H, et al (2017). "Meal Frequency and Timing Are Associated with Changes in Body Mass Index in Adventist Health Study 2." *The Journal of Nutrition.* Vol 147, Issue 9, 2017, pages 1722-1728.

3. Stephen Logsdon (2021) "William Beaumont's Momentous and Unethical Experiments" Bernard Becker Medical Library, Washington University. August 26, 2021 <https://becker.wustl.edu>

Dr Michael Mosley, in his book, *Fast Diet*, talks of allowing the stomach to rest between meals. He refers to this as Time Restrictive Eating (TRE). It involves eating twice in a six hour period out of the 24-hour day, which allows the stomach to have about an 18-hour fast.

Breakfast is at 7:30am, and lunch is at 1:30pm. 9am and 3pm could also be chosen, it all depends on what works for you. This program has proven to increase insulin sensitivity in the cell, improve the metabolic rate, give better quality sleep, and be a powerful tool in weight loss.

For this distance between meals to be achieved with ease, a high fibre plant-based diet is essential. Generous amounts of protein, such as legumes, nuts, and seeds, must be included, as well as healthy fats, such as nuts, seeds, avocado, coconut and olive oils.

Most foods that are high in fibre or protein are typically good for promoting the feeling of fullness, sometimes referred to as satiety. Foods that are highly processed or high in sugars often only satisfy hunger for a relatively short time. These foods are usually low in nutritional content and have few health benefits.[4]

If still hungry between meals, this is usually an indicator of thirst.

4. Medical News Today (2019), "What are the most filling foods?" <https://www.medicalnewstoday.com/articles/324078>

5. Dr Reynolds, A (2020). "Higher fibre saves lives, but food processing may remove benefits" University of Otago. 19 May 2020 <https://www.otago.ac.nz>

## COMPARING THE FIBRE

Fibre has many health benefits, such as helping you feel full between meals. Dietary fibre is only found in foods of plant origin and is best taken in the natural package it was grown. Highly processed food loses much of its fibre content, limiting their ability to help the digestion process.[5]

| MINIMALLY PROCESSED | REFINED FOOD |
|---|---|
| 3.8 | 0.4 |
| COOKED BROWN RICE *one cup* | PUFFED RICE *one cup* |
| 2.0 | 1.0 |
| WHOLEMEAL BREAD *one slice* | WHITE BREAD *one slice* |
| 5.0 | 0.1 |
| MEDIUM POTATO *baked with skin* | POTATO CHIPS *120g pack* |
| 3.7 | 0.2 |
| APPLE *one with skin* | RECONSTITUTED APPLE JUICE *one cup* |
| 5.7 | 2.0 |
| WHOLEMEAL PASTA *100g* | WHITE PASTA *100g* |
| 13.3 | 0.5 |
| RAW ALMONDS *100g* | ALMOND MILK *one cup* |

*(Fibre measured in grams)*

## 5) Environment

As an old book states, 'Cast off care and anxious thought when you sit to dine.'

Mealtimes should be relaxed and happy. If rushed or stressed, or if controversial issues are discussed at the table, digestion is suppressed so the body can reroute its resources to trigger fight or flight. The brain effectively shuts down digestion by slowing contractions of digestive muscles and decreasing the release of the hydrochloric acid (HCl) required to process food. That is why the relaxation response is often called 'rest and digest'.[6]

A damaging modern habit is to watch television while eating. Emotional, exciting or violent scenarios in shows stimulate the adrenal system, and this can severely retard digestion.

# CARDIAC SPHINCTER

When eating, the swallowing action closes the trachea (windpipe) and ensures food travels from the mouth, down the oesophagus to the stomach. Guarding the entry to the stomach is the cardiac sphincter, a double-layered muscle which acts like a door to the stomach, opening only in one direction so that food can flow into the stomach and not back up the oesophagus.

This muscle sits directly in the middle of the large muscle that sweeps across and under our ribs called the diaphragm. As with all muscles, the diaphragm maintains its strength with use. Problems arise when the cardiac sphincter malfunctions, causing stomach acid to repeatedly flow back into the oesophagus. This is known as Gastroesophageal Reflux Disease (GERD) which causes acid reflux, also called heart burn due to the pain it causes.

## FACTORS THAT CONTRIBUTE TO GERD

▶ Poor posture, high chest breathing, and weak abdominal muscles can all render the diaphragm muscle weak.

▶ Late evening meals can cause the contents of the stomach to push against the cardiac sphincter as a person lies down to sleep. When this situation continues night after night, it eventually weakens the muscle.

▶ Stress and anxiety tightens muscles, and the cardiac sphincter is no exception. When the cardiac sphincter is relaxed, it is closed, and when it tightens, it opens.

---

6.  Stress Management & Biofeedback Services "Stress and the Digestive System" Brigham Young University <https://caps.byu.edu/stress-and-the-digestive-system> accessed July 2023.

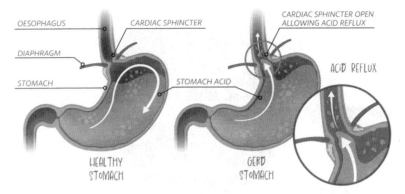

OESOPHAGUS — CARDIAC SPHINCTER

DIAPHRAGM

STOMACH

STOMACH ACID

CARDIAC SPHINCTER OPEN ALLOWING ACID REFLUX

ACiD REFLUX

HEALTHY STOMACH

GERD STOMACH

▶ Allergy to foods, such as wheat, dairy, peanuts, and refined sugar, can exacerbate this condition as well as the acidity of the food.

▶ Low hydrochloric acid can also be part of the cause of GERD, as when the food is not digested efficiently, fermentation may occur, causing gas to push against the cardiac sphincter.

▶ Other risk factors include older age, excessive body mass index (BMI), smoking, and overeating.[7]

## HOW TO HEAL FROM GERD

With the proper conditions and care the body is designed to heal itself, how you can assist this healing process is:

▶ Implement exercises that target abdominal strength, including abdominal breathing to encourage diaphragm strength.

▶ Have your main meal at breakfast and lunch and cut out late-night snacking to allow for an empty stomach at bedtime.

▶ Address any weight issues or stress in your life and take steps to reduce it.

▶ Taking a magnesium supplement with each meal and just before bed can play a major role in healing the cardiac sphincter as it helps muscles to relax and neutralizes the burning from gastric acid.[8]

▶ Boost your hydrochloric acid to increase stomach digestion and reduce the possibility of fermentation. This will be discussed in the next section on the stomach.

▶ If there is any irritation in the oesophagus, slippery elm can be taken just before retiring at night. This will effectively coat, soothe, and contribute to the healing in the lining of the oesophagus.

▶ Quitting smoking.

7.  Clarrett DM, Hachem C. (2018) "Gastroesophageal Reflux Disease (GERD)." *Missouri Medicine.* May-Jun 2018; Vol 115 Issue 3, pages 214-218. <https://www.ncbi.nlm.nih.gov/pmc/articles/PMC6140167>

8.  Gobind, A (2022) "The role of magnesium supplement in laryngopharyngeal reflux disease" *International Journal of Otorhinolaryngology*, Vol 8 Issue 1, Jan 2022.

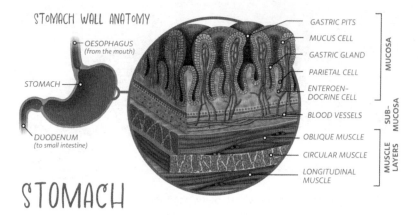

STOMACH WALL ANATOMY

OESOPHAGUS (from the mouth)

STOMACH

DUODENUM (to small intestine)

GASTRIC PITS
MUCUS CELL
GASTRIC GLAND
PARIETAL CELL
ENTEROENDOCRINE CELL
BLOOD VESSELS
OBLIQUE MUSCLE
CIRCULAR MUSCLE
LONGITUDINAL MUSCLE

MUCOSA
SUB-MUCOSA
MUSCLE LAYERS

# STOMACH

Finally, we have arrived at the stomach. The points previously discussed greatly affect what happens here. The stomach begins the digestion process by churning food and breaking it down using digestive acids.

The stomach is the only place in the body that is acidic. The primary active component of gastric acid is hydrochloric acid. The stomach is lined with folds, which contain glands. Two thirds of these glands release mucus, which serves to coat and protect the stomach lining from hydrochloric acid burns.[9]

It is at the very base of the folds where the other third of the glands are situated. These are called the parietal glands, and they release hydrochloric acid, pepsinogen, and intrinsic factor.

The hydrochloric acid in the stomach plays a few roles, it contains antifungal, antibacterial, and a range of antimicrobial properties. This serves to wipe out any unwanted yeasts and pathogens that may have entered the stomach. Hydrochloric acid also connects with pepsinogen in this acidic environment to produce pepsin, which is the enzyme that breaks down protein so your body can absorb the nutrients. Pepsin can only break down protein in an acidic environment.

It takes two to four hours for a healthy stomach to digest food before passing it to the small intestine. However, this can depend on several factors, such as the composition and size of your meal, your hormones, and your sex. Women tend to digest food more slowly than men.[10] Carbohydrates and proteins are processed by the stomach relatively quickly, but fats take longer.

---

9. Forssell, H. (1988), "Gastric mucosal defense mechanisms: a brief review." *Scandinavian Journal of Gastroenterology*, Vol 23, 1988. <https://doi.org/10.3109/00365528809096277>
10. Seladi-Schulman, J (2020). "How Long Does Food Stay in Your Stomach?" *Health Line* <https://www.healthline.com/health/how-long-does-it-take-for-your-stomach-to-empty>

# PROBLEMS THAT CAN ARISE IN THE STOMACH

## Vitamin B12 Deficiency

B12 is a very misunderstood vitamin. Yet, it is not really a vitamin at all. It is more like a bacteria, as all naturally occurring vitamin B12 is produced by microorganisms.[11]

Within the body, cobalamin (vitamin B12) is converted to hydroxocobalamin (an advanced form of B12). The body does not need a lot of it, but cobalamin is essential for proper nerve and blood formation. Demyelination of the nerve cells can result from vitamin B12 deficiency. Cobalamin is also used in DNA formation.[12]

As an airborne bacteria, vitamin B12 is found in rainwater and organic root vegetables, and on organic fruit and vegetables. Cultured foods, such as sauerkraut, also contain traces of B12, which contributes to supplying the body's needs.

What is the least understood, is the way the body absorbs B12.

Vitamin B12 must first be released from polypeptides, which are linked in foods. This release usually occurs through the action of the gastric proteolytic enzyme, pepsin, in the stomach.

Once released from foods, vitamin B12 is absorbed by contact with two proteins: intrinsic factor (IF) and R proteins. Although IF is made and released in the stomach, it functions in the small intestine.

R proteins are found in saliva and gastric juices. Cobalamin, released from food, combines with R proteins, and they unite and travel together from the stomach through to the small intestine. In the duodenum, pancreatic proteases hydrolyse the R protein, which frees cobalamin to travel alone. IF binds to cobalamin, and this complex travels to the ileum where receptor sites for vitamin B are present. Here, cobalamin and IF are absorbed out of the gut and into enterohepatic circulation. B12 is then used by the body as needed.

Vitamin B12 can be stored for long periods of time in the body, even for years. Excess B12 is mainly stored in the liver.[13]

The best B12 supplements are sublingual, which is a method to treat vitamin deficiencies where the supplements are absorbed in the mouth by the

11. Sofia Pineda Ochoa (2017), "Vitamin B12: All Your Questions Answered" Forks Over Knives <https://www.forksoverknives.com/wellness/vitamin-b12-questions-answered-2/>
12. Allen LH. (2012), "Vitamin B-12." *Advances in Nutrition*, Vol 3 Issue 1, January 2012, Pages 54-55.
13. Ankar, A, Kumar, A (2022), "Vitamin B12 Deficiency," StatPearls [Internet]. Available from: <https://www.ncbi.nlm.nih.gov/books/NBK441923/> accessed July 2023.

sublingual glands under the tongue. This removes the need for hydrochloric acid and intrinsic factor. Sublingual B12 bypasses the need for these enzymes, thus overcoming the challenges of injections and should be the first line option for patients with B12 deficiency.[14]

Methylcobalamin is a naturally occurring form of vitamin B12 making it the easiest for the body to absorb and use.[15]

## Low Hydrochloric Acid

When hydrochloric acid (HCl) levels are low, it can affect your stomach's ability to digest and absorb proteins. This can result in a condition called hypochlorhydria. One of the symptoms is slow digestion and bloating as the food begins to ferment. Let us consider what causes this:

1. Drinking with meals, especially large amounts, dilutes HCl. To remedy this dilemma, the body slows digestion, and the stomach endeavors to eliminate the extra fluid by absorption in an attempt to return to the required acid levels. Only then can digesting the protein be resumed. When the habit of drinking with meals continues, HCl levels are gradually depleted.

2. Eating in a stressful environment also effectively blocks hydrochloric acid production.

3. Eating every couple of hours exhausts HCl supplies.

4. Overeating or eating a large meal late at night both contribute to depleting HCl levels.

5. The last two points prevent the stomach from having periods of rest.

Other factors that can cause less stomach acid are stomach surgeries such as gastric bypass; smoking cigarettes and drinking alcohol which can decrease the nutrients in your body; long-term use of antacids and medicines for treating stomach ulcers or heartburn can also cause low stomach acid production.

Encouraged by the legal drug industry, many medical students are not taught that inadequate stomach acid production is simply treatable with unpatentable, natural replacement therapies.[16]

## How to boost Hydrochloric Acid

14. Bensky, MJ, et al (2019), "Comparison of sublingual vs. intramuscular administration of vitamin B12 for the treatment of patients with vitamin B12 deficiency." *Drug Delivery and Translational Research*.

15. Paul C, Brady DM (2017), "Comparative Bioavailability and Utilization of Particular Forms of B12 Supplements With Potential to Mitigate B12-related Genetic Polymorphisms." *Integrative Medicine Clinician's Journal* <https://www.ncbi.nlm.nih.gov/pmc/articles/PMC5312744>, accessed July 2023.

16. Banoo H and Nusrat N (2019), "Implications of Low Stomach Acid: An Update." *Rama University Journal of Medical Sciences*, <https://studyres.com/doc/1966484>, accessed August 2023.

*Bitter* may not be a term that sounds appetizing but such herbs and tinctures can aid and improve your digestion. The basic idea behind bitters is that they stimulate your taste buds to create more saliva, which in turn encourages a release of gastric enzymes. This can be achieved with one third of a hot cup of bitter tea taken just before each meal.

**BITTER TEA RECIPE**

- Mix the following in a jar: one part dandelion, one part gentian, one part licorice, half a part goldenseal
- Next, place one teaspoon of this dried herb mix in a glass saucepan or coffee pot, with one teaspoon of grated fresh ginger. Bring this to a boil in two cups of water.
- After ten minutes of gentle simmering with the lid on, the heat is turned off. Let this sit until cool. Strain and store in the refrigerator.
- Take a third of a cup of this tea (reheated) before each meal.

Little by little, these herbs revive and restore digestive function and boost HCl levels in the stomach.

Other ways to boost Hydrochloric Acid include:

- Drinking a quarter teaspoon of cayenne pepper in a little water just before a meal
- Taking the juice of a lemon in a little hot water before meals

As well as these simple remedies, it is also important to adhere to the dietary and lifestyle principles previously discussed.

## Helicobacter Pylori

Everybody has helicobacter pylori and this is not a problem unless an imbalance is caused. When the HCl levels in the stomach are low, this bacteria can multiply, causing nausea and discomfort.

The remedy is to increase the HCl levels in the stomach, as already described, which will kill off the excess helicobacter pylori, bringing back a state of healthy balance in the stomach. Depending on how chronic the condition is, this may take a few months.

## Stomach Ulcer

There can be a few causes of a stomach ulcer, but too much HCl is not one of them.

One of the main causes is dehydration. The stomach has a thick mucosa wall to protect it from the stomach acid. This mucosa wall is 99% water, and in a state of dehydration, the lining of the stomach is one of the first areas to suffer. The mucus in the lining is lost, causing damage, and the body's own microorganisms can change roles and become part of the clean up team. Having adequate hydration plays an important role in the healing process of the stomach.

Stress can also play a role, as it causes a reduction of HCl.

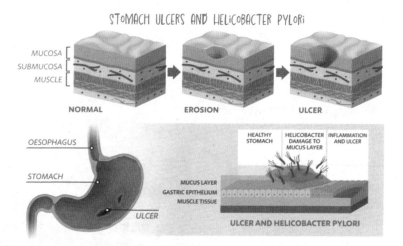

One of the problems with using medication such as Mylanta and other antacids to relieve the pain of stomach ulcers is that they can actually make the whole situation worse by reducing HCl levels, this is not curing the problem.

Implementing the dietary principles at the start of this chapter, and taking slippery elm before each meal and before bed, will help to heal a stomach ulcer. Slippery elm soothes, coats, and heals the lining of the gut, as well as this, slippery elm contains a stimulant for new cell growth.

# ANEMIA

A major issue that can be caused by low HCl is anemia, which is a deficiency in the number or quality of red blood cells in the body. Red blood cells carry oxygen around your body using an iron rich protein named hemoglobin. Anemia means that either the level of red blood cells or hemoglobin is lower than normal.

Our body needs iron to make hemoglobin. Iron is bound up in food and needs HCl to liberate it. The body stores iron in the liver in a protein called ferritin, the level of ferritin is used as a diagnostic test for iron-deficiency anemia.

## SYMPTOMS OF ANEMIA

Some of the symptoms of anemia are fatigue, nausea, hair loss, breathlessness, and cold feet and hands.

When oxygen is present at the cellular level, the energy cycle can deliver 18 times more energy. A lack of available oxygen creates the symptoms of fatigue, breathlessness, and nausea. As the blood's ability to carry necessary nutrients is greatly diminished, there is compromised blood delivery to the extremities, leading to the additional symptoms of cold feet and hands.

Causes of Anemia

- Blood loss is a common cause of anemia, especially for women who experience heavy periods every month.
- Low HCl limits the body's ability to access the iron in our food. Some health conditions affect how much iron you can absorb from your stomach and bowel, such as celiac disease.
- Low HCl compromises protein availability, which inhibits effective iron storage capacity.
- Protein deficiency interferes with iron stores.

## SOLUTIONS

Investigating the cause of anemia is the first step, as the cause can differ person to person.

- If the cause is heavy periods, wild yam cream stimulates the body to restore hormone balance. I will cover this more in depth in the section on natural treatments for Women's Health on page 226.
- If the cause is low hydrochloric acid, the causative factors need to be remedied, see the section on How to Boost Hydrochloric Acid on the previous page.

## Foods to Reverse Anemia

Including generous protein in the daily diet provides the body with the nutrient necessary to store iron. This includes well-prepared legumes and whole grains. It might include eating eight to ten nuts and a quarter cup of seeds at every meal.

Iron-rich foods that can be helpful include:

- Dark green or red vegetables, such as beets, tomatoes and kale
- All red berries
- Dark legumes such as kidney beans and black turtle beans
- Seeds, especially pumpkin seeds, which have the highest levels.

Initially, it may be necessary to take iron tablets, if levels are very low.

Choose a chelated iron with vitamin C, as the acid helps iron release.

# TESTIMONY
## MY STORY

When I was much younger, in my early 40's, I suffered from anemia for 13 years. My hair was thin and didn't grow very long. I experienced breathlessness very easily. My feet were often cold. The iron tablets helped to just keep me above a dangerous level.

The desired range was 11–15. When first tested at the age of 40, my hemoglobin level was eight. My doctor friend suggested FAB iron tablets. I took six a day, which increased my levels to ten in a month. I wasn't as tired. After remaining on the tablets for a few months, I felt quite good and ceased taking them.

Life was busy as a single mum with six children. We moved to Queensland, and after being a single mum for four years, I remarried.

Life was great, but when I mentioned to my sister that I was feeling tired, she suggested I have my iron levels checked again. A few days later, the doctor rang and told me to go straight to hospital as my hemoglobin levels were dangerously low at five. The ferritin levels, which should not be under 26, were three. As there was a crisis, I was given a blood transfusion.

My anemia experience over the next eight years was up and down. I was required to be constantly vigilant about this. My life was very good, and I could have easily missed the symptoms.

There were times when I had to, once again, be on iron tablets, sometimes for up to eight months of the year. I visited hematologists and had a colonoscopy and esophagoscopy, but no one could understand why I couldn't hold my iron levels.

Eventually, I decided I had to work this out for myself, and I studied iron in the body. I studied how it breaks down, is used, and is stored. This is where I discovered that iron is bound up in food and needs acid to liberate it, and protein to store it.

**This is where I discovered that iron is bound up in food and needs acid to liberate it, and protein to store it.**

Before leaving my mountain home in 1993, my first husband was a drug addict and alcoholic, and life was not easy. The stress had gradually depleted my HCl. Even though I left that stressful environment and was a single mum for four years, the residue of that time haunted me. As a single mum, we had a lot of fun, and life was good, but my stomach had developed a habit of making low levels of HCl.

Even though I remarried in 1997, and life was excellent, digestion took a long time after each meal. Without me realizing it, my stomach was not making adequate HCl.

With my new discovery, I made two changes. I drank the bitter tea before each meal, and I began to have legumes every day, sometimes twice daily.

Menopause also happened around this time. This meant there was no more monthly blood loss. After six months, I decided to have a blood test. My hemoglobin level was 15, and my ferritin levels were 35. My vitamin B12 levels were very generous. I had never known such high levels.

My anemia was first discovered in 1993 when I was 40. I was 55 when I implemented the two changes and received the impressive blood results. My hair grew to my waist, I could run up hills with no more breathlessness, my feet were no longer cold, and digestion was vastly improved.

As I write this, I am 70 and still run up hills. I thank God every day for the simple, and yet profoundly effective, natural remedies I applied to my body. Everybody has an inbuilt ability to heal themselves.

# CONNECTING WITH THE COLON

On our journey through the gastrointestinal tract we quickly pass the small intestine and come to the colon.

Dr John Harvey Kellogg, of Kellogg Cornflakes fame and the director of the Battle Creek Sanitarium in the mid-1800s, wrote many books on health. He is on record as stating that three intakes of food a day should equal three evacuations. Once a day is described as constipation.

**The cells lining the colon can develop unhealthy habits but the good news is they can be encouraged to develop habits of regularity.**

Even when the following lifestyle and dietary principles are implemented, some colons remain sluggish or overactive. The cells lining the colon can develop unhealthy habits but the good news is they can be encouraged to develop habits of regularity.

The colon has a mind of its own and will not follow your commands! Gentle stimulation can encourage regular movement and re-establish habits of daily evacuation.

# IMPROVE PROPER COLON FUNCTION THROUGH 'SUSTAIN ME' PRINCIPLES

**SUNSHINE:** The sun stimulates blood supply wherever it touches. Allowing the sun to touch the abdomen and thus penetrate deep into the colon stimulates blood supply to the whole colon.

Expose the abdomen to the sun for at least 15 minutes, as often as possible. Studies have shown that skin exposure to sunlight can rapidly strengthen the gut microbiome without any dietary changes, this can be of great importance for people with immune dysfunction.[1]

**USE OF WATER:** Dehydration can be a considerable contributing factor to a compromised colon.[2] One of the main functions of the colon is to take water out so that stools can be formed, and the contents be passed with ease. On average, the body loses two and a half liters of water a day. Two liters must be replaced, while the other 500ml can be supplied from fruits, vegetables, and herbal teas.

In a state of dehydration, the body takes more water from the colon in an attempt to maintain full blood volume in the arteries. As a result, the contents of the colon lose their much-needed moisture and can become dry and hard, making it difficult to pass stools and contributing to constipation.

**SLEEP:** All organs of the body work in cycles. They love regularity, and the colon is no exception. We have one stomach, which averages three and a half to four hours to digest the food we eat. Leaving five hours between meals gives the stomach and colon time to rest.

Eating lightly and early, or not at all, in the evening allows the stomach to sleep when we sleep. This colon rest helps to restore regularity. To achieve this, we need to eat breakfast like a king (insulin sensitivity is at its height in the morning). We continue with eating lunch like a queen and dinner like a pauper.

Between the hours of 9pm and 2am, the hormone melatonin is released in response to darkness hence the nickname, *hormone of darkness*.[3] This hormone is responsible for rest and healing every cell in the body, and is an important part in the digestion process and moderating stomach pains.

---

1. Bosman, ES (2019), "Skin Exposure to Narrow Band Ultraviolet (UVB) Light Modulates the Human Intestinal Microbiome," *Frontiers in Microbiology*, <https://doi.org/10.3389/fmicb.2019.02410>.
2. Arnaud, MJ, et al (2003), "Mild dehydration: A risk factor of constipation?" *European Journal of Clinical Nutrition*, 18 December 2003, < https://www.nature.com/articles/1601907>.
3. Arendt J, Aulinas A. (2000) "Physiology of the Pineal Gland and Melatonin." *Endotext* <https://www.ncbi.nlm.nih.gov/books/NBK550972/> accessed December 2022.

The circadian rhythm is the rhythm that our brain runs on. It is set by early morning light and sleeping between 9pm and 2am. Artificial light in the hours we should be sleeping, especially from short-range screens, disrupts our circadian rhythm.

The gut is circadian. Evening bugs are different to morning bugs (friendly flora), and they all have different functions.[4]

**TRUST IN DIVINE POWER:** "Tight mind; tight colon," said Margaret Wright, who was one of Australia's leading experts in colonic irrigation therapy. Your emotional state can affect your stomach and the rest of your gastrointestinal tract. Studies have shown that stress and anxiety may cause irritable bowel syndrome (IBS) and gastroesophageal reflux disease (GERD).[5]

*"A merry heart does good, like medicine, But a broken spirit dries the bones."* (and the colon!) Proverbs 17:22

Laughter, love, joy, and peace relaxes the colon. *"You will keep him in perfect peace, whose mind is stayed on You, because he trusts in You."* Isaiah 26:3. Peace of mind relaxes the colon.

Stress in life needs to be addressed and managed in order to heal all bowel problems.

**ABSTAIN:** Caffeine, alcohol, cigarettes, refined sugar, chemicals, and drugs are all risk factors for colon cancer.[6] These substances can also inhibit the action of healthy bacteria, and in some cases even kill it off. Glyphosate, antibiotics, painkilling medication, statin drugs, birth control medication, and refined sugar have a devastating effect on gut flora, which can inhibit colon function.

Meat, dairy, and refined foods lack fibre—which is necessary for stimulating peristalsis—and contribute to diseases of the colon. Refined foods are also fibre deficient.

In the process of hybridizing wheat in the 1950's, the gluten or protein structure was changed. The result is a complex structure, making it very difficult to break down in the gut.[7] Constipation or diarrhea can be the result.

---

4.  Voigt RM, et al (2016). "Circadian Rhythm and the Gut Microbiome. International Review of Neurobiology." Vol 131, 2016, pages 193-205 <https://pubmed.ncbi.nlm.nih.gov/27793218>.
5.  Qin HY, Cheng CW, Tang XD and Bian ZX. (2014), "Impact of psychological stress on irritable bowel syndrome." *World Journal of Gastroenterology.* 21 October 2014.
6.  Martha L. et al (1990), "Tobacco, Alcohol, Coffee, and Caffeine as Risk Factors for Colon Cancer in a Low-Risk Population," *Epidemiology,* Vol. 1, No. 2, page 141-145.
7.  de Lorgeril, Michel and Salen, Patricia. (2014). "Gluten and wheat intolerance today: Are modern wheat strains involved?" *International Journal of Food Sciences and Nutrition.* February 2014.

An integral part of conquering any bowel problem is to cease eating wheat and gluten products.

 **INHALE:** High chest breathing can contribute to colon problems. Abdominal breathing using the diaphragm creates a gentle massaging action felt by internal organs like the intestines and stomach, which can reduce abdominal pain, urgency, bloating, and constipation. The habit of high chest breathing robs the muscles covering the colon of necessary stimulation.

The abdominal muscles were designed to aid in the breathing process. Weak abdominal, pelvic floor, and diaphragm muscles; poor posture; tight belts and clothing around the waist, all inhibit abdominal breathing. This means less oxygen delivery to the cells, thus less energy.

Diaphragmatic breathing can be used while sitting on the toilet to encourage bowel movements by calming and massage the system. The result may be a more complete bowel movement.

 **NUTRITION:** As previously mentioned, meat and refined carbohydrates contain no fibre.

Fibre is required to not only stimulate peristalsis (the relaxation of the intestine muscles) but it is also is needed to sweep the many little grooves and folds that make up the structure of the colon.

The highest fibre foods are vegetables and fruit. All plant foods contain fibre, so this includes whole grains, legumes, nuts, and seeds. Fibre also encourages the growth of the healthy bacteria in the gut, called prebiotics.

The process of rinsing and slow cooking (or pressure cooking) legumes, increases the body's ability to digest them effectively.

Nuts and seeds are an important component of a healthy diet, they just need to be chewed to a cream state to be easily digested.

Whole grains are best cooked in a slow cooker to ensure a thorough breakdown of the starch granules or ground to a flour and cultured with the sourdough method of making bread. This predigests the starch and protein in the grain.

Cultured foods such as sauerkraut, yogurt, kefir and miso, ensure a proper balance of microbes in the gut. An imbalance dramatically affects colon function.

**MODERATION:** Even healthy fats and unrefined sugars need to be taken in moderation.

**EXERCISE:** Daily exercise is essential for effective colon function. This movement increases blood flow to the colon. The most effective exercises are rebounding, Pilates, swimming, and brisk walking, as all these movements involve the core or abdominal muscles, which cover the internal organs causing a massage of the colon.

The deep breathing that results from HI exercises also strengthens the diaphragm, which directly affects the colon, as the diaphragm is situated at the top of the core muscles.

HIIT takes all the exercises to a higher level and has a more profound effect on the colon.

# POSITION MAKES A DIFFERENCE

Throughout Asia and Africa, for thousands of years, squatting was the position commonly used when passing a bowel movement. Today, in many areas of these countries, the toilets are tiled and flush, but often, they are nothing more than a hole in the floor.

Science shows why this is a superior position. In the last section of the colon, there is a slight kink. This kink is the result of the muscle, puborectalis, which holds the final part of the colon up. The puborectalis serves an important role in preventing 'accidents'.

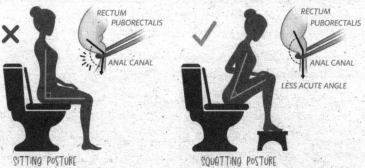

SITTING POSTURE        SQUATTING POSTURE

When sitting on the 'throne', the puborectalis remains firm, but in the squatting position, this muscle relaxes, which causes the colon to open wider, allowing the full evacuation of the rectum with greater ease.

As this position prevents unnecessary pressure on the anus, it not only aids in the healing of all colon problems but also prevents and helps to heal hemorrhoids.

# NATURAL TREATMENTS

The human body has been designed to heal itself, and it will heal, if given the right conditions.

We have discussed the conditions that the colon requires for healing regarding diet and lifestyle through following the SUSTAIN ME principles. Until these lifestyle changes kick in there several other natural treatments that can be used to bring relief. Now, we will explain some treatments for specific diseases in the colon.

## AILMENTS: Constipation and Diverticulitis

Unfortunately, constipation is often a result of the fast food age and is too common today. It is usually caused by a lack of fibre and exercise, as well as dehydration. Irregularities in lifestyle and an inability to deal with stress can be contributing factors.

In the SUSTAIN ME principles the ABSTAIN section lists the main dehydrators that can play a part in constipation. As mentioned earlier, Dr Kellogg stated, "Three meals a day should equal three evacuations a day. Two meals a day should equal two evacuations a day."

Chronic constipation can cause diverticulitis, this is a condition where small pouches called diverticula can form in the large intestine. When inflamed, they can cause pain and discomfort. These simple treatments can do much to bring relief and healing.

We will now look at how the colon can be encouraged to reset the regularity pattern.

### ■ TREATMENT: Promptly Answer Nature's Immediate Call (PANIC)

An important part of returning regularity in the colon is to listen to the body and resist the temptation to delay answering the body's call to evacuate.

### ■ TREATMENT: Colon Tea

This tea is a combination of herbs that gently restore and revive colon function.

The dose changes from person to person. Some need half a cup a day, while a severely constipated person may even need three cups a day. If three cups are required, they are best taken in the morning, at noon, and in the evening. Most people find that a cup taken before retiring at night will help encourage morning evacuation.

> ## HOW TO MAKE COLON TEA
>
> ▶ One part cascara sagrada
>
> ▶ Two parts licorice
>
> ▶ Three parts buckthorn
>
> These roots and barks are mixed in a jar. One teaspoon of this mixture is gently simmered in a cup of water for 15–20 minutes. Drink as required.

Taking this tea regularly, combined with the lifestyle and dietary principles discussed, can reduce and even eliminate constipation.

As these points are implemented, the person will find they need less and less of the tea. This may take four to six months, depending on the severity of the situation.

## ■ TREATMENT: Castor Oil Compresses

Castor oil has powerful natural healing properties and is most well known as an internal laxative. However, people can often experience abdominal cramping, vomiting, bloating, and dizziness from taking castor oil internally.

An external application through a compress is a far more effective and gentle treatment to decrease straining during defecation and to give a feeling of complete evacuation after a bowel movement, thus reducing symptoms of constipation.[8]

> ## HOW TO MAKE A CASTOR OIL COMPRESS
>
> Moisten a few layers of cloth with castor oil, this oil is quite thick so can take about 20 minutes to soak through. This cloth pad is then applied to the abdominal area (hip bone to hip bone, belly button to pubic bone). When in place, cover with a sheet of plastic to protect clothing. Often, our underwear, pants, or skirts can hold the compress in place. Keep in place for least five hours a day and repeat for five days, have a two day break and then repeat the process until the problem resolves.
>
> As a compress, this can be reused perhaps a dozen times before being discarded. This is because it is not absorbing anything from the body but rather acting as a vehicle to hold the castor oil, enabling it to penetrate the skin. It moves past the skin, deep into the body. Each day, a little more castor oil may need to be added.

---

8.  Arslan G, and Eşer I (2011), "An examination of the effect of castor oil packs on constipation in the elderly" *Complementary Therapies in Clinical Practice*, Vol 17 Issue 1, February 2011, pages 58-62.

Castor oil compresses can be applied to the abdominal area for a minimum of five hours a day, at least five days a week.

This oil penetrates deeper than any other oil and has the ability to break up lumps, bumps, and congestion, as well as adhesions and scar tissue. Wherever castor oil penetrates, it cleanses and stimulates healing making it a great natural solution for constipation, or diverticulitis.

### ■ TREATMENT: Contrasting Sitz Baths

Sitz baths have been used for centuries, especially across Europe, as an effective way to increase healing in the pelvic floor area. Two tubs are required that are big enough to sit in, one for hot water, and one for cold, with ice cubes.

1. Sit in the hot tub for three minutes, then the cold tub for 30 seconds.

2. Repeat the whole procedure twice more, ensuring that the hot water is kept hot.

Sitz baths and how to use them are described in more detail in the Hydrotherapy chapter on page 291.

### ■ TREATMENT: Colonic Irrigation

Colonic irrigation is a bowel treatment using warm water that is gently inserted into the anus. The treatment takes 45–50 minutes, in which warm water gently runs in and out through a network of tubes. This softens old buildup on the walls of the colon and cleans out old pockets of accumulated waste. The colonic can also loosen the hard covering on diverticulitis, and little by little, they can clean the pockets out, allowing them to shrink and resolve.

The NUTRITION suggestions in the SUSTAIN ME principles for colon health will work alongside this treatment to nourish and return the colon wall to health.

This treatment requires a trained therapist with the necessary equipment. Colonic irrigation can aid in the healing of all colon problems. Three treatments are often advised over a two week period. The level of chronicity influences the recovery time.

### ■ TREATMENT: Enema

An enema kit can be purchased from a chemist for use at home. To use, one and a half cups of warm water are placed in the enema can/bag and then inserted into the colon via a catheter. After the water is taken into the colon, the person can lie on their back and massage their abdomen, endeavoring to hold the water for approximately ten minutes. They can then sit on the toilet to evacuate. This can quickly relieve constipation.

Four enemas in a row at 15-minute intervals can have a similar effect to a colonic irrigation in that the water can reach the whole of the colon or large intestine.

# TESTIMONY
## SUE'S STORY

Sue came to the retreat to improve her health. She had worked as a psychologist for 40 years and had been plagued by constipation most of that time. To help manage her condition, she would take medication once a week to cause an evacuation.

Every day at the retreat, for five days, Sue had a colonic irrigation treatment. Each night, she applied a castor oil compress to her abdomen. To produce two evacuations a day, Sue found she needed to take three cups of Colon Tea over the day. By the third day, the whites in Sue's eye lightened to white from a dull off-white colour. The skin on her face lost the gray look and became pink. Sue testified that she felt better than she had for years. Even her mind was clearer. She said it made her wonder how many of her depressed patients might be constipated!

**Sue testified that she felt better than she had for years. Even her mind was clearer. She said it made her wonder how many of her depressed patients might be constipated!**

Sue left our retreat a very satisfied customer, looking forward to her future instead of considering retirement. The effect of diet and lifestyle was an eye-opener, and Sue was keen to implement what she had learned when she returned home.

Four months later, Sue sent us an email with some fascinating news. When she had left the retreat, three cups of Colon Tea a day produced two bowel movements a day. After six weeks, she began to have four a day. She dropped back to two Colon Teas a day. This brought her bowel movements back to two a day. Six weeks later, she began to experience four bowel movements a day. She brought the tea back to one cup a day, and this caused two bowel movements a day. Approximately six weeks later, Sue again had four bowel movements a day, so she decided to stop drinking any Colon Tea. With great excitement, Sue told me that she was having two bowel movements daily with no help, a fact that, four months before, she was sure was an impossibility.

## AILMENT: Diarrhea

Diarrhea is recognized by loose, watery stools, the need to use the toilet more frequently than usual, and often stomach pains. Diarrhea is usually short-lived, lasting no more than a few days. When diarrhea lasts beyond a few days into weeks, it usually means that there's another problem.

### ■ TREATMENT: Water and Herbs

While diarrhea may seem like it occurs because of an excess of fluids, it actually can have a dehydrating effect on the body. When you have diarrhea, drink 8-10 glasses of clear fluids such as water or herbal tea.

Several herbs and plants that can effectively treat diarrhea include goldenseal, peppermint, red raspberry leaves, and slippery elm.

In a crisis, if a person has chronic diarrhea, slippery elm can be taken every half hour. As the frequency of bowel movements ease, so can the dose. The body's response is the best guide.

To take slippery elm, stir one teaspoon of the powder quickly into half a cup of warm water to ensure there are no lumps. It is best drunk immediately, as it thickens. More water can be added if it is too thick.

Psyllium, a soluble fibre that comes from the husks of the seeds of a plant called Plantago ovata, is a bulk-forming agent that treats diarrhea by soaking up water in the colon, helping to slow down colon transit and firming up the stool.[9] Take psyllium with a large amount of water as needed.

### ■ TREATMENT: Probiotics

Cultured foods such as sourdough bread, sauerkraut, fermented vegetables, milk kefir, and yogurt all contain the natural probiotics *Lactobacilli* and *Bifidobacteria*. Including these foods in your diet can help a great deal in maintaining the correct microbial balance in the bowel and have been used successfully for the prevention of traveler's diarrhea.[10]

---

9.  Bliss D. et al. (2001), "Supplementation with dietary fiber improves fecal incontinence." *Nursing Research*. Vol 50, Issue 4, July 2001, pages 203-212.
10. McFarland I.V. (2007), "Meta-analysis of probiotics for the prevention of traveler's diarrhea." *Travel Medicine and Infectious Disease*, Vol 5, Issue 2, March 2007, pages 97-105

## AILMENT: Hemorrhoids

Hemorrhoids are often a result of pressure overload on the last part of the colon, resulting in swollen and inflamed veins in the rectum and anus. Constipation, obesity, and pregnancy are the main causes. This is very uncomfortable and can be quite painful. Sometimes, it is accompanied by bleeding.

Drinking more water and consuming more fibre in your diet will soften the stools and can help prevent constipation and encourage the healing process. Suppositories and sitz baths are another way to treat these issues, as they bypasses blockages that would usually stop remedies moving through the digestive system.

My son Peter also makes an essential oil designed to relieve the effects of hemorrhoids, he calls it 'Peace Please', learn more at www.earthbless.com

### ■ TREATMENT: Suppositories

Suppositories are typically about two inches (five centimeters) long and molded to have a rounded tip for easy administration into the body, often through your bottom. Once inside, it melts or dissolves to release its beneficial treatment.

---

**HOW TO MAKE SUPPOSITORIES**

**1. Castor Oil Suppositories**

Soak a cotton ball with castor oil and mold it into a shape the size of a little finger. Freeze the suppository, which may take two to three days, then insert into the anus as far as possible just before retiring at night.

**2. Aloe Vera Suppositories.**

An aloe vera leaf is peeled, and strips are cut approximately the size of a little finger. These are frozen, and when solid, they can be inserted into the anus just before retiring at night.

The suppositories are expelled in the morning evacuation. You can use these two suppositories on alternating nights. Alternatively you can use the suppository method described on page 312

---

### ■ TREATMENT: Contrasting Sitz Baths

Contrasting sitz baths not only speed the healing of hemorrhoids but can also reduce pain and swelling, and help increase blood flow and relax the muscles. This treatment is explained on the previous page in the Natural Treatments for Constipation and Diverticulitis section, and described in more detail in the chapter on Hydrotherapy on page 291.

These can be taken at least once a day—even twice, if possible.

## AILMENT: Irritable Bowel Diseases

The term Irritable Bowel Syndrome (IBS) covers irritation of the whole gastro-intestinal tract, diseases that fall under this term include:

- **Crohn's Disease**, which occurs in the large intestine or colon
- **Colitis** and **Ulcerative Colitis** are indications of inflammation in the colon
- **Gastritis** refers to inflammation in the stomach

All these conditions are an indication that there is inflammation in the lining of the gastrointestinal tract, and the same diet and lifestyle conditions as previously discussed, will encourage healing.

It is vital to eliminate anything that may irritate the colon wall in its inflamed state. The most common substances that do this are alcohol, caffeine, peanuts, wheat, oats, dairy, and refined sugar. It can take at least two months to see good results once these foods are eliminated.

### ■ TREATMENT: Herbs

Herbs that can do much to bring relief and healing from irritable bowel diseases include:

> **Slippery Elm**

Slippery elm is the powdered bark of the slippery elm tree. It is slightly glutinous when mixed with water. This is one of the reasons that it soothes and heals as it lines the gut. Slippery elm also contains a growth stimulant, which stimulates rapid healing in the lining of the gut.

Taken before each meal and before retiring at night is the usual dose, until the gut is healed.

One teaspoon is stirred quickly into half a cup of warm water to ensure there are no lumps. It is best drunk immediately, as it thickens. More water can be added if it is too thick.

Often, slippery elm is enough, but for some more severe cases, a few other herbs can be added.

> **Myrrh**

Myrrh is known as a healer of mucous membranes.

> **Goldenseal**

Goldenseal has the nickname 'king of tonics to all mucous membranes'. The active ingredients in goldenseal have a tonic effect on the mucus lining of the gut. This herb also supplies a broad range of antimicrobial agents.

> **Gut Repair Recipe**
>
> Mix these proportions for the gut repair mix:
>
> - 80% slippery elm powder
> - 10% myrrh powder
> - 10% goldenseal powder.
>
> **DOSE:** Stir one teaspoon of the mixed powders into half a cup of warm water and drink immediately before meals and bed, as often as needed.

> **Marshmallow**
This common herb is rich in slimy mucilage, a tea can be made by pouring boiling water onto the leaves, let it sit for ten minutes, and strain. This tea can be very soothing for an inflamed gut.

> **Ginger and Peppermint**
Both of these herbs have anti-inflammatory properties and can be drunk freely as teas to help relieve inflammation.

> **Aloe Vera**
This is another 'slippery' herb that coats and soothes the lining of the gut. It also contains a growth stimulant.

Aloe vera juice can be bought, or a leaf from the plant can be peeled and blended with a little water or juice.

## ■ TREATMENT: Contrasting Hot and Cold Sitz Baths
Sitz baths can aid recovery by increasing the blood supply to the area, at least once a day and twice if possible. The reason sitz baths are important in relieving irritation and increasing healing in the colon is due to the way the different water temperatures increase the blood supply to the area.

## ■ TREATMENT: Castor Oil Compresses
Castor oil compresses allow the oil to penetrate deep and encourage cleansing and healing. The compress can be worn for at least five hours a day, five days a week. See page 98 for more details.

## ■ TREATMENT: Probiotics
When there is an imbalance in gut flora, a probiotic supplement may be needed. *Lactobacillus acidophilus* and *Bifidobacterium* are the two permanent bacteria in the gastrointestinal tract. All other bacteria develop from these two. A supplement containing at least five billion of each should be taken approximately three quarters of an hour before breakfast.

Fermented foods containing lactic acid bacteria, such as sourdough breads, sauerkraut, miso, kombucha, kefir, and yogurt, are a great source of these microorganisms. Including these cultured foods into your diet can help regulate intestinal health and even treat or prevent Irritable Bowel diseases.[11]

Kefir and yogurt can be made with organic soy and coconut milks.

## ■ TREATMENT: Food

**The YES FOODS:** Eating a diet rich in foods that aid the growth of beneficial gut bacteria will improve your general digestive health. This includes most vegetables and all fruit (though not in large amounts), examples are:

- Olives and avocados
- Red lentils, lima, and red kidney beans, use in small amounts and make sure they are well soaked, rinsed, and pressure cooked
- Root vegetables are good, such as sweet potato, pumpkin, cassava, taro, carrots, and beets
- Leeks are usually better tolerated than onion or garlic
- Well-cooked, fresh rice, millet, and quinoa are good
- Seeds and nuts can be blended, ground, or very well chewed
- Organic eggs are good, if well tolerated

**The NO FOODS:** Some foods have been shown to cause inflammation in your body, which may promote the growth of unhealthy gut bacteria that is linked to many chronic diseases. Initially, no potatoes, bell pepper, eggplant, or tomato should be consumed. These foods are high in lectins, which can increase inflammation.

- High-lectin grains are wheat, oats, and barley
- Peanuts and dairy products, especially aged cheese, should be eliminated from the diet
- Avoid processed junk foods, alcohol, sugary beverages, refined oils, and artificial sweeteners

Each person can fine-tune foods to what suits them, but generally, we find that these guidelines bring the best results.

11. Singh RK, et al. (2017), "Influence of diet on the gut microbiome and implications for human health." *Journal of Translational Medicine.* Vol 15, Article 73. <https://doi.org/10.1186/s12967-017-1175-y>.

# WHAT TO DO FOR
# FLARE-UPS

A flare-up is the name given to acute inflammation, sometimes resulting in pain, cramping, frequent diarrhea, and even some bleeding. This is a time when the treatments you normally rely on to control your disease don't seem to work.

Quick action can bring relief:

- Slippery elm or the gut repair mix can be taken every two hours
- Only vegetable soup or steamed vegetables should be eaten at this time. Often, relief can be experienced within a few hours.

As the pain, cramping, and diarrhea ease, the frequency of slippery elm doses can reduce to four times a day.

This simple diet is not forever—just until the gut heals.

# TESTIMONY
## PUTTING TOM'S FIRE OUT

Tom had suffered with gastritis for ten years. He was 40 and dealing with a recent flare-up. He was aware that the drugs he was taking were not healing him but just bringing temporary relief. Tom was concerned that each drug had side effects, especially the prednisone.

He came to the retreat to see if he could conquer his condition without the drugs.

It came as a surprise to Tom that the foods he had been eating were contributing to his inflamed gut. He loved bread and ate it with every meal. As a vegetarian, he also ate a lot of pasta. Milk and refined sugar were taken in cups of tea, on cereal, and in the form of cookies and cakes.

While at the retreat, Tom learned how to enjoy foods that were in their natural state. Initially, Tom only ate cooked food, mainly comprising vegetables, a little white rice, avocado, and olives. As he improved, he introduced a few legumes, grains, fruit, and nuts, little by little, as his body allowed.

Before each meal, the evening broth, and going to bed, Tom was given a mix of 80% slippery elm, 10% myrrh, and 10% goldenseal. A teaspoon of this was mixed with half a cup of warm water and stirred well.

Within 24 hours, Tom's bowel movements had gone from ten a day to five. Within 48 hours, all cramping in the abdominal area and bleeding from the colon had ceased. As his bowel movements had begun to take some form by day three, and considering how quickly Tom's colon had responded to what he was doing, he decided to begin reducing his prednisone. There was no negative reaction to this at all, and so, by day five, Tom decided to stop taking his anti-inflammatory medication. He was so excited at his body's response, as he had never experienced such results so quickly.

There were no side effects at all to him stopping taking his anti-inflammatory medications and reducing his dose of prednisone.

Tom was now convinced diet was the major cause of his condition and was committed to continuing the diet and lifestyle he had learned about at the retreat. He was committed to allowing his body to continue to heal.

Within six weeks, Tom was medication-free and enjoying a quality of life that he had not known for 15 years.

Tom went back to work and was very happy with the results. He now knows how to manage and heal his colon and be medication-free.

As these principles are introduced into daily life, the colon will begin to revive and restore its function. Remember, we are creatures of habit, and the colon can develop habits, too.

> "Nature's process of healing and upbuilding is gradual and to the impatient it seems slow. The surrender of hurtful indulgences requires sacrifice: but in the end it will be found that nature, untrammeled does her work wisely and well." page 127, *Ministry of Healing* by Ellen White.

# WHAT SHALL I FEED MY BABY?

This is the question on many parents' lips, as there is much information available, including seemingly contradictory advice.

Let's look at this subject historically and scientifically and seal the matter with common sense.

## HISTORY

### › Milk

Historically, babies were breastfed, and if the mother was unable to do so for a variety of reasons, goat's milk was usually the milk of choice.

In Europe, with less land available for grazing animals, goats were easier to tether in the backyard. Cow's milk was usually the choice in the Northern European countries, where cows have been used for many generations, and the land is not as steep.

Both milks were usually drunk in a raw state. This only proved a problem if hygiene and sanitation were compromised.

If you lived around the equator in the South Pacific islands, the milk of choice for babies who could not have their mother's was milk from an immature or green coconut.

## ⟩ Food

Feeding babies food is a fairly new phenomenon. Solid food was usually avoided until teeth were present and the baby could manage chewing. Often, it was two or three years before a baby was fed solid food.

## SCIENCE
### ⟩ Milk

In many ways, breast milk is superior to any other milk[1] for a variety of reasons. The closeness, bonding, and mothering hormones are enhanced in a mother when she breastfeeds and this cannot be overlooked. Let us look at breast milk, concentrating on the nutrition.

In the first three days of their lives, babies receive a very rich mixture of fats and microbes essential for their developing brains and gut flora. This plays a vital role in the establishment of their immune system. On the third day, the milk begins to be released. It is still fairly rich in fats, but as the days and weeks pass, the fat content lessens. Breast milk changes from month to month to adjust to the needs of the developing baby.[2]

> # In many ways, breast milk is superior to any other milk for a variety of reasons.

There is controversy about the adequacy of breast milk in maintaining optimum iron status of exclusively breastfed babies. The World Health Organization (WHO) expresses concern that some exclusively breastfed infants may become iron deficient[3], leading to the recommendations that exclusively breastfed infants receive iron supplements beginning at four months, and that formula-fed infants receive iron-fortified formula. However, further studies[4,5] have proven that exclusively breastfed infants neither developed iron deficiency nor

1. Martin CR, et al (2016). "Review of Infant Feeding: Key Features of Breast Milk and Infant Formula." *Nutrients*, Vol 8 Issue 5 < https://doi.org/10.3390/nu8050279>
2. Gao, X, McMahon, R, et al (2012). "Temporal Changes in Milk Proteomes Reveal Developing Milk Functions" *Journal of Proteome Research*, American Chemical Society, 8 June 2012.
3. Butte, NF, et al (2002). "Nutrient adequacy of exclusive breastfeeding for the term infant during the first six months of life" World Health Organization Handout.
4. Dewey, KG, et al (2002). "Iron supplementation affects growth and morbidity of breast-fed infants" *The Journal of Nutrition* Vol 132, Issue 11, November 2002, Pages 3249-3255
5. Pisacane A, et al (1995) "Iron status in breast-fed infants." *The Journal of Pediatrics*, Vol 127 Issue 3, pages 429-431, September 1995

iron deficiency anemia. Iron supplements can have adverse effects on a baby's health, affecting growth and development, increasing diarrhea risk, and may also increase risk for certain infections.[6]

It is hard work for a baby to massage the milk out from a nipple with the thrust of their tongue and their top lip. This action plays an essential role not only in the development of the jaw and head but also the roof of the mouth and placement of teeth.

For women who aren't able to breastfeed, or who are having trouble producing enough breast milk, infant formula is meant to serve as a substitute. Although infant formula is meant to mimic the nutritional composition of breast milk, it actually doesn't, as infant formula contains higher levels of protein, lactose, and casein than what breast milk supplies and most of their health claims have little or no scientific substantiation.[7]

Lactose is a type of sugar found in cow's milk and dairy products that is difficult for many people to digest. Around 75% of the world's population is lactose intolerant,[8] which means digesting milk properly might be difficult if your baby doesn't have sufficient lactase enzymes in your body. Science shows that goat's milk, which is lower in lactose than cow's milk, is a great alternative and is much closer nutritionally to breast milk than cow's milk.[9]

Coconut milk is another excellent choice as it contains no lactose and the milk from green coconuts is very close in nutritional value to breast milk.[10]

## > Food

To understand the science behind eating, we need to do a quick study of the anatomy and physiology of digestion, beginning in the mouth.

The first eight teeth to appear in a baby's mouth are four on the top of the jaw and four on the bottom, all at the front. These teeth take approximately six months to appear. The average age when they begin to show is between seven and 12 months. There are always exceptions to the rule, but on average, this is what happens.

6.  McMillen, SA, et all (2022). "Benefits and Risks of Early Life Iron Supplementation" *Nutrients*, Vol 14 No 20. <https://doi.org/10.3390/nu14204380>
7.  Cheung K Y, et al (2023). "Health and nutrition claims for infant formula: International cross sectional survey" *British Medical Journal* <https://www.bmj.com/content/380/bmj-2022-071075>
8.  Mattar R, et al (2012). "Lactose intolerance: diagnosis, genetic, and clinical factors." Dove Medical Press Ltd *Clinical and Experimental Gastroenterology*, Vol 5, pages 113—121.
9.  Leong, A (2019). "Oligosaccharides in goats' milk-based infant formula and their prebiotic and anti-infection properties." *British Journal of Nutrition*, Vol 122 Issue 4.
10. Michelle Levitt, MD (2018) "Stages of Nutrition for Babies + Best Baby Foods" <https://draxe.com/nutrition/nutrition-for-babies> accessed July 2023.

Traditionally, these teeth are called milk teeth, as that has always been babies' main nourishment at this age.

The three requirements for a baby beginning solid food is that they can sit by themselves, are able to feed themselves, and have teeth to chew.

The first teeth are considered 'tearing' teeth because of their sharpness. This can also be considered 'taste' time when a baby begins tasting different foods.

Begin with one food at a time, for example, cucumber, the stem of a cabbage, a lettuce leaf, tomato, apple, pear, any berries, banana, or a small cob of corn with the corn nibbles removed. Many mothers have found that placing a piece of apple in a net bag is enjoyable for babies and prevents lumps being swallowed. Chewing is a very important part of digestion, and giving babies whole foods as their first food encourages their chewing reflex.

Chewing is inhibited if a baby is only ever given purée.

The renowned Scottish doctor and dentist from the 1930's, James Sim Wallace published several books showing the deleterious effects of soft foods on our mouths and breathing.

"An early soft diet prevents the development of the muscle fibres of the tongue, resulting in a weaker tongue which cannot drive the primary dentition out into a spaced relationship with fully developed arches which will lead to more crowding of permanent teeth" page 131, *Breath*, by James Nestor.

After a baby has had a few months of eating like this, they can be given pieces of steamed vegetables. This allows them to recognize and connect the various colors, textures, and tastes of the different foods.

Between 14 and 20 months of age, the molars begin to make their way through the gums. These are the biggest teeth, in a square shape with four corner points. The molars are the grinders. When the molars are fully through, the glands in the mouth release the salivary amylase called ptyalin, which is the enzyme that breaks down starch. Now, babies can begin eating starch foods, including potato, cereal, pasta, bread, cookies, grains, legumes, nuts, and seeds.

As the hybridized wheat of today possibly contributes to many allergic reactions,[11] it is advisable to introduce toddlers to the ancient grains first. Einkorn, Spelt, and Kamut are from the original wheat and haven't been hybridized.

Mothers will find that as more food is introduced and eaten, their baby has less and less interest in milk.

A hesitation that many parents have to feeding solid, non-puréed food to their baby is the possibility of them choking. Let us define the difference between gagging and choking. Gagging is a very natural response to a piece of non-chewed food going down the throat. The gagging reflex will cause the lump to be expelled. There is usually noise and a cough or two, and the child goes red. Noise is good.

However, choking is when a large lump is stuck, and help is needed. Choking is silent, and the child may turn pale. A parent should always be near at hand when a child is eating, this is another reason why eating together as a family is important.

> **Timing**
Breast milk digests very easily, as it is perfectly designed for babies' digestion. Within approximately two to three hours, the milk is digested.

Some babies feed every three hours; others seem happy with four-hourly feeding. Even though breast milk is easily digested, it helps babies' stomachs if they have a gap between meals.

Some babies sleep through the night, and others wake to feed a few times. Traditionally, in many countries, mothers slept with their babies, and the night

11. Pes, G, Bibbò, S & Dore, M. (2019), "Celiac Disease: Beyond Genetic Susceptibility and Gluten. A Narrative Review." Annals of Medicine. Vol 51, Issue 1, pages 1–47.

feed was less disruptive. It is best for each mother to establish a routine that brings her the most comfort.

As the stomach needs a rest between meals, it is best to leave four to five hours between eating times when babies begin eating solid food. Larger meals can be eaten at breakfast and lunch. Evening meals are ideally the lightest of the day to ensure children sleep well.

Babies and children work well with routine. This also helps mothers to organize their days. Try to establish a routine early on, for both baby and mother.

Weaning a baby from the breast can change from baby to baby, and mother to mother. When a baby's teeth are through, and they are able to eat a balanced diet, there is no real need for milk any more. Some mothers choose to wean their babies at around 12 months. The babies would then be given goat's milk until all their teeth are through.

Some mothers find their baby is no longer interested in the breast after the age of two. Some mothers and babies happily continue breastfeeding for three to four years. So, weaning depends on whatever works best for mum and baby. Slowly and gently works best for the child and the mother's breasts.

It is a very personal decision.

## FURTHER READING

▶ Luka McCabe and Carley Mendes (2020), *Milk to Meals: A guide to inspire, inform, nourish and nurture you and your baby's journey to food*

▶ James Nestor (2020), *Breath: The New Science of a Lost Art*

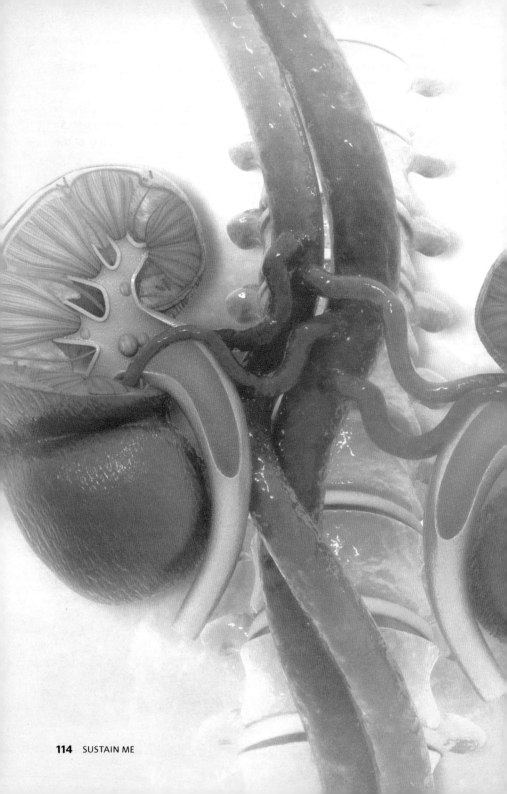

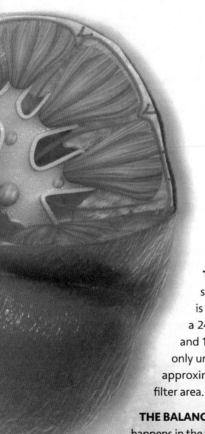

CHAPTER 6

# BE KIND TO THE KIDNEYS

The kidneys are constantly filtering the blood, and between one and two liters are filtered every two minutes. The nephron in the kidneys have two main functions, to filter and balance the blood. Let us look at how this filter works and how to take care of it.

**THE FILTER:** The Bowman's Capsule is a cup-like sac at the beginning of the tubular component and is the first step in the filtration of blood to urine. In a 24-hour period, 1,800 liters of blood are filtered, and 180 liters of filtrate or waste are filtered, but we only urinate one and a half liters a day. This means that approximately 160 liters of filtrate is reabsorbed in the filter area.

**THE BALANCE:** Another important function of the kidneys that happens in the tubular area of the nephron, is homeostasis. This is a self-regulating process by which our body can maintain internal stability while adjusting to changing external conditions. We see this function in the balancing of acid/alkaline levels, sodium and water proportion, and blood pressure.

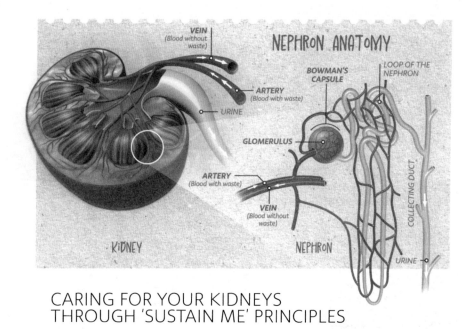

VEIN
(Blood without waste)

ARTERY
(Blood with waste)

URINE

ARTERY
(Blood with waste)

VEIN
(Blood without waste)

KIDNEY

NEPHRON ANATOMY

BOWMAN'S
CAPSULE

LOOP OF THE
NEPHRON

GLOMERULUS

COLLECTING DUCT

NEPHRON

URINE

## CARING FOR YOUR KIDNEYS
## THROUGH 'SUSTAIN ME' PRINCIPLES

**SUNSHINE:** One of the roles of the kidneys is to convert vitamin D from the sun (or supplements) to the active form of vitamin D that is needed by the body. To do this the kidneys must be kept warm. There are several ways to keep them warm, one is sun exposure.

Allowing the sun to rest on the skin of the lower back penetrates deep into the kidneys and stimulates blood supply to the area, which brings more oxygen, nutrients and water. It sparks healing and increases waste elimination.

For dark skin, at least half an hour a day in the sun is recommended, and for light skin, begin with five minutes and slowly build up to 15 minutes. The hotter the sun, the less time is needed.

Warmth from sunshine may not always be possible. So that the blood will not be slowed in its constant journey to the nephron, the kidneys must be kept warm. Keeping the kidneys covered, especially in cold weather, and ideally with natural fibres, helps to maintain the body temperature. Nepalese women bind fur strips around their kidneys to ensure they are kept warm. Allowing the kidneys to become cold on a regular basis forces the body to self-insulate by increasing the fat cells in the area, producing what is known as the 'muffin top'. Chilling the kidneys can be the source of many kidney disruptions and problems today.

**USE OF WATER:** To perform their important monitoring role, the kidneys must have the right conditions, with hydration being paramount.

The kidneys are made up of 79% water and use this water to remove waste from your blood in the form of urine. If you become dehydrated, it's harder for this delivery system to work. Some studies have shown that frequent dehydration, even if mild, may lead to permanent kidney damage.[1]

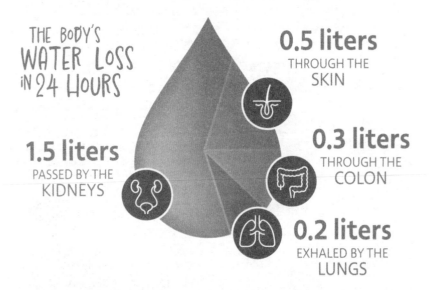

THE BODY'S
## WATER LOSS
IN 24 HOURS

**0.5 liters**
THROUGH THE
SKIN

**1.5 liters**
PASSED BY THE
KIDNEYS

**0.3 liters**
THROUGH THE
COLON

**0.2 liters**
EXHALED BY THE
LUNGS

Each day the body expels two and a half liters through either urine, the skin, colon, or lungs. Two liters must be replaced with pure water. No other fluid will do what pure water does. The other half a litre can be made up by the fluid in our fruits and vegetables, herbal teas, and juices.

Water, and water alone, will cleanse every cell in the body. To best utilize water, it is recommended to take it in little by little. Just as a plant becomes better hydrated if it is given water by a sprinkler or dripper system, so our cells prefer to take in water in a similar way.

Notice how God waters the planet: in showers. When torrential downpours occur, the soil can be washed away into the rivers. Take half a glass at a time over the day, or a mouthful every few minutes. A lot of water can be consumed in this way.

---

1.  Roncal-Jimenez C, et al. (2015), "Mechanisms by Which Dehydration May Lead to Chronic Kidney Disease." *Annals of Nutrition & Metabolism*, Vol 66, Issue 3, June 2015, pages 10–13.

For compromised kidneys, drinking 500ml all at once creates a strain, but they can handle that same amount if given it little by little.

To protect the dilution of stomach enzymes needed for digestion, many find it is preferable to cease drinking water half an hour before a meal and resume drinking one and a half to two hours after a meal.

> **The Relationship between Water and Salt.**
Before each glass of water, a small crystal of Celtic salt can be placed on the tongue. Celtic salt contains 82 minerals, while seawater contains 92. It is inevitable that a few minerals are lost in the evaporation process.

There are three kinds of magnesium in Celtic salt. Magnesium is a water-hungry molecule; this explains why Celtic salt is so moist, especially in rainy or humid weather.

When a crystal of Celtic salt is placed on the tongue, the mucous membranes begin to absorb the minerals, and the blood transports them to the cell membrane. Following the salt, we drink water, and the magnesium from the salt pulls the water into the cell. This is the quickest way to hydrate the body.

In his book, *The Calcium Lie*, Dr Robert Thompson states that when we do this at least eight times a day, we are only replacing the minerals we lost the day before.

Mineral deficiency and imbalance both disrupt kidney function.

> **Water Treatments**
Water is essential internally, but water can also be used externally to enhance kidney function. Hot and cold sitz baths can be implemented to boost healing in the kidneys, and the whole urinary system.

This includes sitting in a hot tub for three minutes, then a cold tub for 30 seconds, repeating three times in a row.

This can be done once twice a day, if possible. Every treatment extends the effect of the previous treatment. Ideally, this is done for 30 days, then a break is taken.

**SLEEP:** At night while we sleep, the kidneys run at a slower rate. Even though they are still running (at a lesser pace) they are effectively resting. The whole body runs on cycles, this resting cycle in the kidneys is vital in preparation for the faster pace it must function at throughout the day.

A growing body of evidence suggests that sleep disturbances, or poor sleep quality, has a negative affect on the kidneys and may be a factor is the development of kidney disease.[2]

**TRUST IN DIVINE POWER:** Fear and stress can have a damaging affect on the whole body and the kidneys are no exception. In a state of fear or stress, incontinence and frequent toilet visits to release the urine is not uncommon. On the other hand, an inability to urinate can also be experienced under extreme stress.

The Bible advises us to live in the now, this effectively causes past pain to fade and future worries not to seem so overwhelming. It is a matter of trusting that God has our future in His hands.

**ABSTAIN:** As animal protein is metabolized, it gives off high sulphur waste, which is very acidic and irritating to the kidneys. If animal foods are eaten, they need to be a small part of the diet and accompanied by many vegetables, which help the body to alkalize.

Alcohol, drugs, glyphosate, refined sugar, caffeine, and tobacco all have an irritating, and thus damaging, effect on the kidneys.

In 2015 the Sri Lankan president banned glyphosate after many farmers using it developed kidney problems, including cancer.[3] Due to lobbying from Sri Lanka's tea industry, the ban was lifted in 2022. Monsanto has settled over 100,000 Roundup lawsuits relating to damages to health from the use of glyphosate, paying out about $11 billion as of May 2022.[4]

As this toxic poison has only recently been acknowledged as such, there are still many foods that contain it. Wheat is one of them.

Another aspect of wheat is not only the poisons it was grown with, but that is was hybridized in the 1950's and went global in the 1970's, so by the 1990's, all wheat products were made with this strain of wheat. The hybridization of

---

2. Calero K, Anderson WM. (2019), "Can poor sleep cause kidney disease? Another step closer to the answer." *Journal of Clinical Sleep Medicine,* Vol 15, Issue 03, pages 371–372.
3. "Sri Lanka bans use and sale of five pesticides," *Ag News* 8 January 2015 <https://news.agropages.com/News/NewsDetail---13923.htm>
4. "Monsanto Roundup Lawsuit Update," Lawsuit Information Center <https://www.lawsuit-information-center.com/roundup-mdl-judge-question-10-billion-settlement-proposal.html>

wheat changed its protein or gluten structure, which created a food that is very difficult to break down in the body, thus putting a strain on the kidneys. Since these new cereal hybrids were introduced into human foods, a significant increase in gluten sensitivity and celiac disease has taken place worldwide.[5]

**INHALE:** Kidneys require optimal amounts of oxygen for energy to function effectively. Inhaling and exhaling, through the nose, long, slow and deep, ensures that the kidneys receive this valuable oxygen.

**NUTRITION:** The kidneys love water foods, which are all fruits and vegetables. Raw food delivers what cooked food doesn't, and cooked will deliver what raw doesn't, ideally,, we aim for 50% cooked and 50% raw food.

As long as legumes are soaked, rinsed well, brought to a boil, and rinsed again, and have a long, slow cooking time or are pressure cooked, they are a great form of protein for the kidneys.

Whole grains need a long, slow cook, such as in a crockpot or slow cooker. Another way to increase digestibility and make life easy for the kidneys, is to grind the grain into flour and bake it with a sourdough culture, increasing the digestibility of the food. This makes light work for kidneys. Nuts and seeds, when raw and well chewed, are another form of easily digestible protein.

Cultured foods, such as sauerkraut, kefir, yogurt, sourdough bread and miso, are very easy to digest and much kinder to kidneys.

Two foods that contain plant chemicals that have a tonic effect on the kidneys are celery and parsley, but they must be non-hybridized, non-genetically modified, and organically grown. Parsley expels an overabundance of water from the body, and scrubs the kidneys and liver, which keeps the body working at it's ideal performance and helps in weight reduction.[6] These should be daily fare for people with any form of kidney problem.

**MODERATION:** Not allowing for eight hours of rest at night can contribute to compromised kidneys, studies have confirmed this link with too short (less than five hours), or long (more than ten hours) sleep duration being associated with a faster decline in kidney function.[7] It is not the odd night when you don't sleep eight hours, and it is not the odd night you do sleep for eight hours, it is what happens every night that matters.

5.  de Lorgeril, M and Salen, P. (2014), "Gluten and wheat intolerance today: Are modern wheat strains involved?" *International Journal of Food Sciences and Nutrition.* Vol 65, Issue 5, pages 577-581.

6.  Ajmera, P, Kalani, S and Sharma, L (2019), "Parsley-benefits and side effects on health" *International Journal of Physiology, Nutrition and Physical Education* , Vol 4 Issue 1, pages 1236-1242.

7.  McMullan CJ, Curhan GC, Forman JP (2016), "Association of short sleep duration and rapid decline in renal function." *Kidney International—Clinical Investigation.* Vol 89, Issue 6, pages 1324-30.

If a person does not have kidney problems, eating wheat in moderation will not be damaging.

**EXERCISE:** The kidneys need exercise. One of the most powerful forms of exercise is rebounding, and everyone can do it. If balance is unstable, a frame can be purchased for the rebounder to hold onto while bouncing.

Rebounding increases blood flow to the kidneys as the heart increases its pumps, and as you bounce, your kidneys bounce, too. This has the effect of strengthening and toning them.

As you become proficient in rebounding, you can bounce even higher, increasing the power of the bounce!

Begin with three minutes, three times a day. This can be done like interval training, as fast as possible, with intervals of rest. One minute on with two minutes rest is recommended, and spread out the exercise over the day.

## PROBLEMS ASSOCIATED WITH COMPROMISED KIDNEYS

### 〉 Water Retention

As one of the kidneys roles is management of fluid and sodium levels, water retention in the tissues can be a sign that the kidneys are struggling. Water retention is usually manifested in swollen ankles and legs.

To remedy this, the dietary and lifestyle principles previously outlined need to be implemented with special focus on herbs and exercise.

▶ **HERBS:** The herb dandelion, is a very effective diuretic in that it stimulates the kidneys to help eliminate excess or built-up fluid in the tissues of the body.

This can be taken as a capsule, tablet, or glycerine tincture, these provide a concentrated higher dose than if taken as a tea. Taking the suggested guidelines on the bottle is usually sufficient. The dose can be doubled if required, as this is a very safe herb.

▶ **REBOUNDING:** The lymphatic system is particularly stimulated by rebounding, and as the swelling in the tissues with water retention is lymphatic fluid, this gentle form of exercise can help relieve water retention. One minute every hour can greatly relieve the swelling in the legs and ankles. Begin slowly with a gentle bounce.

## ❯ Incontinence

The urethral muscle can be strengthened to prevent and reverse incontinence. Rebounding, as previously discussed, is able to strengthen the urethral muscle. Those with a weak bladder need to do this exercise with an empty bladder for three minutes, three times daily.

For women, wearing a yoni stone can also help reverse incontinence by strengthening the pelvic girdle, of which the urethral muscle is part. This is discussed in depth on page 242 in the Yoni Stones section.

Daily contrasting hot and cold sitz baths bring blood to the area, which helps strengthen the urethral muscle.

## ❯ Kidney Stones

The causes of kidney stones can be varied, a high acid diet is one of the most common contributing factors. In the chapter on Arthritis on page 271, the acid/alkaline foods are defined. Specific herbal and health treatments that can assist in shrinking and expelling kidney stones include:

▶ **HERBAL TREATMENT:** A simple, yet effective, remedy to eliminate kidney stones is juniper berries. The volatile oils of juniper increases the rate of kidney filtration[8] which increases urine flow and helps to flush out bacteria. Juniper berries can be ordered dried from a health food shop. Begin the treatment by chewing one berry on day one, two berries on day two, then three berries on day three. One more berry is added to the daily dose until 14 berries are chewed on day 14. On day 15, 13 berries are chewed, and on day 16, 12 berries are chewed. One berry is reduced from the dose every day, until, on day 28, one berry is chewed.

This is the one-month treatment and may be sufficient. The treatment can be repeated a month later if desired. When used in conjunction with a castor oil compress, it is even more effective.

8.     Barnes J, Anderson LA, Phillipson JD. (2007) *Herbal Medicines*. Third Edition, London, England: Pharmaceutical Press; pages 186-188.

Some texts warn that juniper oil may be a kidney irritant, but there is no real evidence that this is the case. This reputation possibly stemmed from the old practice of distilling the needles (a known irritant), branches and unripe berries with the ripe berries, this practice no longer occurs, today only the ripe berries, which are full of health benefits, are used.[9]

▶ **COMPRESS:** Apply a castor oil compress over the kidney area for at least five hours a day, for five days of the week. Castor oil penetrates deeper than any other oil and has the ability to break up the stones. How big the stones are and how long they have been there will influence the time it takes to dissolve them.

This compress may need to be worn until the kidney stones are passed.

## 〉 Urinary Tract Infection (UTI)

The symptoms of Urinary Tract Infections are often frequent and burning urine, sometimes accompanied by an offensive smell. Occasionally pain in the kidneys can be felt. Drinking three liters of water, little by little, over the day and taking a small crystal of Celtic salt before the beginning of each glass can often be enough to flush out a UTI.

It is also important to implement the dietary guidelines already discussed and eliminate known irritants.

Specific herbal and health treatments that can assist conquering a Urinary Tract Infection include:

▶ **SITZ BATHS:** Taking evening sitz baths for 30 days will boost recovery from a UTI. See page 295 for details on this water treatment.

▶ **HERBAL TREATMENTS:** Cranberries are well known to aid recovery from a UTI. There are plant chemicals in cranberries that cause a slippery coating to develop on the lining of the bladder, which can successfully prevent an infection developing. This is a very safe herb and can be taken in high doses.

Goldenseal has the nickname 'king of tonics to all mucous membranes' and has strong antimicrobial properties. This root can be bought in a tablet or capsule form and can be taken three times a day until relief is experienced.

The bladder is lined with a mucus coating. Goldenseal tones this and can kill any harmful pathogens that may be contributing to a UTI.

---

9. Richard Whelan, Mecial Herbalist, "Juniper Berries" <https://www.rjwhelan.co.nz/herbs%20A-Z/juniper_berries%20.html> accessed August 2023.

## › Dialysis

At Misty Mountain Lifestyle Retreat[10], we have been able to help several people who were recommended to go on dialysis. After adhering to the dietary and lifestyle principles outlined in this article, their blood tests revealed an increase in kidney function, showing there was no need for dialysis. Treatments that specifically help include:

▸ **HERBAL TREATMENTS:** Herbal teas such as parsley, celery, dandelion, couch grass, or corn silk have the specific effect of toning and strengthening the kidneys. Rule of thumb for herb teas is a teaspoon of dried herbs or four teaspoons of fresh herbs in a cup of hot water.

At Misty Mountain Lifestyle Retreat, when guests have compromised kidneys, we make a litre of kidney tea, which they drink little by little over the day. Ginger is added for flavor and to help reduce inflammation.

# TESTIMONy
## FRAN'S STORY

Fran came to the retreat as a very resistant customer. Her mother and sister had paid for her visit, and she was about to go on dialysis, as her kidney function was quite low. Both her mother and sister had experienced improved health after their visits to the retreat and were hoping for the same for Fran. As a registered nurse, Fran knew that her future did not look good. Her BP was high, her legs were swollen, and at 58 years old, she knew it may end her career.

The night before the health program was due to begin, Fran called and was very concerned about her visit and what may happen if her condition deteriorated while she was on the detox. We assured her that we would monitor her closely and seek medical assistance if required.

Early Sunday morning, we prayed for God's guidance with Fran. God brought to my mind the fact that our parsley and celery were going to seed, and both are excellent kidney herbs. Couch grass is also abundantly available at the retreat and is another kidney herb.

In the initial consultation, it was revealed that Fran only drank four glasses of water a day at the most and often only had two to three glasses. She also consumed three cups of coffee a day. Fran exhibited all the symptoms of gluten

---

10. Discover more at www.mmh.com.au

intolerance and a hormonal imbalance, as well as carrying 20kg of excess weight. With her legs being so swollen, she never exercised.

We advised Fran not to follow the guests on the morning walk but rather join in the initial stretches, then spend a little time on the rebounder and exercise bike. She was asked to rebound for one minute every hour throughout the day to stimulate the lymphatic system, as this would help reduce the swelling.

Fran was advised to drink one litre of water, little by little, over the day, taking a tiny crystal of Celtic salt on her tongue as she began every glass. She was also instructed to drink a litre of tea over the day, made with celery, parsley, couch grass, and ginger—always in small amounts.

Within 24 hours, Fran's swollen legs had halved in size. After several days, she even joined the guests on the morning walk. Applying wild yam cream helped with her hormone imbalance by the end of the week.

**Fran emailed the retreat with the exciting news that she did not need to begin dialysis. Her kidney function was almost back to normal.**

Fran left a very excited lady with hopes for a much brighter future. She was now armed with the tools to conquer her health problems. The things she learned made sense, and she saw how her lifestyle and eating habits had greatly contributed to her health problems.

Three months later, Fran emailed the retreat with the exciting news that she did not need to begin dialysis. Her kidney function was almost back to normal. Her inflammatory markers were way down, and her liver function was the best it had been for years. She had lost 10kg in weight, and even her blood pressure was more normal. Fran was able to return to full time work with energy she had not experienced for many years.

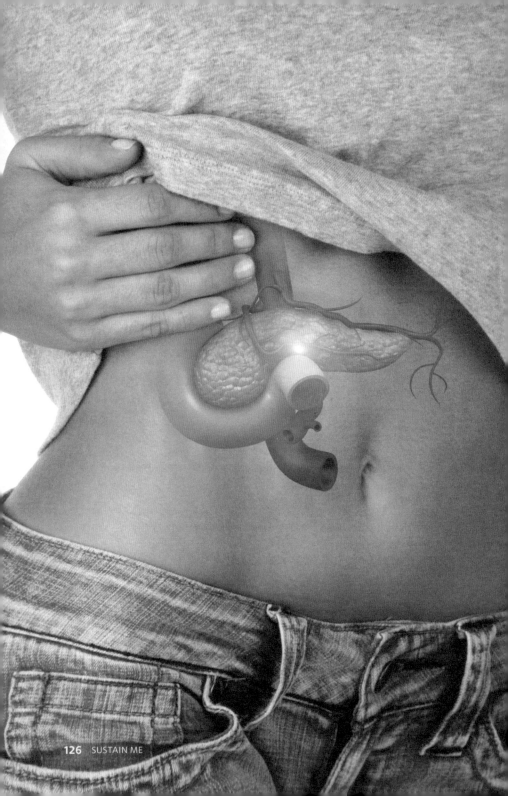

CHAPTER 7

# PONDERiNG THE POWER of THE PANCREAS

Around 1.3 million people were newly diagnosed with type 2 diabetes in Australia between 2000 and 2020. This was around 60,000 people each year, or an average of 166 new diagnoses a day.[1] Type 2 Diabetes is fully acknowledged to be a modern lifestyle disease. Hippocrates, who in 400BC was called the father of medicine, made no mention of diabetes.

In his excellent book on the history of sugar, *Sugar Blues*, William Dufty proved that diabetes began to appear when refined sugar became part of the Western diet.

Now, something else has appeared in the modern diet that has contributed to the explosion in diabetes.

In his book, *Wheat Belly*, Dr William Davis explains how wheat went through intensive crossbreeding in the 1950's. The goal was to produce a plant with a higher yield of grain to help food shortages, especially in Mexico, India, and Africa. Dr Norman Borlaug, a Minnesota-trained geneticist, received a Nobel prize in 1970 for hybridized wheat, which can produce six to eight times more grain than the original wheat plant. What was never addressed was the effect of the hybridization on the wheat's various nutritional components and the corresponding effect on those who eat it. So urgent was the cause of world hunger that these products of agricultural research were released into the food supply without human safety concerns being part of the equation.

1.  https://www.aihw.gov.au/reports/diabetes/diabetes/contents/summary accessed April 2023.

One great change happened to the wheat's starch structure: the intense cross-breeding enabled it to raise blood glucose levels even higher than refined sugar levels. This starch is identified as amylopectin A.

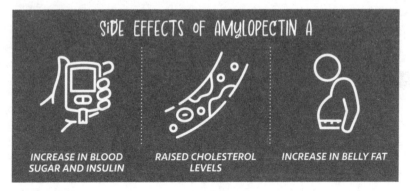

To compare:

Amylopectin B is found in potatoes and bananas, and is relatively high on the glycemic index (GI) chart.

Amylopectin C is found in legumes, which are low on the GI chart.

Considering this, when one contemplates how many foods contain wheat and sugar—especially how many fast foods—it is no wonder we are seeing a pandemic of diabetes.

Sometimes the cause of diabetes can be linked to pharmaceutical drugs such as blood pressure medications, the oral contraceptive pill or large doses of body building anabolic steroids.[2] Every drug has a side effect, and some medications compromise the pancreas. In the four decades I have been helping people manage their diabetes, I have seen it develop after vaccinations and after a course of antibiotics. This does not always occur, of course, but it can create health problems for some.

There can be numerous causes of diabetes, including the refining of sugar and hybridization of wheat. Coupled with the overuse of these products and the side effects of many drugs, diabetes has become prevalent in our society.

Investigation in every case is necessary to ascertain the cause. Sometimes, it is obvious, and sometimes, it is not. While the SUSTAIN ME principles can sustain optimal health, the neglect of these principles can cause disease.

---

2.  Ferner, RE. (1992), "Drug-induced diabetes." *Baillière's Clinical Endocrinology and Metabolism*. Vol 6, Issue 4, October 1992, pages 849-866.

# CARING FOR YOUR PANCREAS THROUGH 'SUSTAIN ME' PRINCIPLES

While type 2 diabetes is a lifestyle disease, we have found type 1 diabetics also respond positively to these principles.

 **SUNSHINE:** When the skin over the pancreas is directly exposed to the sun's rays, the warmth increases blood flow. The increase in blood flow to the pancreas means more oxygen, fuel, and water. These are the very elements required by the pancreatic cells.

The sun's rays penetrate deep into the body, stimulating life, vitality, and health in every cell touched by its healing rays. Over-exposure to the sun burns and damages the skin, so discretion is needed. Light skin should only have very brief exposure. Dark skin needs ten times the sun exposure that light skin does.

As the UVB rays hit the skin, a form of cholesterol just under the skin is converted to vitamin D. Vitamin D has 2,500 receptor sites on the DNA of every pancreatic cell, which boost pancreatic function. Studies have revealed that patients with pancreatic cancer, as well as type 1 and type 2 diabetes have a better survival when they get more sunlight exposure.[3]

**USE OF WATER:** Water supplies the main ingredient for the pancreatic cells to manufacture insulin and glucagon.

These two hormones balance blood sugar levels:

- **Insulin** increases the cellular uptake of glucose, thereby reducing blood sugar levels

- **Glucagon** raises blood sugar levels when they drop too low

In a state of dehydration, the production of these two hormones is impaired, thus compromising the balancing of blood sugar levels, as less water is in the body the concentration of blood sugar also increases.[4]

Often, the body cannot differentiate between hunger and thirst. The hunger sensation many experience between meals is often thirst. Unfortunately, many people today are dehydrated. This is not only from a lack of water but also because of the dehydrating results of coffee, tea, and the many sodas and caffeinated soft drinks on the market.

3.  Altieri, B, et al (2017), "Vitamin D and pancreas: The role of sunshine vitamin in the pathogenesis of diabetes mellitus and pancreatic cancer," *Food Science and Nutrition*, Vol 57, No 16, pages 3472-3488.
4.  Rowden A, (2023), "Does dehydration impact blood sugar levels?" *Medical News Today*, <www.medicalnewstoday.com/articles/can-dehydration-cause-high-blood-sugar> April 2023.

Water enables access to glycogen (quick release glucose) stores between meals, which helps to maintain the status quo in blood sugar levels. This explains why only water should be taken from one meal to the next. Keep the pancreas well hydrated with at least eight glasses of water a day.

 **SLEEP:** Every organ of the body goes through rest and work cycles. These cycles are set by:

▶ **Temperature**—the coolness of the evening tells the body that sleep is near.

▶ **Light and dark**—these signals are carried through neurochemical pathways to the brain's body clock. The setting sun is an indication to the body that night and sleep are approaching. Melatonin is a hormone that your brain produces in response to darkness and causes sleepiness.

▶ **Sleep pressure**—this slowly builds through the day, and as the day nears its end, the sleep pressure in the body produces the tiredness that invites sleep.

Sleep is vital for the regeneration of pancreatic beta cells, the release of melatonin protects the pancreatic tissue from the damage caused by acute inflammation,[5] and this only happens when we sleep at the right time. Being exposed to artificial light at night can block melatonin production, this includes the use of iPads, computers, mobile phones, and televisions in the evening.

In his book, *Why We Sleep*,[6] Dr Matthew Walker quotes studies that show the average person in an industrialized country today has five to six hours of sleep a night. He shows how eight hours is imperative for every function of the body to work effectively.

Further compromising the pancreas, the average bedtime is between 11pm and midnight. The most important hours for sleep and regeneration are the hours before midnight.

This lack of sleep is an important factor in discovering why the pancreas is compromised and thereby failing to function efficiently.

It is at night, while we sleep, that healing accelerates.

To encourage healing in the pancreas, we should sleep from 9pm to 5 am, a good eight hours. Depending on your lifestyle 8pm to 4am or 10pm to 6am may be more attainable.

To protect our cells, especially the brain, and of course, the pancreas, WiFi

5.  Jaworek J, et al (2012). "Protective effect of melatonin on acute pancreatitis." *International Journal of Inflammation*. Vol 2012,  Article ID 173675 <https://doi.org/10.1155/2012/173675>

6.  Walker, M (2017), *Why We Sleep: Unlocking the Power of Sleep and Dreams*, Scribner

should be turned off in our homes no later than 8pm. This deters the damaging habit of being on computers, iPads, and mobile phones close to sleep time.

 **TRUST IN DIVINE POWER:** Worry compounds all problems. Stress, anxiety, and worry cause the release of certain hormones, which can raise blood sugar. Long-term stress may lead to high blood sugar, which can cause health problems.[7]

These emotions place a heavy fuel load on the body, easily exhausting supplies of a well-functioning pancreas, whose job is to adjust and adapt to demands. A compromised pancreas is often unable to meet the increase in required fuel, which can result in hypoglycemia (low blood sugar).

Learning to value each moment helps to fade future fears and dissolve past pain. God has just given us this one day, and tomorrow, He will give us another.

In fact, He has just given us one moment, and soon, we will have another. Practice valuing each moment and be thankful that you have been given a body with an inbuilt ability to heal itself, when given the right conditions. In a nut shell, it is trust in God.

*"Behold, God is my salvation; I will trust, and not be afraid: for the Lord Jehovah is my strength and my song; he also is become my salvation."* Isaiah 12:2 KJV

**ABSTAIN:** There are some articles that must be eliminated to effectively conquer diabetes.

> **Refined Sugar**
In his book, *Sugar Blues*, William Dufty showed that there was no diabetes until sugar was refined.

Sugarcane in its natural state does not cause a dramatic rise in blood glucose levels, as the fibre slowly releases the glucose. Refined sugar does not contain anything to slow the release of high amounts of glucose into the blood. This dramatic rise in blood glucose levels demands a corresponding high release of insulin.

This constant whiplash of blood glucose levels is one of the main things that overstimulates the pancreas, contributing to diabetes.

Initially, even unrefined sugars need to be used very sparingly, if at all, until the pancreas begins to function properly. These include maple syrup,

---

7.  Sissons, B (2023), "Stress: Can it cause blood sugar levels to spike?" *Medical News Today,* <www.medicalnewstoday.com/articles/can-stress-raise-blood-sugar>, accessed August, 2023.

palm sugar, and honey. Artificial sweeteners are dangerous and should never be used.

> **Caffeine**
The effects of caffeine on the nervous system are similar to those in a crisis. In the book, *Caffeine Blues: Wake Up to the Hidden Dangers of America's #1 Drug*, the author, Stephen Cherniske, likens having a cup of coffee to coming across a tiger: a crisis!

In a crisis, the pancreas releases glucagon, which is insulin's partner in controlling blood sugar levels. Insulin increases glucose entering the cell, which causes a drop in blood sugar levels, while glucagon causes a release in stored glucose to raise blood sugar levels. When a crisis arises, glucagon is released to raise blood sugar levels, supplying the needed fuel in a state of heightened activity. Taking caffeine mimics a crisis response; therefore, glucagon levels increase. This is a further drain on the pancreas.

Caffeine is often found in combination with refined sugar, giving momentum to the whiplash in blood glucose levels.

> **Wheat**
As previously noted, Dr Norman Borlaug is credited with developing the exceptionally high-yielding dwarf wheat of today. The starvation crisis certainly was relieved, but these new hybridized strains of modern high-yielding wheat have never had safety tests for consumption by animal or humans.

The intensive crossbreeding of the wheat produced a starch structure (amylopectin A) that raises blood glucose levels very high and very fast. As a result, the hybridized wheat of today has a disastrous effect on people with diabetes.

Refined sugar and wheat go hand in hand in many foods, such as cereals, cakes, doughnuts and cookies. These are like kerosene to a fire.

> **Dairy**
In his book, *The China Study*, Dr Colin Campbell reveals how cow's milk can contribute to diabetes.

This research shows that some people are unable to break down the large protein molecules in milk. Some of these molecules get into the blood. The body then creates antibodies to deal with them. The problem is that these milk molecules are very similar in size and shape to the beta cells in the pancreas. The antibodies have been found to begin attacking the beta cells. This contributes to a reduction of insulin production, as the beta cells are those in the pancreas that produce insulin.

 **INHALE:** Pure air contains 79% nitrogen and 21% oxygen. Oxygen is the most vital element needed for life.

Every one of our 100 trillion cells requires oxygen to produce energy. When the energy cycle has oxygen, it can deliver 18 times more energy than when it is deficient in oxygen. Depriving our pancreatic cells of oxygen inhibits its ability to produce insulin and glucagon—the two hormones that control our blood sugar levels.

It is important to ensure that the air taken into the body is of the highest quality by assessing and eliminating exposure to chemicals, mold, stale air, and waste from industry and motor vehicles.

This is particularly true in the bedroom, where we spend a third of our life. Not only bedding needs to be checked, but also the quality of air that comes in through the window. An open window is a must for good health. In areas that have snow and extreme cold, an air purifier or negative ion machine may be necessary, rather than an open bedroom window.

Always inhale and exhale through the nose. Our nose purifies, warms, humidifies, and pressurizes the air.

 **NUTRITION:** The glycemic index (GI) assigns a numeric value to measure food based on how quickly the glucose, the natural sugar found in food, is released into the blood stream. GI is recorded on a scale of 0 to 100, the lower a food's GI, the slower blood sugar rises after eating that food. Targeting low GI foods allows maintenance of optimal blood sugar levels.

High fibre, generous proteins, and healthy fats cause a steady, consistent delivery of fuel to every cell, which prevents crisis calls to the pancreas.

Eating low GI foods can make a big difference to diabetics, as it prevents surges in blood sugar levels. Such surges, if they continue, can effectively wear out the pancreas, the organ responsible for controlling blood sugar levels.

**MODERATION:** Stevia is a safe, natural plant-based sweetener that does not cause an insulin response, but must be used in moderation.

Unrefined carbohydrates need to be taken in moderation especially whole grains and fruits, which are all excellent sources of fibre but high in natural sugar.

**EXERCISE:** Any exercise wakes up the pancreas! The most powerful way to oxygenate the body is exercise.

Exercise contributes to conquering diabetes and heals the pancreas from other diseases in a few ways:

▶ The increase in muscular activity increases the demand for glucose in the cell. To accommodate this rise in glucose requirements, the membrane around the cell develops extra insulin receptor sites. As insulin is the key that unlocks the door to glucose's entry, more insulin means more glucose and more energy.

▶ Stimulates the liver to release glycogen stores. These are small molecules of glucose stored in the muscle cell, and when released, they supply fuel to the cell, which helps maintain blood sugar levels.

▶ Increases blood flow in the entire body. The increase in blood flow to the pancreas means more oxygen, more water, more nutrients, and an expulsion of more waste products. Inactivity is a contributing factor to diabetes.

▶ Exercise such as High Intensity Interval Training (HIIT) decreases ectopic fat in healthy, prediabetic and type 2 diabetic people.[8] Ectopic fat is a hidden fat that accumulates in the internal organs, including the pancreas, and is a key factor in obesity and the development of type 2 diabetes.

▶ Aerobic exercise restricts pancreatic tumor growth by enhancing anti-tumor immune system to attack foreign invaders like bacteria, and helping it recognize cancer cells as abnormal.[9]

**In our high tech society today, many people spend long hours sitting. Not only do the muscles become sluggish, but also the internal organs, including the pancreas.**

In our high tech society today, many people spend long hours sitting. Not only do the muscles

---

8.  Heiskanen MA, et al (2018). "Exercise training decreases pancreatic fat content and improves beta cell function regardless of baseline glucose tolerance: a randomized controlled trial." *Diabetologia.* Vol 61, Issue 8, pages 1817-1828.

9.  Kurz E, et al (2022), "Exercise-induced engagement of the IL-15/IL-15Ra axis promotes anti-tumor immunity in pancreatic cancer" *Cancer Cell,* Vol 40, Issue 7, pages 720–737.

become sluggish, but also the internal organs, including the pancreas. Lack of activity can also compromise the uptake of glucose at the insulin receptor sites on every cell.

# TESTIMONY
## DAN'S DIABETES DILEMMA

Dan's journey with diabetes began at the age of 15 when he was given two courses of strong antibiotics to try and heal a severe chest cold. The doctor told him the antibiotics had damaged the beta cells in the pancreas that make insulin.

When Dan booked into our health retreat, he was 19 and arranged to stay for four weeks. The plan was two weeks health program and two weeks helping in the vegetable garden.

At the time of his arrival, Dan was injecting 90 units of insulin a day.

Later, Dan related his experience with his blood sugar levels. If he experienced a blood sugar low in the night, he would take a sweet candy. This would always give him a headache as this caused the blood sugar to rise rapidly. On the second week, he chose instead to eat an apple if blood sugar was low. No headache, but it took a while to eat the apple. Third week Dan decided to try something else, if blood sugar levels were low in the night, he would do thirty push-ups. This always caused a release of glycogen stores which raised his blood sugar levels enough to restore balance.

By the end of the third week, Dan had reduced his insulin to ten units a day. Dan was encouraged and excited at the incredible results he had experienced in just three weeks of implementing the SUSTAIN ME principles.

When leaving, Dan told me he had been diagnosed as a type 1 diabetic, told that his pancreas was dead and that he would never conquer this disease. In only three weeks Dan had proved that this diagnosis was not correct.

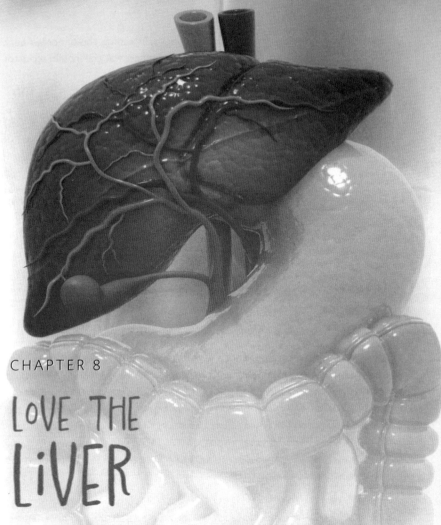

CHAPTER 8

# LOVE THE LIVER

Situated under the right rib, the liver is the only organ in the body with the ability to regenerate. It is the largest internal organ in the body.

It is often called the master chemist because of its ability to break various substances down into different forms. It is also called the *project manager* because it orchestrates everything that goes into the body.

The liver produces bile, which is the enzyme that breaks down mono- and polyunsaturated fats. Bile is stored in the gall bladder and when required, bile travels down the bile duct and is released into the duodenum, which is the first section of the small intestines.

Environmental poisons are stored in fat cells, if the necessary nutrients are present in the diet, the liver converts the fat-soluble toxins into a water-soluble state to be released out of the body via the organs of elimination.

## FATTY LIVER

As food is broken down in the gut, the carbohydrates are broken down into either glucose or fructose. They are then absorbed into the blood and transported to the liver via the portal vein.

Here, the glucose is either sent to the cell to be burnt as fuel, stored in the cell as glycogen, or kept in fat cells as stored fuel.

The liver is the only organ in the body with fructose receptor sites, meaning this is the only organ that can use fructose. The fructose is converted into glucose in the liver and then sent to the cells.

If a high-fructose diet is consumed, it will be too much for the liver to convert to glucose. The liver must instead store it as fat in the liver. This causes the condition known as fatty liver disease.

**Examples of dietary elements that could cause this are:**

1. Breads/pastries/cookies that have been sweetened with high-fructose corn syrup

2. Coffee sweetened with sugar, or soda and commercial fruit juice that is also sweetened with sugar

3. Chocolates, lollipops, candies, or other sugar-sweetened foods

Sugar breaks down in the body to glucose AND fructose. When foods like this are eaten day after day for weeks and months, the fat is stored in the liver, making it fatty.

## CARING FOR YOUR LIVER THROUGH 'SUSTAIN ME' PRINCIPLES

The SUSTAIN ME principles outlined for the pancreas on pages 129–134, can also be applied to the liver. The best solution is to eliminate all foods and drinks that have been sweetened with high-fructose corn syrup or refined sugar. Fruit is only a problem if it is eaten in large amounts, or if it's the main part of the diet, and taken in conjunction with breads and pastries.

# NATURAL REMEDIES FOR THE LIVER

Give the liver a kick start with a five day liver cleanse. This can be very helpful for hepatitis and other liver problems. If the body is quite ill, this may need to be repeated several times over several months—in some cases, week on and week off will be most beneficial.

As the liver is the project manager of the body it is essential for optimal health to have it working in peak efficiency. The following liver cleanse drinks can be taken when on a fast or while eating a regular diet.

## PART 1: LIVER CLEANSE

- 1 cup of fresh orange and lemon juice
- 1 cup of pure water
- 1 clove of garlic*
- 1 tablespoon of olive oil*
- ½ teaspoon of chopped ginger (this will negate any nausea)

1. Blend all ingredients.

2. Drink upon rising on an empty stomach.

| DAY 1 | DAY 2 | DAY 3 | DAY 4 | DAY 5 |
|---|---|---|---|---|
| Drink upon rising on an empty stomach | Double the garlic and oil in the recipe | Triple the garlic and oil in the recipe | Same as day 2 | Same as day 1 |

**Fifteen minutes after drinking the Liver Cleanse mixture, take one cup of Liver Tea.**

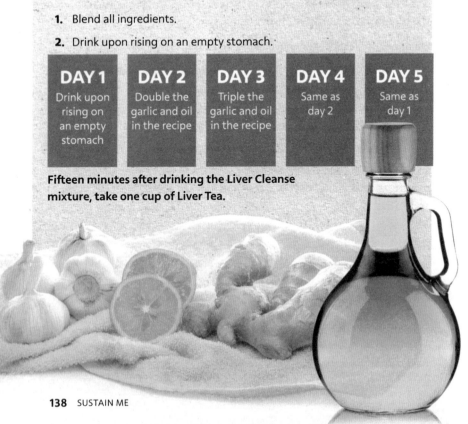

# PART 2: LIVER TEA

**Dried herb mixture**

- 1 part dried dandelion root
- 1 part dried St. Mary's thistle
- 1 part dried gentian
- 1 part dried licorice
- ½ part dried goldenseal

1. Assemble these herbs into a jar in these proportions for use as required.

2. To make the tea, put 1 teaspoon of this dried herb mixture with 1 teaspoon of fresh ginger into 2 cups of water. Gently simmer on the stove with the lid on for 15 minutes.

3. Let cool. Strain and store in the fridge, reheat as needed.

Continue this cleanse for five days. The bowels must be kept regular to allow the liver waste to be eliminated every day. This can be achieved by taking approximately one cup of Colon Tea each night before going to bed, this amount will differ depending on the needs/health of the colon. Ideally, there should be at least two bowel evacuations per day.

# COLON TEA

- 1 part cascara segrada*
- 2 parts licorice
- 3 parts buckthorn

1. Take one teaspoon of this tea mix to one cup of water. Gently simmer for 15–20 minutes with the lid on.

*Cascara sagrada is a natural herbal laxative made from the reddish-brown bark of a tree (Rhamnus purshiana). It contains compounds called anthroquinones, which trigger contractions in the colon, causing the urge to have a bowel movement. Cascara sagrada can be found in various forms such as capsules, liquid extracts, and dried bark, which, when made into tea, can taste very bitter.*

To assist in this cleanse a Castor Oil Compress should be warn (see page 311). Castor oil penetrates deeper than any other oil and has the ability to break up lumps, bumps, and adhesions. As part of this cleanse, it can soften and break down the gallstones, as well as lubricating the bile duct, thus aiding in the expulsion of the gravel/stones.

This compress should be worn around the liver area for at least five hours every day. Ideally, this should be done for the weeks before and after the liver cleanse. The liver is discussed more in depth in my book *Self Heal By Design*.[1]

---

1. Available from Amazon or https://shop.mmh.com.au/collections/books-and-dvds

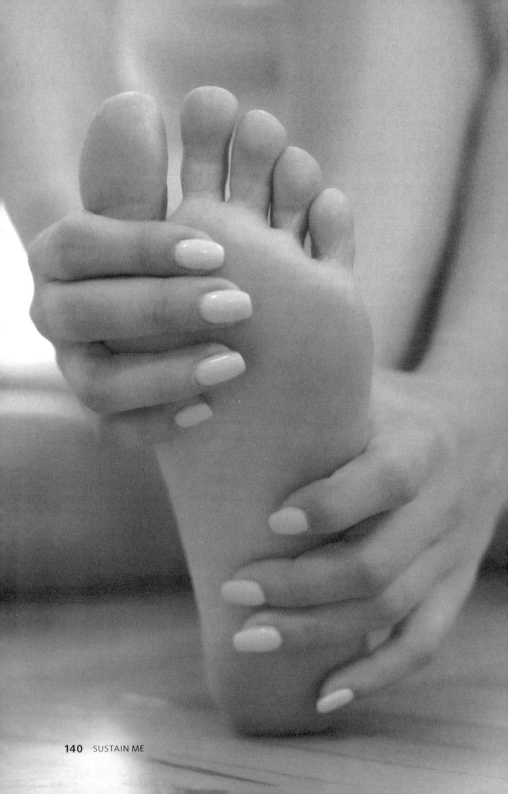

CHAPTER 9

# LEGS AND FEET

Our legs and feet connect us to Earth, so it is of the utmost importance that they work well. With them we walk, skip, dance, run, and hike mountains. We often underestimate the importance of our feet until they are injured. We will look at some of the more common feet and leg problems and how to keep them in good working order, and if necessary restore them.

## VARICOSE VEINS AND SWOLLEN LEGS

Healthy leg veins have tiny one-way valves to help blood flow up to your heart. Varicose veins happen when these valves in the veins become damaged or stop working. This causes blood to flow back down your leg and pool in your veins, stretching and twisting them, causing pain and swelling. While varicose veins are not considered a serious medical condition, they can be uncomfortable and can lead to more serious problems. With varicose veins, there is usually an inherited factor, but remember that although genetics may load the gun, lifestyle pulls the trigger.

This condition can be managed.

## Possible causative factors

> ### Constipation

Constipation can increase a person's tendency to develop varicose veins because of the added pressure on the vascular system in the legs.

"Three intakes of food a day, should equal three evacuations a day. Evacuating once a day is constipation," declared Dr John Harvey Kellogg, a famous doctor from the mid-1800s.

Increasing water consumption and eating a plant-based diet can make a difference by encouraging regular bowel movements.

Alcohol, meat, dairy products, caffeine, refined grains, and sugar all tend to cause constipation, as they lack fibre and have a dehydrating effect.

> ### Carrying extra weight

Carrying excess weight puts pressure on the legs, as does carrying heavy loads, whether it be on the back or shoulders, or in the arms and hands. This practice is always felt in the legs.

> ### Standing for long periods

Standing for extended periods of time, especially on cement floors, adds pressure to lower extremities, namely, the legs and vascular system. Poorly fitting footwear can add to the problem.

> ### Inactivity

The second heart is the calf muscle. This muscle stimulates the vascular system which is the system that delivers blood back to the heart. When the legs are not used the vascular system becomes sluggish.

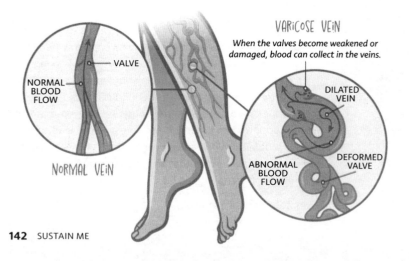

VARICOSE VEIN

When the valves become weakened or damaged, blood can collect in the veins.

VALVE

NORMAL BLOOD FLOW

DILATED VEIN

NORMAL VEIN

ABNORMAL BLOOD FLOW

DEFORMED VALVE

> **Some forms of exercise**

Running, jumping, and skipping are all exercises that have a jarring effect on the body, especially if the heel strikes rather than toe strike. Heel striking mostly happens when wearing padded running shoes. This form of exercise puts a strain on the legs, including the vascular network.

# CARING FOR YOUR LEGS AND FEET THROUGH 'SUSTAIN ME' PRINCIPLES

**SUNSHINE:** Legs love sunshine, depending on skin colour try to expose them as much as possible but don't over do sun exposure. Sunshine does not cause varicose veins, but too much heat can worsen the disease.

The warmth of the sun stimulates blood flow, which is the life of the tissues however too much heat from the sun can cause the veins to dilate and fill with more blood. It is important for the production of vitamin D that our skin receive at least 10 to 15 minutes of sun a few times a week, this can be done safely early in the morning or late afternoon.

**USE OF WATER:** Sufficient water intake is one of the most simple and effective ways to keep your veins in good condition. Drink at least eight glasses of water throughout the day, this will help the blood move a lot freer through the legs bringing with it its life-giving oxygen, nutrients, and water. Herbs may be necessary to encourage regularity.

To bring relief and to help heal varicose veins, water therapy can assist. Ice massages can be applied to the backs of the legs and may bring relief if the veins are swollen and painful.

Massage with ice for ten seconds, then have a ten second break. Keep repeating this until the area is chilled and a numbing sensation is experienced.

**SLEEP:** Early nights, allowing for at least eight hours of sleep a night particularly in the early hours of the night, give the legs a break. Sleeping during these hours doubles the healing powers that are inbuilt in the body.

Having a half hour nap in the late morning or early afternoon with the legs elevated can bring great relief to aching legs.

**TRUST IN DIVINE POWER:** While medical assistance may be necessary in a crisis, only God can bring about true healing. The Bible speaks of King Asa who had a serious foot disease and failed to seek God's help, relying only on his doctors, which ultimately led to his death.

*"Asa developed a serious foot disease. Yet even with the severity of his disease, he did not seek the Lord's help but turned only to his physicians. So he died".* 2 Chronicles 16:12–13 NLT

**ABSTAIN:** Stop taking all stimulants which inhibit healing the body. Alcohol, cigarettes, caffeine, and drugs all have a dehydrating affect on the blood, and quality blood is vital for healing in the legs.

**INHALE:** Every cell in our legs and feet require oxygen for energy. Practicing deep breathing will help to get sufficient oxygen into the bloodstream. When we breathe using our diaphragm it increases our blood circulation.

**NUTRITION:** Peak nutrition is vital to ensure that the cells that line the veins have integrity. A diet high in organic vegetables will deliver adequate minerals. Protein supplies the building blocks for the cells that line the veins. Well prepared plant-based proteins are the most efficient.

Natural fats, as found in olives, avocados, nuts and seeds, keep the cells lining the veins strong and supple.

Ensure regular bowel movements by eating a non-refined, plant-based diet.

**MODERATION:** Though it is required for us to often stand and use our feet and legs, moderation in the amount of time we are on our feet is vital. Likewise sitting for too long can seize up or pinch the veins.

**EXERCISE:** If possible, weekly massages to the legs and feet boost the muscles and blood flow through the vascular system in that area. Investing in comfortable, well-fitting shoes made of natural fibres is worth every cent and helps encourage better blood flow through the legs.

Weight management is ensured when the main meals are taken at breakfast and lunch, carbohydrates should be greatly reduced, and an exercise program implemented.

One needs to implement forms of exercise that strengthen the muscles and vascular network in the legs, but do not add pressure. Some examples are swimming, using an exercise bike, and rebounding. Walking can be helpful, but not for long periods. Exercise must be done daily to ensure strength, not only in the main muscles, but also the tiny muscles that surround the venous system.

Consistency is key. Little by little, day by day, healing takes place when the right conditions are applied.

# HERBS TO HELP

› **Cayenne pepper**

Cayenne pepper is well known for its tonic effect, not only in the blood but also the blood vessels. Taking this herb strengthens the walls of the arteries and veins from the inside. Begin by taking a quarter of a teaspoon in a little water three times daily.

› **Witch Hazel**

The herb witch hazel is an astringent and so is able to tighten and even shrink the varicose veins externally. This can be bought as a cream and applied topically to varicose veins.

# FRIENDLY FEET FOREVER

The biggest pores in the whole body are on the soles of our feet. Traditionally, in many cultures, this area has been used as an avenue into the blood for medicines. Historically, these would mostly come in the form of oils infused with herbs.

When I was in my 20s, a 90 year old lady told me an old remedy to help with colds. She said to bind fine slices of garlic wrapped in a cloth, to the soles of my baby's feet (don't grate or crush the garlic as this will blister the skin), within a few minutes, I could smell the garlic on my baby's breath, and soon her nose and chest cleared up.

Lavender-infused coconut oil massaged into the soles of the feet has helped induce sleep in babies and grand-mas alike.

We must be mindful of where and what the soles of our feet touch. Walking barefoot on sand or grass, or in a forest or mountain stream not only gives a remedial massage to the soles of our feet but also enables them to absorb the elements of nature. There is much literature available on the benefits of walking barefoot on the grass to be revitalized from the Earth's energy. It is often called *earthing* or *grounding*.

If you have always worn shoes, begin walking barefoot on sand or soft grass. Do not walk barefoot where your feet could be damaged or where the soles may absorb poisons.

## SHOES

Our shoes directly affect our feet, so it is important to ensure we buy shoes that fit well and are made from natural fibres. We must only wear shoes that will allow the feet and toes to move, and let the feet breathe.

Such shoes are usually more expensive but well worth the money paid, and they often outlast cheaper shoes.

Since the book *Born to Run* by Christopher McDougall became a bestseller, barefoot running shoes have become popular. McDougall shows how important it is to toe strike when running. The toes and ball of the foot are designed to have a shock absorber effect as the weight is taken with jumping and running. Most padded running shoes encourage heel striking, which can cause pelvic, back, and hamstring problems.

Rubber and leather are the two most common natural materials that shoes are made from, ideally shoes should be made from these items.

Socks must be made with natural fibres, with bamboo, cotton, and wool being the most common. Always wash new socks first before wearing them, to make sure they do not contain residue chemicals from the manufacturing process.

# FOOT PROBLEMS

## AILMENT: Cold Feet

Feet should not be cold! Perfect health requires perfect circulation, which is indicated by a warm body, including feet and hands.

Blood is the life of the body, and the presence of blood brings warmth. Cold feet show compromised blood flow to the feet. The long-term effect of cold feet can result in the toes losing feeling and even a development of gangrene.

Blood carries oxygen, nutrients, and water to every cell, including nerve cells. Blood also carries away waste. This is why the toes eventually lose feeling, as the nerves die from a lack of nourishment and oxygen.

## ■ TREATMENT: Hydrotherapy

Cold feet can NOT be put into hot water, as the tissues could sustain further damage. It is best to place cold feet in lukewarm water and slowly add hot water as they warm up. Keep the feet in the hot water for at least ten minutes and finish by lifting them out and briefly pouring cold water over them.

This quick cold water exposure equalizes circulation and has a tonic affect by drawing more blood to the area. Dry the feet well and put on natural fibre socks, such as wool, bamboo, or cotton. Genuine sheep skin slippers can maintain the warmth of the feet once the feet have been warmed.

## ■ TREATMENT: Cayenne Pepper Compresses

Since cayenne pepper is a circulatory stimulant, using it in a compress on the feet draws blood to the area, thus warming it. This compress can be used when the hydrotherapy can not, and can be worn every second night until feeling returns.

Cayenne pepper compresses can be placed on the soles of the feet overnight. These gently increase blood supply; the feet warm up little by little, and by morning, they are warm. With chronically cold feet, this may take two or three nights.

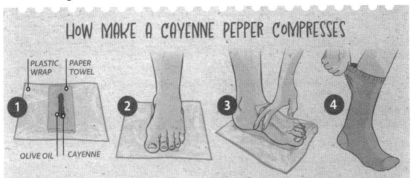

HOW MAKE A CAYENNE PEPPER COMPRESSES

PLASTIC WRAP | PAPER TOWEL

OLIVE OIL | CAYENNE

**STEP 1** Put a piece of paper towel on some plastic wrap. Smear a small amount of olive oil over the paper towel, then sprinkle half a teaspoon of cayenne pepper over that. **STEP 2** Place your foot onto the paper towel so the sole of your foot is touching the cayenne pepper. **STEP 3** Wrap your foot in the plastic wrap. **STEP 4** Hold the compress in place with a sock. Both feet can be treated at the same time.

In the morning, the compress is removed and discarded. Wash or wipe over the feet with a moist cloth.

## ■ TREATMENT: Exercise

Exercise is the best circulation booster, as the heart beats faster and pumps the blood more effectively through the whole body.

HIIT is the best exercise and is the exercise of choice for most trainers today. This is discussed in chapter four in The Heart on page 65.

For those with swollen feet and legs, or knee or ankle problems, the best exercises are rebounding, using an exercise bike, or swimming. These exercises take the weight off the legs and feet yet boost the blood and lymph circulation to those areas.

## ■ TREATMENT: Massage

Regular foot massages encourages blood flow to the feet and frees up tension. Tension in the feet is often a result of poorly fitting and restrictive shoes.

Prevent the feet from getting cold by taking steps to keep them warm. Never let them be cold. Warm them up by wearing warm socks and shoes or slippers. Australia is famous for its sheepskin ugg boots, which are an excellent way to keep feet warm.

## AILMENT: Peripheral Neuropathy

Peripheral neuropathy is a condition that effects the extremities, particularly the feet. This results in numbness and pain in the feet and sometimes the hands.

The causes can include chronic cold feet and diabetes, and often are the side effect of some medications, particularly chemotherapy.

## ■ TREATMENT: Same as Cold Feet

The solutions for cold feet also help to manage, and in some cases, even reverse peripheral neuropathy. Much depends on the age of the person, the severity of the problem, and their ability to implement the solutions.

## AILMENT: Planter Fasciitis

The plantar fascia is a thick band of tissue that connects the toes to the heel. When inflamed, the condition is called plantar fasciitis.

This can cause heel pain and discomfort when walking as pain is often experienced under the heel. This is usually caused by changing to a different form of exercise, which can strain this part of the foot. Being overweight, standing for long periods, and wearing poorly fitting shoes can aggravate the condition.

### ■ TREATMENT: Foot baths

Hot and cold foot baths can accelerate the healing of plantar fascia. Two buckets are needed. The foot is immersed in hot water for three minutes then in a cold bucket with ice in cold water for 30 seconds.

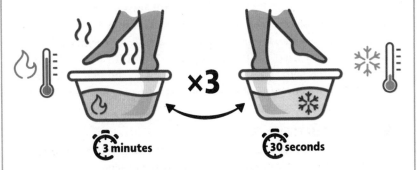

This is repeated twice more, resulting in three hot (ensure the water stays hot) and three cold baths. Even though this treatment only takes 15 minutes at the most, it can reduce pain dramatically while contributing to healing.

The key is consistency, and this should be done at least once a day—twice, if possible. See page 292 for more about this treatment.

### ■ TREATMENT: Exercise

To boost healing, simple exercises, such as pulling/stretching the toes toward the ankle every day, can help. Arch supports can make a difference as well as wearing shoes such as Birkenstocks.

### ■ TREATMENT: Castor Oil

Castor oil compresses overnight can help to reduce the inflammation, refer to the poultice section of this book on page 311.

Plantar fasciitis is not quick to cure and may take several months, but if the above treatments are implemented, it will be cured.

## AILMENT: Plantar Warts

Plantar warts are hard, grainy growths that usually appear on the heels or balls of the feet and are said to be a viral infection caused by the Human Papilloma Virus (HPV).

The virus loves warm, moist environments, so is often picked up from communal areas such as public showers and pools where it can enter your body through a cut or a break in the skin. It is common to experience pain from a plantar wart, particularly if it is on weight-bearing area of your foot as your body weight places pressure on the wart making it uncomfortable.

## ■ TREATMENT: Herbs

Thuja is an evergreen cypress tree native to north America. The leaves and leaf oil have been traditionally used as medicine for breaking down fine protein, which makes these hard formations. A clinical case in 2013 demonstrated the successful eradication of the Human Papilloma Virus with Thuja extract.[1] You can purchase this herb in the form of Thuja cream or ointment, which can be applied to the wart every night and covered with a bandage or tape. This may take several months to heal.

## ■ TREATMENT: Foot Baths

Implementing the alternating hot and cold foot baths, as previously recommended for planter fasciitis, will also accelerate the healing.

Application should be daily to take effect. The time it will take for the wart to break down depends on how long it has been there and the consistency of the treatment application.

## AILMENT: Tinea or Athlete's Foot

Tinea infections are known by several names, depending on the part of the body that is affected. The kinds that affect feet are typically Athlete's foot and nail fungus (onychomycosis).

Tinea is a highly contagious fungal infection of the skin, and the symptoms include redness, itching, and stinging or peeling skin between the toes, it can also appear as yellow or white discoloration of the nails. Tinea can be spread by skin-to-skin contact or indirectly through towels, clothes, or floors.

## ■ TREATMENT: Diet

As this is systemic, meaning it comes from within, a strict diet and lifestyle program can be implemented to conquer this and other fungal infections and diseases.

The use of broad spectrum antibiotic treatment kills off *L. acidophilus* and *Bifidobacterium*, these are the good bacteria that protect us from yeast over colonizing our body, without this protection, Candida can multiply at an aggressive rate making us more susceptible to fungal infections such as tinea.

---

1.  Joseph R, Pulimood SA, Abraham P, John GT. (2013) "Successful treatment of verruca vulgaris with Thuja occidentalis in a renal allograft recipient." *Indian journal of Nephrology*. Vol 23, issue 5, pages 362–364. doi: 10.4103/0971-4065.116316.

The human body will heal itself, if given the right conditions. One of the most important conditions is the right fuel (food). This is covered in more detail in my book, *Self Heal by Design*.[2]

There are a few other remedies that can bring quick relief and boost healing in the toes:

### ■ TREATMENT: Ice
Ice is the best anti-itch and anti-inflammatory agent. If itchy toes are scratched, the skin can be broken, and infection may develop. Ice will effectively kill the itch and prevent damage to the skin. It can also stop the spread of the tinea to other areas on the foot. Icing the affected areas can often bring relief for several hours.

### ■ TREATMENT: Vinegar
Bathing the toes with apple cider vinegar after a shower every day can reduce discomfort and arrest the spread of tinea.

### ■ TREATMENT: Soak
Soaking the foot in a mix of a quarter cup of sodium bicarbonate and two liters of warm water for ten minutes can ease discomfort, and contribute to conquering tinea.

### ■ TREATMENT: Herbs
Tea tree oil is extracted from the leaves of *Melaleuca alternifolia*, a tree native to Australia. The oil is a powerful natural germicide, and quite effective for treating tinea, as well as other fungal infections of the skin and nails.

After a soak, the feet can be well dried with a clean towel, and tea tree oil can be lightly applied to the area using a cotton ball.

### ■ TREATMENT: Breathe
Allow the feet to breathe by wearing sandals made of natural fibres. If the weather is cold, and the feet need to be covered, ensure that the socks and shoes are also made of natural fibres.

Look after your anchors to Earth. You won't be disappointed with the results.

---

2.   Available from Amazon or https://shop.mmh.com.au/collections/books-and-dvds

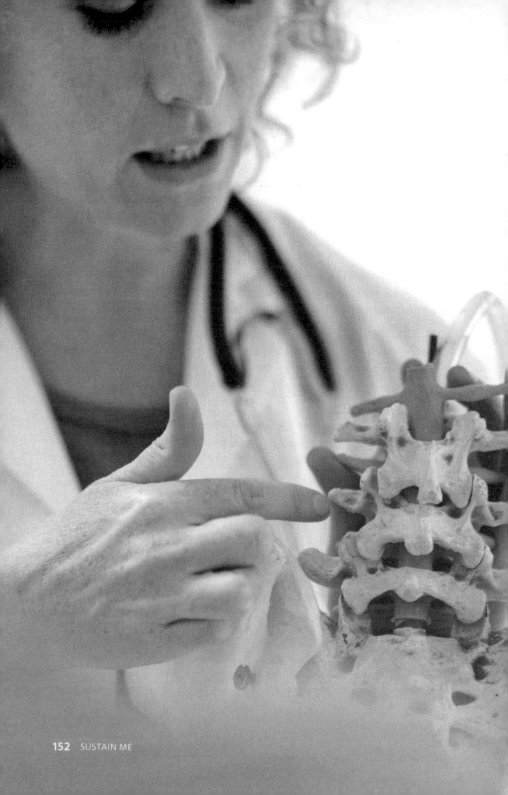

# CHAPTER 10

# BuilDing BETTER BONES

Our skeletal system is made up of over 200 bones. Each bone plays a very important role in making all the mechanics of our body function properly. Bones work with muscles and joints to hold our body together and form our shape, they protect our internal organs, cause us to stand upright, and allow us to move. This is the foundation of our body, but unfortunately today, bones are deteriorating at an alarming rate. We will now look at some common bone problems and solutions.

## OSTEOPOROSIS

Osteoporosis is the most common bone disease. It develops when bone mineral density and bone mass decreases, or when the structure and strength of bone changes, making the skeleton more fragile.

Our skeletal system is comprised of two main types of cells: osteoblasts and osteoclasts. Osteoblasts are the cells that cause new growth. Osteoclasts are responsible for the breaking down and absorption of the old or worn-out cells. Ideally, there is a balance between the two types of cells, and in the right conditions, they work well together. Bones break down;

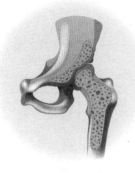
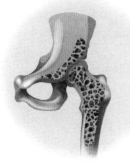

NORMAL BONE                    SEVERE OSTEOPOROSIS

the old cells are eliminated and replaced with the new, this function is called 'bone remodelling'. It takes the body approximately three months using these two processes, to create a new set of bones.

Normally, the rate of bone deposit and absorption are equal to each other, except in growing bones. This action continues throughout life so that most of the adult skeleton is replaced about every 10 years.[1]

## OSTEOPENIA

Osteopenia is a condition where bone mineral density is lower than normal, leaving you with fewer minerals in your bones than you should have, which makes bones weaker, but not so low as to be considered osteoporosis. Certain lifestyle changes can help you preserve bone density and prevent the condition from progressing into osteoporosis.

## RICKETS

In infants and children, vitamin D deficiency results in rickets, which is characterized by the failure of bone to mineralize. In vitamin D deficient infants, epiphyseal cartilage continues to grow and enlarge without replacement by bone matrix and minerals. The long bones of the leg bow and the knees knock as weight-bearing activity, such as walking, begins. The spine becomes curved, and pelvic and thoracic deformities occur. Rickets can have severe consequences for all ages, including obstructed labor, myopathy, seizures, pneumonia, lifelong deformity and disability, impaired growth, pain and even death from heart failure caused by hypocalcemic cardiomyopathy.[2]

1.  Langdahl B, et al (2016). "Bone modeling and remodeling: Therapeutic targets for the treatment of Osteoporosis." *Therapeutic Advances in Musculoskeletal Disease.* Vol 8, Issue 6, pages 225–235

2.  Munns CF, et al (2016). "Global Consensus Recommendations on Prevention and Management of Nutritional Rickets." *Journal of Clinical Endocrinology & Metabolism.* Vol 101, Issue 2, page 397.

# THE SOLUTIONS
## STEP ONE: IDENTITY THE CAUSES

In the first half of the 19th century sixty percent of children in London had rickets,[3] a disease that inhibits bone development. In the early 1900s, it was finally acknowledged that rickets was caused by a vitamin D deficiency. Very little sunshine hits the streets between the closely built multi-story houses.

The UVB rays from the sun hit the skin and cause a form of cholesterol under the skin to make vitamin D. Vitamin D is essential for the absorption and utilization of calcium.

Recent studies have revealed a resurgence in rickets and vitamin D deficiency, even in developed countries, despite education and the free availability of sunshine and supplements.[2]

Like children in the 19th century, children today are not getting enough sun!

The sun can be over- and under-used. The amount of sun needed depends on the colour of the skin and the time of day and season. Sunburnt skin is a clear sign of overexposure and needs to be prevented, as six to seven sunburns in a lifetime can double the risk of skin cancer.

Sunscreen and wearing long sleeve UV protective clothing and hats can affect the UVB rays that are necessary to make vitamin D. To lower the dangers of skin cancer while still achieving adequate sun exposure, it is safer to go outside without sun protection in the early morning and late afternoon, unless you are at high altitudes, near highly reflective surfaces like snow, work outdoors, or are outside for extended periods.[4]

The darker the skin, the more sun is needed to achieve optimum vitamin D levels. Lighter skin requires a shorter duration. Short, frequent exposure enables lighter skin to develop a tan, which will allow for longer time in the sun.

Since cholesterol is a precursor of vitamin D, cholesterol-lowering medication and fat-free diets can interfere with the body's ability to make vitamin D.[5]

Vitamin D deficiency can be a contributing factor in osteoporosis.

---

3.  Chesney RW. (2012), "Environmental Factors in Tiny Tim's Near-Fatal Illness." *Arch Pediatr Adolesc med*, Vol 166, No. 3, page 271.
4.  "Vitamin D, How much sun do we need?" Cancer Council of Australia, https://www.cancer.org.au/cancer-information/causes-and-prevention/sun-safety/vitamin-d
5.  Wakeman M. (2021), "A Literature Review of the Potential Impact of Medication on Vitamin D Status." *Risk Management and Healthcare Policy*. Vol 2021: 14, pages 3357—3381.

# MALNUTRITION

In his book *The Calcium Lie*,[6] Dr Robert Thompson shows that bones are not made of calcium. Bones are made of 12 minerals and 64 trace minerals. The 12 minerals are boron, calcium, chromium, iron, magnesium, manganese, potassium, phosphorus, selenium, silica, sulphur, and zinc.

Thompson also shows that calcium supplements do not strengthen bones and can even make the situation worse as only supplementing calcium leads to relative deficiencies in the other minerals needed for healthy bones.

Bones require the full range of minerals, not just calcium. This mineral balance and proportion is found in organic, dark green leafy vegetables, and Celtic salt, which contains 82 minerals. Himalayan salt is a close second with 75 minerals.

Mineral deficiency through dietary deficiency can contribute to bone loss, as the body simply doesn't have the building materials to build new bone.

# CALCIUM LOSS

Calcium loss can occur when a high proportion of acid-forming foods and drinks are taken into the body. The body runs according to a precise balance, and a high intake of acid-forming foods can disrupt the acid/alkaline balance.

The blood's pH must always sit between 7.35 to 7.45 and the lungs and kidneys are ever working to maintain that balance. When an overload of acid occurs, pH can drop. In an attempt to remedy the situation as quickly as possible, calcium phosphate is released out of the bones to obtain the excess calcium output required to maintain the delicate balance.[7] Calcium is an alkaline mineral, and the body uses this process as a last resort to maintain a correct pH in the blood. If this becomes a regular occurrence, the bones suffer, and this can potentially contribute to osteoporosis.

Acid-forming foods include meat, cheese, refined sugar, caffeinated foods and drinks, wheat, oats, rice, kidney beans, chickpeas, walnuts, cashews, and peanuts. The body can cope with a few acid-forming foods, but it is an overload of them that tips the scales. Drugs, alcohol, and tobacco also have an acidic effect on the blood.

Cow's milk is not a good source of calcium for humans. Cows have five stomachs and are better able to access the calcium in the milk, but cows get their

---

6. Thompson  R (2008), *The Calcium Lie: What Your Doctor Doesn't Know Could Kill You*, InTruthPress.
7. Buclin, T., Cosma, M., Appenzeller, M. et al. (2001), "Diet Acids and Alkalis Influence Calcium Retention in Bone." *Osteoporosis International*, Vol 12, June 2001, pages 493–499.

calcium from eating grass. Cow's milk is very high in protein, and animal protein leaves a high sulphur waste when it is metabolized. This sulphur waste has an acidic effect on the blood and the body uses the calcium in the milk to negate the acid residue. As a result, there is no calcium available for the body.

Research shows that dairy products have little or no benefit for bone health.[8]

A deterioration of bones can occur if a person's diet is mineral-deficient and contains a high proportion of acid-forming elements.

## FOOD FOR BONES

The most healthful sources of minerals for bones are green leafy vegetables and legumes. Broccoli, brussels sprouts, collards, kale, dandelion greens and other greens are excellent alkaline forming foods for the body. These are loaded with highly absorbable calcium and magnesium and a host of other healthful nutrients required to build bones.

Beans also contain calcium, fibre, protein, and micro-nutrients, including iron, zinc, folate, magnesium, and potassium, all needed for healthy bones.

Dairy products do contain calcium, but it is acid-forming in the body and is accompanied by animal proteins, growth factors, lactose sugar, occasional drugs and contaminants, and a substantial amount of unhealthy fat and cholesterol.[9]

8.  Bolland MJ, et al (2015). "Calcium intake and risk of fracture: systematic review." *British Medical Journal*, 2015; 351:h4580 <https://www.bmj.com/content/351/bmj.h4580>
9.  Calcium and Strong Bones, *Physicians Committee for Responsible Medicine*. <www.pcrm.org/good-nutrition/nutrition-information/health-concerns-about-dairy/calcium-and-strong-bones> accessed September 2023.

# HORMONE IMBALANCE

A hormone imbalance can affect bone strength. Chemicals and plastics that contain nonylphenol and bisphenol A, and the well-known herbicide, Roundup, or glyphosate, all create the estrogen mimickers called xenoestrogens. Exposure to any or all of these xenoestrogens raises levels and results in a depletion of progesterone.[10]

Progesterone boosts osteoblasts, which are bone-building cells, and estrogen boosts osteoclasts, which are bone-depleting cells. This hormone imbalance, which is sadly too common today, causes bones to deteriorate too fast. With the rise in osteoclasts, more of the aging bone is removed. With a drop in progesterone, the new cells aren't being generated quickly enough to replace the old ones. This hormone imbalance is another contributing factor in osteopenia and osteoporosis.

*What Your Doctor May Not Tell You About Menopause*, by Dr John Lee and *Hormone Heresy*, by Sherryl Sellmen both explain this phenomenon.

Wild yam creams are able to revert hormones back to their correct balance by stimulating the body to make more progesterone. This may take several months, but can bring healing and balance. This is discussed more in the chapter on Women's Heath page 213.

# LACK OF USE

Osteoporosis causes unstable bones, which is why the risk of injury is significantly higher in those affected. Avoiding exercise, however, is the wrong approach. Exercise not only strengthens muscles but also bones. Many bones deteriorate because of a lack of use and effective weight-bearing activities.

Compared to 80-plus years ago, people spend far more time sitting in front of screens. Whether this is watching television or using a computer, iPad, or cell phone, our bodies are not physically active like they used to be.

Strength comes by defying gravity, and the bones need this pressure created by regular exercise to prevent them from degenerating even further. Many people today are not performing the necessary bone-strengthening activities. The best gravity defying activity is rebounding. With every leap every cell is challenged and thus strengthened, bones included.

Many people—and bones—age and deteriorate because they stop jumping!

10. Vandenberg LN, Najmi A, Mogus JP. (2020), "Agrochemicals with estrogenic endocrine disrupting properties: Lessons Learned?" Molecular and Cellular Endocrinology. Vol 518, 1 December 2020.

# SLEEP DEFICIENCY

Osteoblast (bone builders) activity is most prominent while we sleep.

In his bestselling book, *Why We Sleep*, Dr Matthew Walker shows, through extensive research, why we must sleep for eight hours every night. He explains that rebuilding predominantly occurs between 9pm and 2am.

Sleep problems are a modern phenomenon and can be directly attributed to most people's evening pastime of watching screens. See my chapter on Sweet Sleep (page 179) for tips on how to get a better night rest.

# STEP TWO: STRENGTHENING YOUR BONES THROUGH 'SUSTAIN ME' PRINCIPLES

**SUNSHINE:** Vitamin D is essential for the absorption and assimilation of calcium and it also stimulates osteoblast cell formation. Without sufficient vitamin D, bones will not form properly. You can obtain this vital nutrient from three main sources: the sun, food, and supplements.

Sun exposure is the best way to achieve this. Bone health experts recommend short periods of 5-15 minutes of unprotected exposure of the face, arms and hands to sunlight, four to six times per week to prevent vitamin D deficiency.[11] In winter, up to 40 minutes of skin exposure may be needed.

Although overexposure to UV from the sun can cause negative health effects such as sunburn, exposure to the sun 'little and often' is a safe way to supply our daily vitamin D levels, which is essential for skeletal health.

The required amount of sunshine we need varies from person to person and can be affected by the time of day, clothing, excess body fat, and skin colour. The darker the skin, the more exposure is required as the darker pigment in the skin reduces UV penetration.[12]

If you're taking a vitamin D supplement, you probably don't need more than 600 to 800 IU per day, which is adequate for most people. Too much vitamin D from supplements can be toxic, however you cannot overdose on vitamin D that is created from sun exposure. That's because your body regulates the amount of vitamin D produced by sun exposure.

---

11. Nowson CA, et al (2004). "Vitamin D in Australia. Issues and recommendations." *Australian Family Physician*. Vol 33, Issue 3, pages 133-138.
12. "Vitamin D, How much sun do we need?" Cancer Council of Australia, https://www.cancer.org.au/cancer-information/causes-and-prevention/sun-safety/vitamin-d

**USE OF WATER:** Dehydration can actually damage your bones. All cellular functions, including bone remodelling, require water. Full hydration is necessary for strong bones.

If dehydrated, the endocrine system produces cortisol, this hormone interferes with osteoblast formation and blocks calcium from entering your bones. This dramatically decreases the body's ability to repair and build new bones.

Take at least two liters of water daily between meals. A small crystal of Celtic salt can be placed in the mouth before each glass of water. The 82 minerals in the Celtic salt will:

- Aid in replenishing daily mineral loss
- Enable the water to enter the cell
- Trigger a tiny motor in the cell membrane to produce energy
- Contribute to the correct mineral ratio in the bones

**SLEEP:** Early nights. 'Early to bed and early to rise makes a man healthy (including strong healthy bones!), wealthy, and wise.'

'The early bird catches the worm.' The early bedtime catches and utilizes the bone-building cells.

New evidence suggests that both sleep timing and duration may be important for optimal bone health, with the disruption of the circadian rhythm and sleep restriction being the most detrimental to bone health in early adulthood.[13]

When the natural sleep rhythm is disrupted this impairs bone formation as osteoblast cells are most active while we sleep, particularly during the early hours of the night. It seems plausible that all these factors can compound causing an increase risk of falls due to fatigue or loss of balance, and may make a fracture more likely to occur.

**TRUST IN DIVINE POWER:** 'Trust in the Lord with all thine heart, and lean not unto thine own understanding. In all thy ways acknowledge Him, and He shall direct thy path. Be not wise in thine own eyes, fear the Lord and depart from evil. This shall be health to thy navel and marrow to thy BONES.' Proverbs 3:5–8

Bone marrow is the spongy tissue in the hollow center of our long bones. It is the support and strength of the bones. In the same way, trust in God is the support, strength, energy, and salvation we need for our soul.

---

13. Swanson CM, et al (2018). "The importance of the circadian system & sleep for bone health." *Metabolism.* Vol 84, page 28–43, July 2018

**ABSTAIN:** Eliminating acid-forming foods and drinks, especially caffeine, wheat, refined sugar, meat, alcohol, sodas and other sweetened beverages, will protect the body from a lowered pH.

Caffeine is deleterious to bone health. Caffeine has been shown to negatively alter calcium homeostasis and decrease calcium absorption.[14]

**INHALE:** Bones are made up of cells, and every cell requires a balance of oxygen and carbon dioxide to guarantee the presence of oxygen in the cells. Oxygen and glucose provide the energy for the osteoblast and osteoclast cells to function. Inhaling and exhaling through the nostrils is the most effective way to maintain this balance.

**NUTRITION:** A diet containing a balance of 80% alkaline-forming foods and 20% acid-forming foods will help to maintain a correct pH balance in the blood, preventing a leaching of calcium from the bones. The acid/alkaline foods are defined in the Arresting Arthritis and Gout chapter, page 271.

**MODERATION:** Ensure hormones are correctly balanced by applying a wild yam cream twice daily for three weeks a month.

Ideally, the cream is applied for at least one year to ensure progesterone levels are high and to guarantee healthy osteoblast (the bone-building cells) activity.

**EXERCISE:** Daily exercise will strengthen bones, especially weight-bearing exercises. The best weight-bearing exercises are those that defy gravity, such as trampolining or rebounding. Every gravity-defying bounce strengthens the bones.

Rebounding is unique in that it affects every single cell in the body. NASA discovered that this was the only form of exercise that reduced the loss of bone and muscle strength when astronauts were in outer space. Rebounding proved to be effective in restoring bone loss upon their return to earth.[14]

"Increasing the G-force by rebounding, sends a message to the bone cells telling them the entire skeletal system needs to be mineralized, dense and strong. This reduces the chance of, or even reverses the effects of Osteoporosis. The bone cells are intelligent enough to recognize an increased G-force demands stronger bones and they simply set about producing a stronger skeleton."[15]

Carter suggests as little as three minutes of rebounding three times daily can produce this effect.

---

14. Bhattacharya, A. et al, NASA Ames Research Center (1980), "Body acceleration distribution and O2 uptake in humans during running and jumping" *Journal of Applied Physiology.* ID 19810029519
15. Albert Carter. *The Miracles of Rebound Exercise.*

# CHAPTER 11

# THE SKIN
## OUR PROTECTIVE COAT

The skin is the largest organ of the body and is made up of water, protein, fats and minerals. It protects us from microbes and the elements, helps regulate body temperature, and permits the sensations of touch, heat, and cold.

As the skin is the exterior covering of our bodies, it is prone to many problems, including skin cancer, acne, wrinkles, and rashes.

All skin problems are systemic, which means they come from the inside. When the right conditions are implemented, the skin will respond, either negatively or positively, depending on the conditions. Enhancing colon function is the first place to start when dealing with any skin issue as it takes pressure off the skin as an organ of elimination.

Let's take a look at some of the more common ailments and how the SUSTAIN ME principles can help.

# SKIN CANCER

There can be multiple causes of skin cancer with all of them typically presenting as a small patch of dry, scaly skin. The three common types of skin cancer are squamous cell carcinoma, basal cell carcinoma and melanoma.

Melanoma is the most serious form of skin cancer. It begins in cells in the skin called melanocytes (the cells that produce pigment and cause your skin to tan) when the melanocyte DNA can get damaged causing cells to replicate out of control and even spread to other parts of the body. Melanoma is the leading cause of death from skin disease.

MELANOMA

EPIDERMIS

DERMIS

HYPODERMIS

ASYMMETRICAL MOLE WITH IRREGULAR COLOUR

SQUAMOUS CELLS

BASAL CELLS

MELANOCYTE

CANCEROUS MELANOCYTES

To prevent skin cancer's occurrence or aid in the healing process, we must adhere to the SUSTAIN ME principles of health. In addition to these natural health laws, the following simple remedies have helped thousands conquer skin cancer.

### ■ TREATMENT: Aloe Vera

Many can attest to the beneficial healing properties of the aloe vera plant for a large range of skin ailments, including using the gel from the inside of the aloe vera plant to help eliminate some skin cancers. This must be applied twice daily and may take several months, depending on the severity. Research supports the fact that aloe vera, particularly certain components in the plant, have striking anticancer effects and can suppress cancer cell proliferation.[1]

### ■ TREATMENT: Castor Oil

Others have found that regular application of castor oil will eventually remove skin cancer. Consistency is key. This is not a quick remedy; it is slower and gentler than many conventional treatments.

---

1.  Chang X, et al (2016) "Aloe-emodin suppresses esophageal cancer cell TE1 proliferation by inhibiting AKT and ERK phosphorylation." *Oncology Letters*. 2016 September; 12(3):2232-2238.

# ■ TREATMENT: Cansema or Black Salve

For skin cancer, one of the most prominent alternative therapies is Black Salve, commonly marketed as Cansema. This cream is not hard to find, as the recipe is on the internet. The number one ingredient is bloodroot, a flower native to the woodlands of North America.

Black salve comes as a black paste, and a SMALL amount is applied to the suspect area ONCE. The salve is then covered with a low-allergy tape and left on for 24 hours. A clear sign that there are positive cells is that the person experiences a slight stinging sensation in the first few hours after application.

After 24 hours, the tape is removed. If there are no positive cells, there will be no reaction.

If positive cells are present, the area will be red and raised with a pus center. Often, the wound will become more inflamed over the next 24 hours.

After 24 hours, the swelling and inflammation will begin to subside. The inside pus dries out and forms a scab of dead tissue. This slowly happens over the next few days. By day ten, a dry core usually falls out. This may leave a small hole, but many can testify that this fills up in a matter of weeks with proper wound treatment. Applying castor oil daily can speed the healing process.

WARNING: While Cansema is the quickest way to eliminate skin cancer, it is **important to note that one application is often enough.** If you suspect that there are still some cancer cells present, a second application can be done, but this must not happen any earlier than two to three months later when the initial wound has fully healed. Incorrect use of this herbal treatment can result in serious complications.

Improper use can be as simple as using too much or too often, as the main ingredient, bloodroot, can have powerful effects on the body. Although bloodroot compounds have strong antioxidant and antimicrobial effects, incorrect use has been tied to the formation of scars and contact dermatitis, which has lead to this treatment receiving a lot of negative press.

# ■ TREATMENT: Oregano Essential Oil

One drop of oregano essential oil can be applied to cancerous cells once a day. This may take a few weeks, but eventually, they will fall off. Much depends on how advanced the cancer is, and the type of skin cancer.

# HERPES

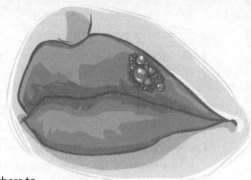

Herpes is caused by the herpes simplex virus and is characterized by regular outbreaks of small, painful, fluid-filled blisters. They normally manifest around the mouth or genital area.

Many people have this virus, and it is there to stay. It is believed to be primarily spread by skin-to-skin contact. The good news is that it can be managed.

Adhering to the SUSTAIN ME principles of health is fundamental in boosting the body's ability to heal itself, and herpes is no exception. People have testified that as their overall health improves, the outbreaks become far fewer, and the severity is greatly diminished.

### ▣ TREATMENTS: Ice

Applying ice to the area until the site is numb (as soon as the tingling feeling arises) can often arrest the development of a herpes wound. Ice may need to be applied every few hour.

Inflammation feeds the development of herpes, and ice is the ultimate anti-inflammatory. It can be applied for even just five minutes every few hours for the first few days. Not only does this bring great relief but it also speeds recovery.

Washing the area with one teaspoon of sodium bicarbonate to one cup of water can bring relief and boost healing.

### ▣ TREATMENTS: Vitamin C

Clinical studies have shown vitamin C has healing benefits in patients with infections of herpes viruses.[2] 5,000 mg of vitamin C can be taken every four hours to help reduce the effects of an outbreak of herpes.

### ▣ TREATMENTS: Lysine

Cold sores are from the herpes virus. L-Lysine appears to be an effective agent for reducing the occurrence, severity and healing time of recurrent herpes infections.[3] Lysine tablets can be easily purchased and, if taken at the first sign of discomfort, can prevent cold sores.

---

2. Biancatelli RMLC, Berrill M & Marik PE (2020) "The antiviral properties of vitamin C," *Expert Review of Anti-infective Therapy*, Vol 18, 2020, Issue 2, <https://doi.org/10.1080/14787210.2020.1706483>

3. Griffith RS, et al (1987). "Success of L-lysine therapy in frequently recurrent herpes simplex infection. Treatment and prophylaxis." *Dermatologica.* Vol ;175, Issue 4, pages 183-190.

## ■ TREATMENTS: Cayenne Pepper

A lady from Jamaica contacted us regarding her genital herpes, which she had suffered from for five years. She decided to try a cayenne pepper compress. A light sprinkle of olive oil was applied on a panty liner, then a light dust of cayenne pepper. She wore this for eight hours through the day while at work. She reported that there was a slight burning, but it was certainly bearable, and she was able to work. She repeated the process to wear the compress overnight.

Within 16 hours, the lesion had healed, and the pain had gone. This usually takes five to seven days. One half teaspoon of cayenne pepper in one cup of water was also drunk twice a day.

Her inability to perspire (hypohidrosis) was another problem that was resolved as a result of consuming cayenne pepper daily. For years, this had caused her much discomfort, including cold feet and hands. She believes she has a new lease on life because of her positive experience with cayenne pepper.

# WARTS

Warts are a skin infection, and there are a few theories as to why warts develop. Some theorize that they are viral and others that they are fungal. Warts most commonly appear on the hands, but they can also affect the feet, face, genitals and knees.

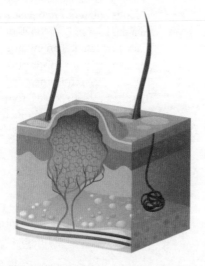

## ■ TREATMENTS

Several remedies have been suggested. One woman told me she found that wrapping green banana skins on a wart overnight for a week caused it to disappear. Other solutions are:

- ▶ Thuja herbal cream is highly effective for treating warts as well as tinea and fungal symptoms of any type or location on the body.

- ▶ Regularly applying castor oil can cause warts to dissolve. Castor oil has antibacterial and antimicrobial properties that can help speed wound healing.

- ▶ Applying apple cider vinegar or a drop of oregano oil a couple of times a day has been known to eliminate warts.

# ECZEMA/PSORIASIS

Eczema is the name for a group of inflammatory skin conditions that cause itchiness, dry skin, rashes, scaly patches, blisters and skin infections. It often occurs in babies and children. Most commonly, it manifests itself in the folds of the skin. In extreme cases, the whole body may be covered. It is estimated that one in ten individuals will develop eczema during their lifetime.[4]

Psoriasis is a similar condition in adults and tends to develop on areas such as the elbows or scalp. Scratching can inflame and worsen both conditions. These are systemic, meaning that the problem comes from within the body and so must be treated from within.

 HEALTHY SKIN

 ECZEMA

Tightly packed skin cells create a natural barrier

Chemicals, solvents and water can enter and cause inflammation

Rough, cracked, partially inflamed skin due to damaged skin barrier.

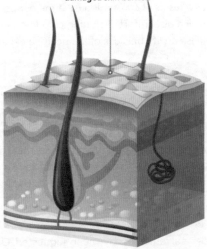

# CAUSES

While the exact cause of eczema is unknown, researchers do know that people develop eczema due to an interaction between genes and an environmental trigger. The most common allergens are chemicals, mold, and food.

The first step is to investigate the cause and eliminate any exposure to chemicals and mold.

Mold releases tiny seeds called spores into the air, which can trigger eczema symptoms. Mold spores are found in any damp place, such as piles of leaves, steamy bathrooms, kitchens and even piles of damp clothes.

> Regarding foods, the most common allergenic foods are peanuts, dairy,

---

4. Eczema Stats <https://nationaleczema.org/research/eczema-facts/> accessed October 2023.

wheat, oats, and refined sugar. It can take at least two months to see a result once these foods are eliminated from the diet.

▶ Vaccinations can have a devastating effect on infant immune systems and can trigger eczema. This is due to the neurotoxins in the vaccines and the damaging effect on the gut flora. Studies carried out in Australia give evidence that diphtheria, tetanus, pertussis, and polio vaccines have been associated with an approximately 50% higher risk of eczema and food allergies in seven year olds.[5]

▶ Antibiotics and so-called 'safe' analgesic use in young babies can disrupt gut flora causing dysbiosis which contributes to eczema. Antibiotic use in infancy is associated with the development of atopic eczema during the first 12 months of life.[6]

▶ Research suggests that mineral-rich tap water, also known as 'hard water,' can negatively impact eczema symptoms and introduce skin conditions early in life.[7] Swimming pools can also irritate eczema as they often contain high levels of chlorine, a powerful disinfectant, and various other chemicals. This can vary depending on the mix of chemicals used in an individual pool.

▶ Cow's milk allergy is the most prevalent type of food allergy among infants, affecting up to 3.8% of small children.[8] Symptoms that can appear within minutes of having a small amount of milk include: raised red bumps of skin, hives, itchy, red, weeping or crusty rash on the skin or eczema.[9]

Gut disruptions that cause low intestinal microbial diversity interfere with the colon's ability to effectively eliminate body waste. This forces the body to increase the elimination of waste via the skin, thus contributing to skin irritation, eczema, and, in adults, psoriasis.

5. Nakajima K., et al (2007). "Is childhood immunisation associated with atopic disease from age 7 to 32 years?" *Thorax.* 2007, Vol 62, Issue 3, pages 270–275.
6. El-Heis S., et al (2023). "Early life exposure to antibiotics and laxatives in relation to infantile atopic eczema." *Pediatric Allergy and Immunology.* Vol 34, Issue 5, <https://doi.org/10.1111/pai.13964>
7. Zarif K., et al (2020). "The Effect of Water Hardness On Atopic Eczema, Skin Barrier Function: A Systematic Review, Meta-Analysis." *Clinical & Experimental Allergy,* 1 December 2020.
8. Maryniak NZ, (2023). "Alternatives to Cow's Milk-Based Infant Formulas in the Prevention and Management of Cow's Milk Allergy." *Foods.* 2022 March 23, Vol 11, Issue 7 <https://doi.org/10.3390/foods11070926>
9. Cow's milk allergy <https://www.betterhealth.vic.gov.au/health/conditionsandtreatments/cows-milk-allergy>

# THE SOLUTIONS

## STEP ONE: BRING RELIEF

Until the skin responds to the dietary and lifestyle changes as outlined in SUSTAIN ME, there are some simple solutions you can use to bring quick relief.

**Don't Scratch:** Scratching will only intensify the situation and make the eczema or psoriasis much worse, to the point of breaking the skin and causing it to bleed.

- **Apply Ice:** This will often bring relief to itching quite quickly. Ice works by freezing and numbing the area, which reduces inflammation. When inflamed, more blood is drawn to the area; thus, there is more heat and more itching. Apply ice for seven seconds, rest for seven seconds, continue this process until the area is numb.

- **Sodium Bicarbonate Baths:** Add four cups of bicarb soda to a full bathtub to bring relief.

- **Oat Baths:** Adding four cups of oats in a full bathtub will soothe the skin. It is helpful to put the oats into a cloth bag, so they are not loose in the water.

- **Aloe Vera and Coconut Oil:** Some have found a cream using natural oils with calendula helps. It is a matter of trying different things to see what your skin responds to best.

## STEP TWO: HEALING SKIN PROBLEMS THROUGH THE 'SUSTAIN ME' PRINCIPLES

In addition to the SUSTAIN ME principles below, proper colon function will also be helpful in improving your skin as outlined on page 92

**SUNSHINE:** Skin needs sun. The sun has an antimicrobial effect on the skin and stimulates vitamin D production used in the production of the important antimicrobial peptides which combat skin infections.

Children living in areas with lower levels of sunlight are at greater risk of developing eczema, compared to those in areas with higher UV.[10] The colour of your skin will dictate the amount of healthy sun exposure. Light skin requires moderation to prevent burning.

---

10. Osborne NJ, Ukoumunne OC, Wake M, Allen KJ. (2012). "Prevalence of eczema and food allergy is associated with latitude in Australia." *The Journal of Allergy and Clinical Immunology.* Vol 129, issue 3, pages 865-7. doi: 10.1016/j.jaci.2012.01.037. Accessed November 2023.

Sunshine on the skin can appear to irritate at times if the skin is inflamed, but overall, the sun's rays penetrate, disinfect, and can help to heal skin irritations.

**USE OF WATER:** Keeping well hydrated keeps the skin soft and supple. Adequate water also allows for perspiration to be self regulated, this is an important part of the body eliminating waste. An adult should have at least eight glasses of water a day, ceasing half an hour before a meal and resuming one and a half to two hours after the meal. This is paramount in keeping the skin cells supple and helps prevent skin drying out.

 **SLEEP:** Not only can eczema and its symptoms interfere with sleep, not getting enough sleep can also decrease skin barrier function recovery.[11] As with any other part of the body, skin needs sleep. This allows periods of rest which results in more efficiency in its many functions. Especially in regards to healing, sleeping at night is vital.

**TRUST IN DIVINE POWER:** Psychological stress and worry can greatly enhance skin disorders.[8] Trusting that God gave us a body with an inbuilt ability to heal itself and giving it time to do that aids the healing process. We can be assured that *"The Lord will hear when I [you] call to Him."* Psalm 4:3.

**ABSTAIN:** There are some elements that must be eliminated to effectively take care of our skin:

> **Smoking**
Smokers are more likely to develop skin cancers, particularly on the lips. Melanoma patients with a history of smoking are on average 40 per cent less likely to survive skin cancer. Damage to cells within the immune system from smoking is believed to be the underlying reason.[12]

> **Chemicals**
There are many hidden chemicals in our food, water, clothes, soaps, skin products, and even furniture. Books such as *The Chemical Maze*[13] can help to identify them. This book has also been converted to a mobile app to make it simpler and easier to recognize food additives and cosmetic ingredients while at the shops.

Only natural fibres should touch the skin. Although cotton is a natural fibre, this crop is heavily sprayed with chemicals, and articles made with

---

11. Altemus M, et al (2001). "Stress-induced changes in skin barrier function in healthy women." *Journal of Investigative Dermatology.* Vol 117, Issue 2, pages 309-317.
12. Cancer Research UK <https://news.cancerresearchuk.org/2019/02/18/smoking-may-limit-bodys-ability-to-fight-dangerous-form-of-skin-cancer>
13. *The Chemical Maze: Your Guide to Food Additives and Cosmetic Ingredients,* By Bill Statham

cotton should be washed and dried in the sun to purify for at least a day before being used.

Lamb's wool, hemp, silk, linen, cotton and bamboo are all natural fibres. Modal is a fabric that has been spun from the cellulose of the birch tree. Rayon, Tencel and viscose are also fabrics that are made from wood pulp. All of these are considered natural fibres

Natural fibres, especially wool, are better at reducing body odor and their moisture-wicking properties can help keep the skin dry. This is especially important for eczema sufferers, as excess moisture can exacerbate their symptoms. That being said, chemicals are often used in the process of making these fabrics, so they should be washed and dried in the sun before wearing.

## › Mold

All exposure to mold must be investigated and eliminated. The bedroom and bathroom are often rooms of contamination. Bathrooms should be well ventilated and contain exhaust fans to help reduce moisture buildup.

In the bedroom, pillows, quilts, blankets, mattresses, and carpets under the bed need to be assessed to ensure they are not sources of mold growth.

In my book *Self Heal by Design,*[14] I explore in detail how to eliminate the presence of mold, yeast, and fungus in the body.

## › Peanuts

Peanuts are an acknowledged allergen and one of the most common food triggers of fatal anaphylaxis worldwide. It is the most common food allergy in children, affecting about 25% of those with a food allergy.[15] It is the presence of mold on the peanut, rather than the peanut itself, that makes them an allergen.

In his bestselling book *The China Study*, Dr Colin Campbell explores the contamination of peanuts with mold.

## › Wheat

Wheat has become a high allergen food for a few reasons.

Australia and North America both grow huge amounts of wheat, which is often stored in silos. Cold, frosty mornings leading into hot, sunny days

---

14. *Self Heal By Design* is available from Amazon or <https://shop.mmh.com.au/collections/books-and-dvds>.
15. Cannon HE., (2018). "The Economic Impact of Peanut Allergies" *American Journal of Managed Care*, Vol 24, Issue 19 <https://www.ajmc.com/view/the-economic-impact-of-peanut-allergies>

cause a moisture buildup inside the silos, resulting in perfect conditions for mold growth. Leaking silo rooftops can also be a causative factor for mold contamination.

The hybridization of wheat contributes to allergic responses in the body. Cardiologist William Davis tells the story of what happened to wheat in his *New York Times* bestseller book *Wheat Belly*. Much of the wheat today is grown with Roundup or glyphosate products, which are considered carcinogenic and acknowledged as disrupting gut microbiome.[16]

Initially, when conquering skin diseases, it is wise to cease eating oats, as they are high in lectins, which can have an inflammatory effect.

> **Dairy**

Cow's milk has been used for centuries in many countries as a staple food. Science reveals that when dairy has been used for several generations, the gut produces lactase, which is the enzyme that breaks down the milk's sugar, lactose. However, when milk has not been a traditional part of the food program, the gut ceases to produce lactase when a baby is weaned. This can lead to lactose intolerance, which is common among many populations affecting up to 75% of people worldwide.[17]

Professor Walter Veith has an excellent presentation on different races of people and their ability or inability to handle dairy products. He has titled his presentation *Udderly Amazing*.[18]

Pasteurization of milk reduces the concentrations of vitamins B12 and E and leads to a significant decrease in vitamin C and folate.[14] While advocates of milk may argue milk is not an important source of these vitamins, this does show that milk is no longer the staple food of the past. In addition to this, and of more concern, pasteurization destroys the natural enzymes and carrier proteins needed to absorb the calcium, folate, vitamins, iron and many other minerals found in milk, leaving milk more difficult to digest.

Cows today are given a lot of antibiotics, which also affects their milk. Some people who have allergies to milk find that organic raw milk is easier to digest for some people.

16. Barnett JA, Bandy ML, Gibson DL (2022). "Is the Use of Glyphosate in Modern Agriculture Resulting in Increased Neuropsychiatric Conditions Through Modulation of the Gut-brain-microbiome Axis?" *Frontiers in Nutrition.* Vol 9, 2022 <https://doi.org/10.3389/fnut.2022.827384>.

17. MacDonald, L & B, et al. (2011). A Systematic Review and Meta-Analysis of the Effects of Pasteurization on Milk Vitamins, and Evidence for Raw Milk Consumption and Other Health-Related Outcomes. *Journal of Food Protection.* Vol. 74, No. 11, 2011, Pages 1814–1832.

18. Watch *Udderly Amazing* online at <https://adtv.watch/truth-about-cancer/is-milk-bad-for-you>

These are some of the reasons why cow's milk can be a causative factor of eczema:

> **Refined Sugar**
Refined sugar causes a huge rise in blood glucose levels, whereas the sugarcane plant slowly releases the glucose. This dramatic rise effectively feeds unhealthy pathogenic bacteria.

In very severe cases of psoriasis, some have been able to conquer the disease by totally eliminating grain and all forms of sugar from their diet.

> **Refined and Altered Oils**
The body doesn't recognize oils that have been damaged, usually through heating, refining, genetic modification and hybridization, such as in refined vegetable oils, fried foods and margarine. Where this poses a problem to the skin, lies in the fact that the body will try to expel these fats and oils through the skin. When this is combined with dehydration, malnutrition and over exposure to the sun, skin damage can result. Cold pressed olive oil and coconut oil do not fall into these categories.

 **INHALE:** The skin is the only organ besides the lungs that is directly exposed to atmospheric oxygen. Like the lungs, the skin breathes, and whatever touches the skin can enhance or inhibit its ability to breathe. Not only does the skin breathe, but it plays an important role in throwing off waste through the sweat glands.

Chemicals should not be allowed to touch the skin as they interfere with its three main functions; breathing, absorbing, and eliminating waste. This includes skin creams and antiperspirant deodorants.

Breathe through your nose. This forces the air through a series of natural filters the body has which cleans the air and adds a gas called nitric oxide. This gas is produced in the sinuses and excreted continuously into the nasal airways when we breathe in, and helps to kill viruses and bacteria, as well as being a vasodilator, meaning it promotes the dilatation of blood vessels.[19] The dilation of blood vessels is probably the most important job of nitric oxide as it improves the delivery of oxygen and nutrients to every organ, including, of course, the skin where it promotes wound healing.

**NUTRITION:** Foods that encourage the skin cells to heal include a large range of colorful fruits and vegetables, legumes, nuts, seeds and natural

19. Lundberg JO, Settergren G, Gelinder S, et al (1996). "Inhalation of nasally derived nitric oxide modulates pulmonary function in humans." *Acta Physiologica Scandinavica*, Vol 158, issue 4, pages 343–7. doi: 10.1046/j.1365-201X.1996.557321000.x. Accessed January 2024.

fats, such as olive and coconut oils. Fruits and vegetables contain powerful antioxidants that help protect skin from cellular damage caused by free radicals. One oil that can be particularly nourishing for the skin when taken internally is flaxseed oil.

Vitamin C promotes radiant skin and helps blemishes heal by producing collagen, the protein that keeps our skin plump and supported, and strengthens the blood capillaries that supply the blood that nourishes our skin. The best sources of vitamin C are blackcurrants, blueberries, broccoli, guava, kiwi fruit, oranges, papaya, strawberries, and sweet potatoes.

Regarding babies with skin ailments, breast milk is best, along with water. Ideally, breastfeeding mothers should cease eating known allergenic foods, such as peanuts, dairy, wheat, oats and refined sugar.

Many babies on cow's milk formula have been helped immensely by changing to goat's milk formula. Goat's milk is particularly high in prebiotic oligosaccharides (a form of carbohydrates) and has six times the concentration of regular cow's milk. These prebiotic oligosaccharides are also structurally closer to breastmilk and research studies suggest that these oligosaccharides help to start your baby's life with a healthy gut flora and are excellent for promoting fewer digestive issues.[20]

Several mothers have testified to their babies healing from eczema after they eliminated these foods from their diet, but it may take two or more months to heal completely.

As the toddler eats more food, their dietary needs are generally the same as an adults', and ensuring the previously

20. "Is bub having tummy troubles? You should consider goat's milk formula" from *The Pregnancy Babies & Children's Expo* <https://www.pbcexpo.com.au> accessed November 2023.

mentioned foods are avoided will help their bowel movements become regular, as well as help their skin to heal. An abundance of fresh fruits and vegetables, and using legumes, nuts, and seeds as the protein source will supply adequate fibre. This aids peristalsis (movement) of the colon, a process that takes excess pressure off the skin as an organ of elimination.

**MODERATION:** Too many sunburns and not enough sun can also be harmful. The darker the skin, the more sun is needed. The whiter the skin, the less sun is needed. Overdoing sun can burn the skin which is when the skin sustains damage.

**EXERCISE:** Exercise is needed to increase blood supply to the skin. Exercise increases the uptake of oxygen in the lungs, which enables an increase at the cellular level including skin cells.

# TESTIMONY
## MATTHEW'S STORY

As a child, Matthew suffered from eczema. He remembers his legs bleeding from his scratching to relieve the itch. His parents would often argue about whether he should use cortisone cream or not. His father was for the medical treatment, but his mother disagreed. The cortisone cream afforded only temporary relief, and the rash always returned, sometimes worse.

In his early 20s, Matthew, a vegetarian since childhood, discovered that his eczema eased immensely if he kept away from wheat, refined sugar, and dairy products.

Matthew experienced a severe flare-up in his mid-20s while living in a condemned house with other young men. The rent was cheap, but it had a serious mold problem.

Having finished his schooling, Matthew moved back to a cooler climate with better living conditions and a more balanced diet. His eczema responded well to the change and again settled down.

Over the next decade, Matthew's eczema had periods of calm with occasional flare-ups. Stress, diet, and exposure to mold were the usual triggers for the flare-ups, and Matthew was not satisfied with his lifestyle. He wanted to be free of this annoying, and sometimes debilitating, condition.

After reading Dr Natasha Campbell-McBride's book, *Gut and Psychology*, Matthew was inspired to give her diet a try. He did this with a vegetarian twist.

Breakfast, lunch, and dinner were all a thick vegetable soup. There were no nightshade vegetables, and it always contained pumpkin or sweet potato, carrots, celery, beets, and leeks. All grains were eliminated initially. He made variations by adding different greens. With the soup, he also ate a legume dish, a few raw vegetables, and some nuts and seeds. This differed from meal to meal. If not legumes, he would have a few organic eggs. Sometimes, he would include goat feta cheese.

As well as this, Matthew either shaved, waxed, or trimmed the hairier parts of his body. His long hair was now short.

Within two months, Matthew experienced a dramatic change in his body. For the first time, he was now totally free of eczema.

# Matthew was not satisfied with his lifestyle. He wanted to be free of this annoying, and sometimes debilitating, condition.

After six months on this regime, Matthew reintroduced a few pieces of fruit and some gluten free grain to his diet. To his delight, he found that his eczema didn't return. By his mid-30s, Matthew was free of the eczema that he had been told was irreversible and incurable.

Today, he is careful, but if he overworks, lacks sufficient sleep, is dehydrated, and eats too much wheat and sugar while being stressed, his eczema can reappear. The good news is, that he knows exactly what to do to conquer these outbreaks.

CHAPTER 12

# SWEET SLEEP

Our body was designed to have periods of wake and periods of sleep. To be able to perform their tasks efficiently and effectively, every cell and every organ, and also every function of the body, requires these cycles to be functioning at specific times in the 24-hour day.

These cycles, both physical and mental, are caused primarily by light and dark, affecting animals, plants and most living things, including microbes.

The purpose of this chapter is to explore these time schedules, and also to investigate what inhibits and enhances these wake/sleep cycles.

Let us begin by looking at the purpose of sleep, and what is happening while we sleep.

We are tired and ready to sleep at the end of the day because of the build up of sleep pressure and our circadian rhythm system that is set by light and dark signals.

# SLEEP'S PURPOSE

## 1 METABOLISM

Metabolism is the name given to the sum total of all the chemical changes which take place in the body. These changes, or actions, can be grouped into two categories, catabolism, and anabolism.

Reactions which involve the breakdown or decomposition of substances into energy is happening all day as we work and move. This is called **catabolism**.

The action involving the building up or synthesis of new material, which is happening while we sleep, is called **anabolism**.

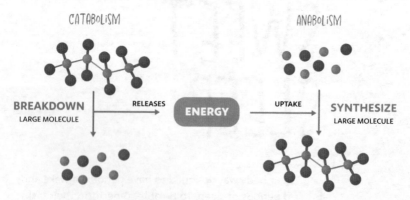

The natural process is for us to become weary and fatigued when catabolism has been active for a while and then it is time for anabolism. Sleep is essential for anabolism to effectively take place. We wake up naturally when it is completed.

## 2 HOUSE CLEANING

The brain is actually a collection of cells. There are two groups of brain cells, *neurons* and *glial* cells. These cells work together to make sure that our brain can do its job. Like all work places, some house cleaning is always required and this happens at night while anabolism is in motion. This cleaning system is called the glymphatic system, which is achieved by the glial cells.

Neurons are often thought of as the main cells in the brain because they have a very important job of communicating between the brain and body. Glial cells are the supportive cells in the brain and are more numerous than nerve cells. They are the second smallest cell in the body, the sperm cell being the smallest. Glial cell's role in the brain is one of basic house cleaning. As our neurons fire all day long, metabolic waste is created and this system effectively executes the elimination of this waste. The energy cycle inside the nerve cells also leaves waste products that require elimination.

More waste is created by negative emotions. In her book *Who Switched off My Brain*,[1] Dr Caroline Leaf explains how entertaining and cherishing negativity can cause thorns to grow between the dendrites (receiving stations) in the nerve cell. These have the potential to damage the tissues and contribute to many psychosomatic diseases.

When we make a decision to forgive all who have ever hurt us in our lives, our glial cells are activated to clean up the thorns while we sleep.

## 3 LIGHT AND DARK
Light and dark signals are fed through the optic nerve in the eye to a control center in the brain where the body clock is located, the suprachiasmatic nucleus, or SCN. The SCN spontaneously generates a near 24-hour rhythm. Sunlight synchronizes it each day. This natural process is called the circadian rhythm.

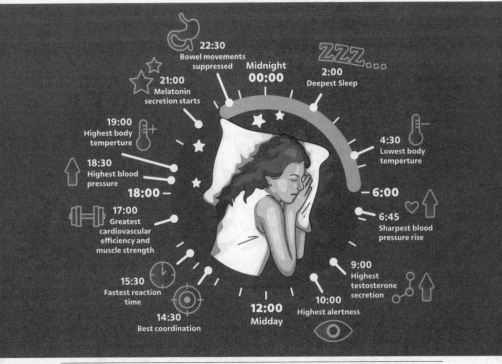

---

1. Who Switched Off My Brain?: Controlling Toxic Thoughts and Emotions, by Caroline Leaf 2009 Thomas Nelson Inc

It is the SCN that communicates with the pineal gland to release certain hormones between the hours of 9pm and 2am. There are four specific hormones that the pineal gland releases through these hours.

> **Serotonin**
This is often called the mood hormone, because of the way it boosts our mood. We are happier people when we sleep in these hours.

> **Epithalamin**
Learning capacity is increased and aging is slowed with this hormone.

> **Arginine Vasotocin**
Called our natural pain killer as it can ease our pain if we have any. Also this hormone is instrumental in causing us to fall into a deep sleep.

> **Melatonin**
This hormone is given the name 'The Fix and Rejuvenate Night Time Hormone' as it is the hormone that activates our glial cells and anabolism while we sleep. Melatonin is the body's biological signal of darkness, meaning, it is dark and time to sleep.

## 4 PROCESSING

While we sleep, everything that we experienced through the day is being processed and filed. This filing system puts our memories in the appropriate filing place, depending on the emotions and thoughts connected with what is being processed.

Since the 1950's, research has revealed that the brain goes through alternating cycles while we sleep. Experts divide these cycles of sleep into four stages, rapid eye movement (REM), when the brain is very active, and three stages of non-rapid eye movement (NREM) which is a much deeper sleep. Each stage plays an important role in repairing and rebuilding the brain and body.

These busy and still times go through 90 minute cycles. These are the nightly 'shifts'. We spend the most time in NREM deep sleep during the first half of the night. During the early sleep cycles, NREM is typically 20 to 40 minutes long but as we continue sleeping, these stages get shorter, and more time gets spent in REM sleep instead.

> **NREM**

> NREM sleep has three stages: **Stage one** (N1) usually lasts 1 to 7 minutes and is the initial stage, this is a very light sleep and can be easily interrupted by noise. **Stage two** (N2) lasts approximately 10 to 25 minutes in the initial cycle and lengthens with each successive cycle, eventually constituting

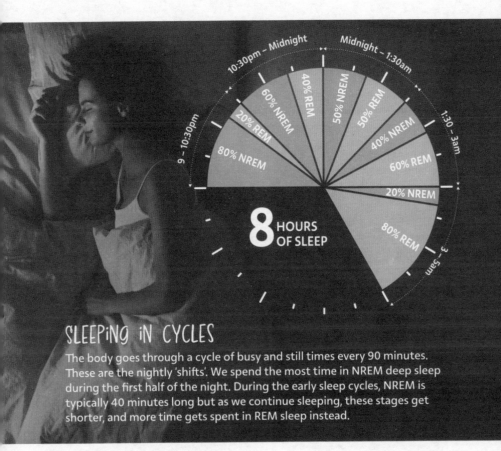

The clock diagram shows, reading clockwise:

9 – 10:30pm — 80% NREM
10:30pm – Midnight — 20% REM, 60% NREM, 40% REM
Midnight – 1:30am — 50% NREM, 50% REM
1:30 – 3am — 40% NREM, 60% REM, 20% NREM
3 – 5am — 80% REM

**8 HOURS OF SLEEP**

## SLEEPING IN CYCLES

The body goes through a cycle of busy and still times every 90 minutes. These are the nightly 'shifts'. We spend the most time in NREM deep sleep during the first half of the night. During the early sleep cycles, NREM is typically 40 minutes long but as we continue sleeping, these stages get shorter, and more time gets spent in REM sleep instead.

between 45 to 55 percent of the total sleep cycle. **Stage three** (N3) is a deep sleep. Muscle tone, pulse, and breathing rate decrease in N3 sleep as the body relaxes even further.

▶ NREM sleep is critical in allowing our body to recover and grow, boosting the immune system. Deep sleep involves greater slowing of bodily processes, allowing the immune system to utilize more energy to fight infection.

▶ During NREM a courier service is instigated, where the memory we take in all through the day is moved. This is our brain's 'house cleaning' event, where our short term memory unit, the hippocampus, is emptied out, and the memories moved to the long term storage unit, the cortex. The cortex refers to the top section of the brain.

> **REM**

▶ During REM sleep, brain activity picks up, nearing levels seen when you are awake. At the same time, the body experiences atonia, which is a temporary paralysis of the muscles, with two exceptions: the eyes and the muscles that control breathing.

- This is when our dreaming happens. Old memories, past events, and recent experiences are all pulled out and molded together to be able to be filed in their correct spot.

- The things we learned and experienced through the day are confirmed and consolidated in our memory at this time.

- During REM we develop creative ideas, it's our inventing time.

For these processes to be fully completed each night, eight hours of sleep are required. Sleep stages are important because they allow the brain and body to recuperate and develop. Failure to obtain enough of both deep sleep and REM sleep may explain some of the profound consequences that insufficient sleep has on thinking, emotions, and physical health.

As you can see, the brain is quite a busy place while we sleep. This also shows how important it is that we do sleep, in the night hours—especially before midnight.

# SLEEP APNEA

Sleep apnea is a common sleep disorder that causes frequent pauses in breathing during sleep. People suffering with this disorder may struggle to properly cycle into these deeper sleep stages, which if left untreated, can lead to potentially serious health consequences. Three of the main causes of sleep apnea are being overweight, allergies, and mouth breathing.

> **Excess Weight**
One of the main components contributing to sleep apnea is obesity. If someone is carrying excess weight, when they lie down, the extra pressure on the neck can cause a narrowing of the airways, which compromises the amount of air passing through to the lungs.

> **Allergies**
The response of the body to allergic substances is to create excess mucus in the Eustachian tubes as a form of protection to the delicate lining of the respiratory organs. This reaction reduces the air flow in the Eustachian tubes, thus contributing to sleep apnea. This phenomenon also encourages mouth breathing.

The most common allergens are exposure to chemicals, mold, and foods. The foods that are the main culprits here are peanuts, dairy, wheat, oats and refined sugar.

Once these allergens are ceased, it can take at least two months to see a response, and experience a reduction of mucus build up in the Eustachian tubes.

> **Mouth Breathing**

Mouth breathing comes with a whole host of potential health issues, from the small (like bad breath, dry mouth, and sore throat) to the much more serious such as sleep apnea, high blood pressure, and impaired brain function. The body is designed to inhale and exhale through the nose. Mouth breathing is recognized as one of the causative factors of sleep apnea in children.[2]

# THE SOLUTIONS
## USING THE 'SUSTAIN ME' PRINCIPLES FOR ENHANCING SLEEP

**SUNSHINE:** As it is light and dark signals that are fed through the optic nerve to the suprachiasmatic nucleus, which in turn communicates with the pineal gland regarding the release of the night hormones, we should be allowing our eyes to experience sun every day. Our eyes tell us not to look at strong sunlight, and so we shouldn't, but just by being outside, the sun's rays are entering our eyes.

Dr Neil Nedley in his book *Depression: A Way Out* shows that the first hour of light in the day is particularly powerful at resetting the circadian rhythm. He found that up to 80% of his depressed patients experienced a disruption in their circadian rhythm.[3]

Even directing your head towards the sun with closed eyes, and allowing the sun's rays to rest on your eyelids for a few minutes has a positive effect.

**USE OF WATER:** Drinking at least eight glasses of water through the day, with a small crystal of Celtic salt on the tongue before each glass, will supply the water the body needs to run efficiently through the night shift.

---

2. Izu SC, Itamoto CH, et al (2010). "Obstructive sleep apnea syndrome (OSAS) in mouth breathing children." *Brazilian Journal of Otorhinolaryngology*. 2010 Sep-Oct; Vol 76, issue 5. Pages 552-556. doi: 10.1590/S1808-86942010000500003.
3. The chapter "Melatonin" from *Proof Positive* by Dr Neil Nedley.

**SLEEP:** Retiring to bed at 9pm in the winter or 10pm if daylight saving time is in place in the summer months will ensure we receive the vital night time release of hormones while we sleep. Even six hours of sleep robs us of our nightly rest and recovery , especially if we neglect the earlier hours of night.

Getting enough sleep isn't only about total hours of sleep. It's also important to get good quality sleep on a regular schedule. Our body likes rhythm and routine so going to bed at the same time every night will reinforce your circadian rhythm, encourage a natural production of melatonin, and help your body run efficiently.

**TRUST IN DIVINE POWER:** Our mind can be our best friend or our worst enemy. Grief, anxiety, discontent, remorse, guilt, distrust, irritation, and annoyance are some of the main sleep stoppers Conversely, lack of sleep can also affect mental health. There's a reason it's said that someone in a bad mood woke up on the 'wrong side' of the bed.

The mind has the ability to resist these emotions and concentrate on all the positive things in our life.

Many do not realize that happiness is a choice. Gratitude is also a choice, and where we are often the most tempted to neglect these healing emotions is when we cannot sleep.

Listing all the things that we can be thankful for is a very beneficial pastime if we are lying awake in the middle of the night!

> *"In everything give thanks; for this is the will of God in Christ Jesus for you."* 1 Thessalonians 5:18

Laughter in the day has been shown to increase the output of the hormones at night.

> *"A merry heart does good, like medicine, but a broken spirit dries the bones."* Proverbs 17:22

To encourage sleep, we must stay out of the 'chat room'! This is the room in our mind where we chat away, commenting on our day and planning the next day. What we can do instead, is focus on all the things for which we are thankful. It can be difficult at times, but remember practice makes perfect.

> *"I lay down and slept; I awoke, for the Lord sustained me."* Psalm 3:5

> *"I will both lie down in peace, and sleep; For You alone, O Lord, make me dwell in safety."* Psalm 4:8

**ABSTAIN:** Sleep pressure is slowly building up all through the day, creating weariness by the time the sun sets. The sleep pressure is created by adenosine. As we sleep, this sleep pressure is released, allowing us to wake refreshed. There are several items that can prevent the release of sleep pressure.

> **Technology**

Not only should we seriously police our screen exposure nearing the hour of 9pm, especially the close exposure, but also what we are viewing. Violent and stimulating viewing makes it very hard for the brain to relax and drift into sleep. We should also critically assess our exposure to electromagnetic fields (EMFs) in the room we are sleeping, EMFs depress melatonin secretion.

If an electric blanket is used, heat the bed, but then turn off and remove the plug before getting into bed.

All electrical devices are best charged in an adjoining room. If the phone is used for an alarm, make sure it is at least two feet from your head, that can reduce exposure by almost two thirds. Ideally the phone can be placed outside the bedroom door.

## The Dark Side of Light

Electronic devices, such as television, computers, and smartphones have become permanent features of our everyday life. The use of such devices, especially at night, is linked to poor sleep. It's like having electrical caffeine right before you go to sleep.

The blue light emitted from these electronic devices acts similar to sunlight, interrupting your circadian rhythm, or sleep cycle. It signals your brain to wake up when it should be winding down. As little as two hours of exposure to blue light at night can slow or stop the release of the natural sleep hormone melatonin. Powering down your digital devices at least three hours before bedtime can help.

## › Caffeine and Other Drugs

Stop caffeine, refined sugar, alcohol, and any drug or substance that has a stimulating effect. These cause an unnatural excitement when the body should be winding down in preparation for sleep. Research has shown that coffee consumption can suppress the production of melatonin produced by the pineal gland,[4] leading to poor quality sleep, and delay of the circadian clock.

Melatonin production is regulated by the body's internal clock, and alcohol disrupts this process. Many associate drinking with passing out or getting tired and falling asleep, but sleep quality during alcohol consumption can be poor and disrupted. Drinking alcohol leads to fragmented and restless sleep. As the body metabolises alcohol, its sedative effects wear off, causing disruptions in sleep stages, particularly REM sleep[5] causing the drinker to wake up with only a half charged battery.

Late afternoon (happy hour) drinking, as much as six hours before bedtime, also disrupts sleep, even though alcohol is no longer in the body at bedtime[6]. This shows the relatively long-lasting change alcohol can have on sleep.

Refined sugar is a stimulant and can interfere with the natural winding down process that happens as the sun goes down. Melatonin has a depressing effect on insulin production, which inhibits the pancreas' ability to process glucose in the evening.

The hybridization of wheat produced a starch that causes blood sugar to rise quicker than refined sugar.[7] The scenario just explained with the consumption of sugar in the evening, can also be appropriately applied to wheat. Not only was the starch structure altered, but so was the gluten or protein structure. This structure is so complex that it is difficult for even the strongest digestion to effectively break it down.

**INHALE:** The body is designed to inhale and exhale through the nose. Breathing through the nose filters the air, warms the air, adds moisture to the air, and pressurizes the air. Oxygen soothes the nerves. Breathing through

---

4.  Park, J, et al (2018), "Lifetime coffee consumption, pineal gland volume, and sleep quality in late life." *Sleep*, Vol 41, Issue 10, 2018 < https://doi.org/10.1093/sleep/zsy127> accessed November 2023.

5.  Stein MD, Friedmann PD. (2005) "Disturbed sleep and its relationship to alcohol use." *Substance Abuse.* March 26, 2005, pages 1–13.

6.  Landolt HP, Roth C, Dijk DJ, Borberly AA. (1996) "Late-afternoon ethanol intake affects nocturnal sleep and the sleep EEG in middle-aged men." *Journal of Clinical Psychopharmacology.* Vol 16 Issue 6, pages 428–436.

7.  William D, (2014), *Wheat Belly: Lose the Wheat, Lose the Weight, and Find Your Path Back to Health.*

the nose and using the abdominal muscles can increase oxygen levels in the cell quite significantly. When lying down to sleep, breathe in deep through the nose, to the count of seven, breathe out to the count of seven. Ideally this is done at least ten times.

The habit of mouth breathing causes noisy breathing, or snoring. In the book *Breath* by James Nestor,[8] many examples are given of those who conquered sleep apnea and snoring by changing over to nose breathing at night.

To encourage nose breathing, a small piece of tape can be placed over the mouth to hold the lips together.

**NUTRITION:** Two factors essential for health are diet and sleep. These may well influence one another. Whole food diets rich in fruits, vegetables, legumes, and other sources high in the dietary amino acid called tryptophan have been shown to predict favorable sleep outcomes.[9] Tryptophan is a key amino acid used in the production of melatonin and serotonin.

Ensure enhanced digestion by the proper preparation of the legumes. This includes soaking, rinsing, and pressure cooking them. The process kills the lectins and increases the gut's ability to access the essential nutrients.

The membrane around the brain cell is 70% fat. Fat is an important nutrient to maintain neuron flexibility and electric communication. Omega-3 is an essential fatty acid that is designed particularly for these functions.

Dark leafy green vegetables such as, spinach, chard, and kale, all contain sleep-promoting minerals like potassium. Minerals literally 'glue' us together.

## HERBS TO HELP

The following herbs are all mild tranquillisers and may help to relax and induce sleep.

- Valerian
- Chamomile
- Skullcap
- Passionflower
- St John's Wort

A hormonal imbalance can also cause insomnia. Many, especially ladies, have found that wild yam cream has helped them to sleep. The herbs in this cream work with the body's own hormone system to return the balance by boosting progesterone, the relaxing, sleep-inducing hormone.

8. James Nestor (2021), *Breath: The New Science of a Lost Art*, published by Penguin Life, Australia.

9. Zuraikat FM, et al (2021). "Sleep and Diet: Mounting Evidence of a Cyclical Relationship." Annual Review of Nutrition, Vol. 41, pages 309–332

Magnesium, found naturally in foods such as avocados, nuts, legumes, and tofu, is especially important as a relaxant to help sleep.

**MODERATION:** Timing and rhythm play a vital role in all body functions. The body loves it when we do the same things at the same time every day. Regularity in every area of our life enhances the routine of sleep.

Moderation and timing in eating can also affect sleep. The research is showing that an eating program with specific times for eating that aids sleep, is eating twice in 24-hours within six hours of each meal. For example, breakfast 7:30am and lunch at 1:30pm. Or it may be breakfast at 9am and the second meal at 3pm. Much depends on what suits your schedule. This has been given the name 'Time Restricted Eating' (TRE).

TRE is modern science discovering the value of the age-old saying that we should 'Eat Breakfast like a King, Lunch like a Queen, and Tea or Supper like a pauper.' Often paupers don't eat!

Insulin sensitivity is at its height in the morning. It takes a lot of energy to digest a meal and the stomach deserves to sleep when we sleep. The evening meal should be the lightest of the day, if we eat then at all. Melatonin stops the release of insulin; no more midnight snacks!

If an evening meal is necessary, a banana or two is a great choice, as bananas are light on digestion and can boost melatonin production. A bowl of soup is also easily digested. While estimates vary, most experts recommend eating should cease two to four hours before bedtime. People who eat meals well ahead of bedtime have enough time to properly digest their food.

Sleeping with very little activity happening in the first part of the small intestines causes this part of the gut to produce tryptophan, a key amino acid used in the production of melatonin and serotonin.

Our gut is circadian, and it repairs at night. The microbial population in our gut or microbiome changes; the microbes at night are different from the microbes present during the day. They all have different functions.

**EXERCISE:** Proper exercise can alleviate sleep-related problems and help you sleep more soundly, conversely insufficient or poor quality sleep can lead to lower levels of physical activity the following day. Exercise in the day, especially the High Intensity Interval Training (HIIT), increases the circulation of the blood to the pineal gland, this can help alleviate daytime sleepiness and, for some people, reduce the need for sleep medications.

Exercise can also improve sleep in indirect ways. For instance, moderate to vigorous physical activity can decrease the risk of excessive weight gain, which can make a person less likely to experience symptoms of sleep apnea. People who are obese often suffer with shorter sleep duration and have twice as many subjective sleep problems compared to non-obese people.[10]

When physically weary, sleep comes much easier.

*"The sleep of a laboring man is sweet"* Ecclesiastes 5:12

If these SUSTAIN ME lifestyle modifications are widely applied, then not only could the consequences of obesity and sleep apnea be reduced, but also the incidence of cardiovascular and other diseases could greatly decrease.

# OTHER HELPERS

- Magnesium supplements can be helpful as magnesium is a muscle relaxant, and can help induce sleep. 500mg of magnesium citrate can be taken before retiring.
- Melatonin supplements have been helpful in some cases but should not be your only solution. Supplements don't make you sleep, they only relax the body to prepare for sleep. Sufficient melatonin to assist in sleep is naturally produced in the body when the SUSTAIN ME principles are followed.

If you suffer from insomnia, your body may be in the habit of not sleeping. Once the above principles are implemented, the mind will eventually break this habit and sleep. This may take time, which is why being thankful for even the smallest periods of sleep helps.

---

10. Jehan S, et al (2017), "Obstructive Sleep Apnea and Obesity: Implications for Public Health." *Sleep Med Disord.* 2017 Vol 1, issue 4.

# CHAPTER 13

# CHRONIC FATIGUE SYNDROME

Chronic fatigue syndrome (CFS), also referred to as myalgic encephalomyelitis, is a complicated disorder. It causes extreme exhaustion after physical or mental exercise, leads to memory problems, severe fatigue, and sleep problems. Fatigue is the end result of the underlying muscle fatigue, which is more commonly encountered than muscle weakness. While the symptoms can vary from person to person, the disorder has one cause, and that is lack of oxygen in the cells.

The ability of cells to extract oxygen from the blood and use it to make energy is essential for a healthy life. When the body has enough oxygen present to allow every cell to run aerobically, the energy-producing pathway in those cells will produce 18 times more energy than an energy pathway that doesn't use oxygen.

In the absence of oxygen, the cell is forced to function anaerobically, which produces a much smaller amount of energy by the process of fermentation. This is a non-oxygen-requiring pathway for breaking down glucose, which the body uses for energy.

Aerobic cells give 36 units of energy.

Anaerobic cells deliver two units of energy.

There can be many different reasons why the cells may be low in oxygen.

## STEP ONE: DISCOVER THE CAUSE

All the systems in our body rely on oxygen to make energy, when the cause or causes (often there can be many) of the low oxygen are identified, then steps can be taken to rectify the problem and improve health. Some of the more common issues are:

### ❯ Lack Of Pure Air

The most obvious place to begin is the air we breathe. A fresh breeze is one of the magic tricks of nature. Fresh air contains 21% oxygen and 79% nitrogen. There is a very small percentage of carbon dioxide.

Country air, with lots of trees all giving off oxygen, is far higher in oxygen than city air.

In the city, there is car, truck, and industry exhaust fumes, and lots of people, all playing a role in depleting the air of oxygen. Being indoors is not much better, most indoor air pollution comes from sources that release gases or particles into the air. Things such as building materials, air fresheners, adhesives in furniture, carpets, and household cleaners, all give off pollution constantly. Many indoor air pollutants have been around for years, but in the past they were often weakened by fresh outdoor air seeping into the home through open windows. Today's more energy-efficient homes don't let as much outdoor air get inside.

## > Mouth Breathing

How we breathe can be a causative factor too. Mouth breathing can result in low oxygen concentration in the blood. It also prevents the purification of the air, and thus dirty air can be taken into our lungs, inhibiting the oxygen supply to the body.

When we breathe out through our mouths we lose too much carbon dioxide.

Contrary to popular belief, carbon dioxide is not just a waste gas because it performs a number of essential functions in the body before being exhaled. These include the maintenance of blood pH and being the catalyst for the release of oxygen from the hemoglobin in red blood cells through a process called oxygen binding and release.[1] Four molecules of carbon dioxide will allow a pick up of four molecules of oxygen by the hemoglobin. If only two molecule of carbon dioxide are present in the transfer, only two molecules of oxygen can be picked up, another reason why our cells may be lacking oxygen.

## > Carbon Monoxide

Carbon monoxide is a dangerous gas for humans, as it competes with oxygen in the blood cells. The blood cells pick up oxygen in the lungs like a parcel. It is an unstable union so that it can be dropped wherever the oxygen is required in the body. Carbon monoxide forms a stable union on the blood cell. It holds tight, preventing the blood cell from picking up oxygen. The blood carries these gases to the cell.

Whenever carbon monoxide is being breathed in, there will be a lack of oxygen in the blood, which means that there will not be enough oxygen for every cell. The cell with no oxygen will produce only two units of energy instead of 36 in the presence of oxygen.

The three main emitters of carbon monoxide are motor exhausts, cigarette smoke, and mold.

> ### Motor Exhausts

When there is regular exposure to the exhaust of motor vehicles, there is excess inhalation of carbon dioxide.

> ### Cigarette Smoke

Whether a person is smoking or breathing in passive smoke, they are breathing in carbon monoxide.

> ### Mold

Living in a moldy house can cause CFS. Even sleeping on a moldy pillow,

---

1. Dr Alan Ruth (2015). "The health benefits of nose breathing—a clinical review" Nursing in General Practice, Issue 1, 2015, pages 40-42. <http://hdl.handle.net/10147/559021>

mattress, or quilt can lead to breathing in mold. We spend a third of our lives in bed, so this area needs to be investigated to ensure there is no contamination while we sleep. Don't forget the carpet under the bed or the air coming in through the bedroom window.

Before making the bed in the morning, the bedding should be aired for at least an hour. Pillows, blankets, and quilts should be washed and hung out in the sun several times a year.

Mold, yeast and fungus are opportunist organisms. You will find them mostly where there is damp, dirt, moisture, and stale air.

⬤ Eating moldy or old food, such as peanuts, may be a source of mold for the body.

⬤ Taking antibiotics is another way that mold can enter the body. Antibiotic use is a risk factor for common fungal infections such as invasive candidiasis.[2] These drugs may save a life in a crisis but are sadly overused today.

## ❯ Chemicals

Chemicals come in many forms and can affect the body in many different ways. They can be on food, in the fabric our clothes are made from, what we wash our clothes in, and personal care products. There are many hidden ways that we can be exposed.

Environmental chemical exposure is associated with the development of Fatty Liver Disease.[3] As the body is unable to properly dispose of these chemicals, the liver is often left with the only option of wrapping them up in fat and storing them. Chemicals are toxic to everybody. Often, it can depend on how many chemicals are already stored as to how severely they affect the person.

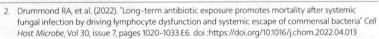

One of the ways the body is affected is by the way chemicals can interfere with the cell's ability to pick up oxygen. As mentioned before, the less oxygen a cell has, the less energy it can produce.

Chemicals can be breathed in, consumed, or enter through the skin.

2.  Drummond RA, et al. (2022). "Long-term antibiotic exposure promotes mortality after systemic fungal infection by driving lymphocyte dysfunction and systemic escape of commensal bacteria" *Cell Host Microbe*, Vol 30, issue 7, pages 1020–1033.E6. doi :https://doi.org/10.1016/j.chom.2022.04.013

3.  Wahlang B, et al. (2019). "Mechanisms of Environmental Contributions to Fatty Liver Disease." *Current Environmental Health Reports.* Vol 6, issue 3, pages 80–94. doi: 10.1007/s40572-019-00232-w.

> **Animals**

Animals in the home may be a causative factor. The worst place to have animals is the bedroom. The emissions from animals are the opposite to fresh air, they often carry worms, and their hair is left wherever they have been. If animals are in the home, they should be away from sleeping and eating areas, and on tile or wood floors.

> **Electromagnetic Fields (EMFs)**

Excess EMFs can contribute to chronic fatigue syndrome.

We are electrical people. There is a spark of electricity in every cell. Our electrical system is our nervous system, and that includes the brain. Overexposure to EMFs coming from microwaves, iPads, iPhones, computers, and smart meters has the potential to disrupt normal bodily functions by interfering with the delicate electrical balancing act that governs every cell. This includes the cell's ability to take in oxygen.

> **Stimulants**

The Catch-22 with stimulants is that they are often taken to give an energy boost but can end up taking more energy than they give! It is like taking out a loan to pay off another loan. The energy they give comes from the adrenal glands, which are sometimes called our energy bank account. This has been designed as a backup in times of crisis. Adrenal exhaustion is the end result if there are continual withdrawals with no deposits.

Highly nourishing food, early nights, exercise, and good recreational activities are all depositors into our energy bank.

Caffeine is the biggest withdrawer of our energy. This explains why Stephen Cherniske titled his book *Caffeine Blues*. Another withdrawer of our energy is refined sugar from sugarcane or sugar beet plants. Like caffeine, it gives an initial lift and is accompanied by a corresponding drop. This is described in detail in William Duffy's book, *Sugar Blues*.

> **Allergies**

Food allergies are known to have a lethargic effect. The most common allergen today is wheat.

One problem with the hybridized wheat of today is that it is quite difficult for the gut to break down or digest. Many people today have compromised gut function, which can further compound the problem.

The complex structure that was created in the intense crossbreeding of the wheat puts an extra burden on the digestive system. Extra energy is called from the brain and muscles to the gut, leaving energy levels in the body somewhat compromised.

Common symptoms of gluten intolerance are brain fog and fatigue.

## > Poor Posture

The abdominal muscles were designed to aid in the breathing process. Abdominal breathing is essential to obtain full lung expansion and allow optimal oxygen intake with every breath.

The abdominal muscles are encircled by one long muscle, the transverse abdominis (TA), which begins at the spine, connects to the pelvis and ribs on either side, then goes back around to the spine in a circle. When these abdominal muscles are strong, they are a powerful aid in pulling the spine erect, allowing full lung expansion with every breath.

Poor posture and a slouching positions while sitting can result in weak abdominal muscles. When the posture is poor, abdominal breathing is inhibited and the diaphragm is unable to fully contract and relax. The body, in a need to breathe, compromises by using high chest breathing, which while supplying the body with oxygen, does so at a reduced level.

As a result of weak abdominal muscles, the transverse abdominis loses its strength to pull the spine erect resulting in a vicious downward spiral of breathing and other posture based health issues.

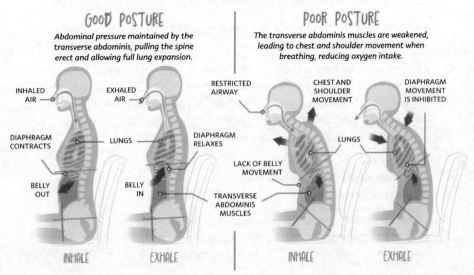

GOOD POSTURE

Abdominal pressure maintained by the transverse abdominis, pulling the spine erect and allowing full lung expansion.

POOR POSTURE

The transverse abdominis muscles are weakened, leading to chest and shoulder movement when breathing, reducing oxygen intake.

INHALED AIR · EXHALED AIR · RESTRICTED AIRWAY · CHEST AND SHOULDER MOVEMENT · DIAPHRAGM MOVEMENT IS INHIBITED

DIAPHRAGM CONTRACTS · LUNGS · DIAPHRAGM RELAXES · LUNGS

LACK OF BELLY MOVEMENT

BELLY OUT · BELLY IN · TRANSVERSE ABDOMINIS MUSCLES

INHALE · EXHALE · INHALE · EXHALE

To feel the transverse muscle first lie on your back and breathe, place your hands on your belly and feel the belly rise and fall with the breath. Observe how the belly falls as the air rushes out and rises as you breathe in. This drawing in is activating the transverse abdominis.

In addition to poor posture, tight pants, skirts, and belts also inhibit the abdominal muscles from being used in the breathing process.

## STEP TWO: IMPLEMENT THE 'SUSTAIN ME' PRINCIPLES TO CURE CHRONIC FATIGUE

**SUNSHINE:** Exposure to sun's rays allows our body to naturally produce vitamin D. In otherwise healthy individuals, fatigue can be a sign of low vitamin D levels.[20] Sunshine boosts the mood and increases blood movement, which equals an increase in oxygen movement through the body. Sunlight also purifies the air, allowing a higher percentage of oxygen in the air.

Low vitamin D may be caused by less exposure to sunlight, application of sunscreen, elevated melanin in skin, or fully covered skin. Allow your bare skin at least 30 minutes of sunlight exposure each day.

**USE OF WATER:** In a well-hydrated body, the blood cells move quickly and freely as they zoom through the arteries, veins, and capillaries. It takes one minute for one blood cell to complete a circuit of the whole body. As these free-moving blood cells pass through the lungs, they pick up oxygen like a little parcel. It is an unstable union, which allows the oxygen to be dropped off easily, wherever it is needed, but in a state of dehydration, the blood cells tend to clump together and move slower.

The clump of blood cells passing through the lungs collects the oxygen, but it has a greatly decreased surface area because of the clumping. The result is that less oxygen is transported around the body. Dehydration can contribute to chronic fatigue syndrome by limiting oxygen delivery to the cells.

Alcohol, tea, coffee, refined sugar, and prescription medication have a dehydrating effect on the body and may contribute to the symptoms of chronic fatigue syndrome.

A hot steam sauna for eight to ten minutes followed by a cold-water rinse gives a mighty shock to the body. The cold could come from having a cold shower, diving into a cool creek or pool, or rolling in the snow, as the Europeans do.

---

20. Roy S, et al. (2014). "Correction of Low Vitamin D Improves Fatigue Study." *North American Journal of Medical Sciences.* Vol 6, issue 8 pages 396-402. doi: 10.4103/1947-2714.139291.

The cold equalizes circulation and prevents chilling. This process of hot and cold is repeated twice more.

A rise in temperature greatly increases metabolism and so greatly increases the oxygen-carrying capacity of the blood at the cellular level, assisting in cell repair and allowing more oxygen to be available for each cell's energy cycle.

The immune system works more efficiently when the body gets hotter, which is why our body will often produce a fever to fight an infection. The heat from a sauna will cause a brief artificial fever resulting in a higher pulse and breathing rate and accelerated elimination of stored environmental poisons.

This hot-to-cold shock is also beneficial in activating Brain-Derived Neurotrophic Factor (BDNF) production (see the section on Nutrition on page 19).

As recovery from chronic fatigue syndrome begins, having at least five session a week in a hot steam sauna is a great kick start.

**SLEEP:** A lack of sleep can cause fatigue. The body has been designed to sleep for a third of our 24-hour day to allow our body to be recharged and regenerated, but there are only five hours out of 24 when the specific hormones that do this are released, and there are certain conditions required for their release. These hours are between 9pm and 2am in the winter, and with daylight saving time, the summer hours change to 10pm and 3am.

Four hormones are released that boost mood, increase learning capacity, heal and, regenerate every cell, and put us into a deep sleep. Energy levels diminish when we don't give the body time to recover and replenish at night.

Sleep expert Dr Matthew Walker shows through his research that eight hours of sleep are required every night to promote the optimal conditions for the following day's energy demands.

See my chapter Sweet Sleep on page 179 for more information on how to get a good night sleep.

**TRUST IN DIVINE POWER:** There is a time factor involved to allow the body time to recover and begin to function aerobically again. An attitude of gratitude plays an important role in recovering from chronic fatigue syndrome. Thanking God for what we have and where we are right now affects every cell.

*"So don't worry about tomorrow, for tomorrow will bring its own worries. Today's trouble is enough for today."* Matthew 6:34 NLT

It can take time to build muscles up to be able to implement the type of exercise that ensures maximum oxygen uptake. Time is needed to retrain the body into an aerobic way of running.

God gives us one day at a time. Value each moment, we will never have it again!

**ABSTAIN:** Stop anything that reduces oxygen in the body.

Stop consuming artificial stimulants like refined sugar, alcohol, drugs, and caffeine.

Stop exposure to allergens and their debilitating consequences. It may take at least two months to free the body from the effect of wheat.

Stop any exposure to environmental poisons, especially in the bedroom as they can harm and disrupt our sleep. This includes EMFs emitted from TV's, WiFi routers, laptops, and digital devices such as mobile phones.

Stop all exposure to mold. Once you move out of a moldy house, it takes time, even several months, to eliminate mold from the body. Much depends on whether the body has been given the right conditions for elimination. My book, *Self Heal by Design*,[5] describes these conditions.

**INHALE:** Oxygen is the spark needed by every cell in the body, more oxygen equals more energy. The best way to receive this oxygen is right in front of your eyes: your nose.

Breathing in and out through the nostrils not only purifies the air, warms the air, and moistens the air, it also pressurizes the air. Nose breathing keeps those vital gases, carbon dioxide and oxygen, in balance. In addition to that, it produces nitric oxide, which improves your lungs ability to absorb oxygen and transport it throughout the body. It relaxes vascular smooth muscle and allows blood vessels to dilate, increasing the oxygen availability for every cell.

Seriously assess the quality of air that is breathed in every area you visit in a day.

**NUTRITION:** Cells need peak nourishment to give energy. As previously discussed, the three essential food groups are fibre, protein, and fat. A fast can give a kick start. One or two days without food has a shock effect on the body, especially one that is used to having daily food.

The absence of food sends the body into survival mode, and it begins breaking up fat stores for the liver to convert back to fuel. In this process, stored environmental poisons are also released, which the body begins to eliminate.

---

5. *Self Heal By Design* is available from Amazon or https://shop.mmh.com.au/collections/books-and-dvds

This explains why a fast is often called a cleanse or detox.

**Brain-Derived Neurotrophic Factor (BDNF):** The lack of sustenance coming into the digestive system triggers a crisis state, and a protein is released in the brain called Brain-Derived Neurotrophic Factor. This protein stimulates neurogenesis, which is the creation of new brain cells. Enhanced production of BDNF is one of the most important neuronal adaptations resulting from intermittent fasting.[6]

It is important to nutritionally support the body at this critical time with fresh fruit and vegetable juices every two hours. Vegetable juices made of 80% carrot, 10% apple, and 10% celery work well.

Having a protein supplement every four hours supports the liver's detoxification pathways.

A fast like this can be done weekly, fortnightly, monthly, or however suits the individual.

A very easy fast is to eat breakfast like a king, lunch like a queen, and eliminate the evening meal. Maybe have a thin soup or a vegetable juice at night with no fibre. That creates an 18-hour fast every 24 hours, called Time Restricted Eating. Nutrition is vital, the food plan needs to contain fruit and vegetables, plant proteins, and healthy fats.

**MODERATION:** As the body recovers from chronic fatigue syndrome, it is important not to push the body too far. While daily exercise is important, it is also important to take it easy and go at the pace the body can cope with, slowly increasing the pace a little more each day.

**EXERCISE:** When the body is not exercised daily, the lungs lose their ability to expand sufficiently to take in adequate oxygen.

The Framingham Heart Study[7] revealed that by the age of 50, most people have lost 40% of their lung capacity. By 80 years old, 60% lung capacity has been lost. This is felt at the cellular level, and as previously explained, less oxygen means less energy.

Lung capacity need not diminish, and if it does, it can be regained. Exercise is the answer because it is the most effective way to oxygenate the body.

The main ways exercise does this is by:

6.  Brocchi, A.; Rebelos, E.; Dardano, A.; Mantuano, M.; Daniele, G. (2022). "Effects of Intermittent Fasting on Brain Metabolism." *Nutrients*, Vol 14, issue 6, article 1275. https://doi.org/10.3390/nu14061275

7.  see <https://www.framinghamheartstudy.org>

- Increasing blood movement, which is the oxygen carrier to the cell.

- Increasing lung capacity, which is responsible for oxygen uptake and the elimination of carbon dioxide.

Thus, exercising in fresh air is important.

When sitting stationary, we breathe in 500ml of air and breathe out 500ml of air with its waste products.

When breathing extremely deeply, as a result of high intensity exercise, we breathe in 3,600ml of air and breathe out 3,600ml of air.

GO for the real stimulating effect of exercise.

GO to the true stimulant, oxygen, which is captured by the expansion of the lungs in EXERCISE.

GO fast with HIIT. This is the exercise that increases fitness and oxygen availability more than any other.

GO with the exercise that suits you, such as rebounding, swimming, or cycling. Start small and build up.

Practice nose breathing. This may be difficult at first, but with practice, nose breathing can be maintained, even through exercise.

Do exercise daily, as exercise is the best oxygen booster. This explains the old saying that 'we receive more energy than we expend on our exercise routine.'


Once the cause has been eliminated, there are three powerful stimulants, or shockers, that can kick start recovery and cause a gear change in how the body runs. These three natural stimulants also activate Brain Derived Neurotrophic Factor (BDNF). BDNF has been shown to stimulate neurogenesis (new brain cells).

1. Finishing every hot shower with 10 to 15 seconds of cold water

2. Regular fasting

3. High Intensity Interval Training

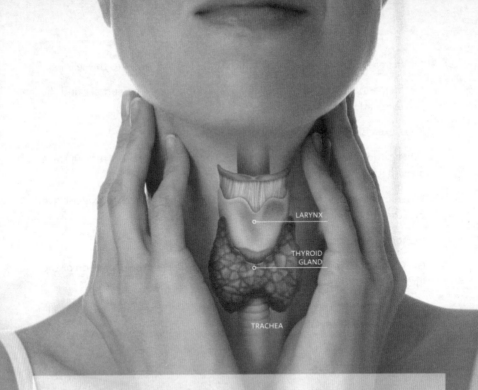

LARYNX

THYROID
GLAND

TRACHEA

CHAPTER 14

# THYROID

The thyroid is a butterfly-shaped gland located in the front of the neck comprising of two lobes that lie on either side of the windpipe. The thyroid gland makes two main hormones: thyroxine and triiodothyronine. These hormones affect every cell in the body, including growth and energy expenditure. They support the rate at which the body uses fats and carbohydrates. They help control body temperature, maintain a healthy heart rate, and control how much protein the body makes.

If your thyroid becomes overactive (hyperthyroidism) or underactive (hypothyroidism), you can experience a range of health problems. Disruption of its function is causing many problems today. There is a reason for this, and we will consider these reasons and their solutions in this section.

# SOME OF THE CAUSATIVE FACTORS

## ⟩ Iodine Deficiency

Iodine is central to healthy thyroid function. The thyroid gland's main food is the mineral iodine. This mineral is used for brain development, growth, healing, and energy. The disruption of iodine levels is a big contributing factor in thyroid problems.

According to studies by the World Health Organization, about one-third of the population are at risk of iodine deficiency disorders.[1]

In his book, *Iodine: Why You Need It, and Why You Can't Live Without It*, Dr David Brownstein states that under and overactive thyroids can both be caused by iodine deficiency.

In her book, *The Iodine Crisis*, Lynn Farrow explains the many reasons for the deficiency. The body does not make iodine, so you need to get it from the foods you eat. Thanks to environmental pollutants iodine deficiency has become a worldwide epidemic. People who live near the coast and eat the food grown there don't usually show an iodine deficiency. As the waves of the sea break, the iodine goes into suspension in the air and goes into the soil. This explains why coastal foods have higher iodine levels. People living hundreds of miles from the coast are more likely to show an iodine deficiency.

Bromide negatively influences iodine uptake by decreasing iodide accumulation in the thyroid and increasing iodide excretion by kidneys.[2] In the past, iodine was used in commercially-made bread as a bread improver, but has been replaced with bromide in the last 20 years. Bromide is often used as an insecticide on berries and a common fire-retardant used in children's sleepwear also contains bromide. Including these items in your home and diet can contribute to iodine deficiency.

## ⟩ Mercury

Selenium is a powerful antioxidant essential for thyroid function and the immune system, mercury acts as a selenium magnet combining the two minerals to produces a mercury-selenium substance that is not absorbable in the human body,[3] this prevents mercury absorption but the process also negatively

---

1.  Hwalla N, et al (2017) "The Prevalence of Micronutrient Deficiencies and Inadequacies in the Middle East and Approaches to Interventions." *Nutrients*. Vol 9, Issue 3, page 229.

2.  Pavelka S. (2004), "Metabolism of bromide and its interference with the metabolism of iodine." *Physiological Research*. 2004; Vol 53 Issue 1, pages 81–90. PMID: 15119938.

3.  Ralston, N. V. C., R. Ralston, and L. J. Raymond. (2016). "Selenium Health Benefit Values: Updated Criteria for Mercury Risk Assessments." *Biological Trace Element Research* Vol 171, Issue 2, pages 262–269. <https://doi.org/10.1007/s12011-015-0516-z> accessed December 2023.

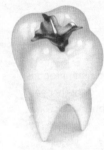

affects the amount of selenium available for the thyroid to use. The main areas of mercury exposure are amalgam fillings in the teeth, and in fish. Mercury is also found in many vaccines, particularly the flu shot.[4]

As mercury is bioaccumulative, the longer the amalgam fillings are in the teeth, the more mercury accumulates in the tissues. The bigger the fish, the more mercury it contains.

### › Hormones

In his book, *What Your Dr May Not Tell You About PreMenopause*, Dr John Lee shows that your body requires the right balance of estrogen, and any deviation can affect the relationship between estrogen and thyroid function.

The birth control pill raises estrogen levels in the body as a side effect of disrupting the hormones to prevent conception.

Several environmental poisons have an estrogenic effect, such as nonylphenols and bisphenol A, which are in many plastics today. In its molecular structure, estrogen has a phenol ring, which acts as a key to allow entry into the estrogen receptors on the cell. These plastics gain entry as they contain the phenol, which explains why they are often called estrogen mimics or xenoestrogens. Dr John Lee explains this in detail in his book.

There are also environmental wastes and chemicals that come under the classification of xenoestrogens.

# THE SOLUTIONS
## STEP ONE: BRING RELIEF

### › Iodine Intake

Iodine deficiency is the most common cause of thyroid disease. A simple test to assess iodine levels is to use Lugol's Solution which can be bought from a pharmacy. This contains iodine and iodide. One drop is applied to the inside of the arm and forms a brown mark. There should be some semblance of colour after five hours, which indicates adequate iodine levels. If the colour fades within the hour, iodine levels are very low. To bring the levels up, a drop of iodine can be applied to the upper inside arm daily until the colour remains for five hours.

---

4.  "Thimerosal in Flu Vaccine", *Centers for Disease Control and Prevention* <www.cdc.gov/flu/prevent/thimerosal.htm> accessed December 2023.

### 〉 Cleansing the Body of Mercury

In dentistry, amalgam fillings (a mixture of copper, silver, tin and about 50% mercury) have been widely used. These are strong and low cost fillings, however they come with potential negative side effects on the thyroid. Mercury levels in our blood and urine decrease after a mercury filling removal. Mercury fillings can be replaced by a biological dentist who is aware of the dangers and can take appropriate measures to remove them safely and replace them with white composite fillings.

Eliminate fish from the diet. If you are a fish lover, stick to smaller fish and make them a rare treat.

Be aware of the dangers of vaccines. We live in bodies that have been designed to heal themselves. We each own a phenomenal immune system, which can very effectively combat disease when given the right conditions.

Chlorella is an algae that has metal-chelating properties, as does fresh coriander. Including oils such as extra virgin olive oil and coconut oil into your diet, as well as fat-rich foods, such as avocado, nuts, and seeds, can help to protect the nerve cells from mercury damage.

### 〉 Supplying Selenium

Brazil nuts are the highest source of selenium. Only five a day will supply the daily requirements of selenium. Your body will use this selenium to convert iodine into thyroid hormones and proteins that protect your thyroid. For those with mercury fillings still in their mouths they may need a 200ug selenium supplement a day.

### 〉 Balancing Hormones

Wild yam creams, when applied consistently over a period of time, are able to stimulate the body to make more progesterone, which reduces estrogen levels.

How long the hormones have been unbalanced for, will influence how long the cream is applied. Most would do well to continue the cream for at least a year.

Eliminating exposure to environmental poisons and hormone disrupters, is important and is discussed in more detail in the chapter on Women's Health on page 213 and The Birth Control Pill on page 217.

# STEP TWO: MANAGING THYROID FUNCTION THROUGH 'SUSTAIN ME' PRINCIPLES

**SUNSHINE:** Vitamin D, received from daily exposure to sunshine, plays a significant role in the running of the immune system, studies have revealed anti-thyroid antibodies and abnormal thyroid function are more frequently elevated in patients with vitamin D deficiency.[5]

In addition to benefiting the immune system, sunshine (especially received through the eyes) stimulates the pituitary gland, which aids in hormone balancing, and positively affects the thyroid. Daily sunshine to the thyroid gland will boost blood to the area, stimulating healing.

**USE OF WATER:** The thyroid cannot function effectively in a dehydrated body. Water loss from the body equals two and a half liters on an average day in an average climate in an average sized adult body.

Two liters must be replaced by pure water, the remaining 500ml can be supplied by the fluid in food. Drinking water that contains fluoride has been shown to impair thyroid function, even in generally low fluoride concentrations.[6] Water purification, such as reverse osmosis, electrodialysis, activated carbon filter, and other adsorption/ion-exchange methods, can help remove fluoride.

For the cells in the thyroid to access the water effectively, a small crystal of Celtic salt should be placed on the tongue before each glass. The three types of magnesiums in Celtic salt pull the water into each of the cells.

**SLEEP:** Between the hours of 9pm and 2am, the pineal gland releases four hormones that are responsible for restoring the cells. This only happens when a person is asleep. For thyroid recovery, sleep must be during these hours. Though these hours are the peak of healing hours, a full eight hours is necessary.

Some studies show that sleeping less than 6 hours a day is associated with disorders of energy metabolism. This indicates that normal sleep is necessary for the regulation and release of thyroid hormones.[7]

---

5. Kivity S, et al. (2011) "Vitamin D and autoimmune thyroid diseases." *Cellular & molecular immunology.* Vol 8, Issue 3, pages 243–247. doi: 10.1038/cmi.2010.73. Accessed December 2023.
6. Kheradpisheh Z, et al (2018), "Impact of Drinking Water Fluoride on Human Thyroid Hormones: A Case-Control Study." *Scientific Reports* Issue 8, 2018, Article number: 2674. PMC5805681.
7. Nazem MR, et al (2021). "The relationship between thyroid function tests and sleep quality: cross-sectional study." *Sleep Science.* Vol 14, Issue 3, pages 196–200. PMCID: PMC8848531.

**TRUST IN DIVINE POWER:** Stress intensifies every disease and the thyroid is no exception. God is able to sustain and bring healing to the thyroid gland when we give it the right conditions and trust Him.

*"Now to Him who is able to do exceedingly abundantly above all that we ask or think, according to the power that works in us."* Ephesians 3:20

**ABSTAIN:** Grains to keep away from are wheat, oats, and barley. These are the hardest grains to digest and are commonly grown with glyphosate, which affects the hormones.

Meat and dairy products are also often affected by contact with chemicals and antibiotics and so are best avoided. If they are eaten at all, they must be organic.

Fruits and vegetables are vital but they must be organic. Keep away from all foods grown with chemicals. Stimulants like alcohol, caffeine, refined sugar, and tobacco need to be kept out of the diet as they over-stimulate and exhaust the thyroid gland.

### Electromagnetic Fields and the Thyroid

Greatly restrict exposure of the thyroid to electromagnetic fields. It is particularly susceptible to the dirty electricity coming out of mobile phones, computers and tablets. Studies have shown a significant correlation between the radiation from mobile devices and thyroid dysfunction.[8] If these devices are used they need to be positioned far away from the thyroid.

**INHALE:** How we breathe matters. The thyroid is made up of cells, and each cell requires oxygen, inhaling in and out of the nose will ensure that supply is met.

Breathing through our mouth produces a lower level of oxygen in the blood and tissues (called hypoxia), if there isn't sufficient oxygen in the cells, the body instinctively preserves the limited oxygen available for critical functions. If this happens consistently over time it can potentially lead to a condition called

---

8.  Baby NM, Koshy G, Mathew A. (2017). "The Effect of Electromagnetic Radiation due to Mobile Phone Use on Thyroid Function in Medical Students". *Indian Journal of Endocrinology and Metabolism*, Vol 21, Issue 6, pages 797-802. <doi: 10.4103/ijem.IJEM_12_17> accessed December 2023.

hypothyroidism.[9] This is where the thyroid gland does not produce enough thyroid hormones to meet your body's needs, resulting in weak respiratory muscles and significantly less lung function. Symptoms of hypothyroidism include fatigue, sensitivity to cold, dry skin, thinning hair, and weight gain.

**NUTRITION:** Often, digestion is compromised when thyroid function is disrupted. Digestion is affected by the health of the thyroid gland. Until the thyroid is functioning well again a supplement may be necessary. Betaine hydrochloride is an extract from beets and can boost HCl levels in the stomach, thus improving the stomach's ability to break up protein. An underactive thyroid (hypothyroidism) can benefit from foods high in iodine, including seaweed, Brazil nuts, and eggs. Berries and cruciferous vegetables also support your thyroid. The thyroid requires optimum nutrition for function and healing.

An overactive thyroid (hyperthyroidism) inversely requires a low-iodine diet and can often be a consequences of untreated vitamin B12 deficiency.

**Goitrogens:** The cabbage family contains a plant chemical named goitrogens. These have the effect of slowing thyroid function. Those with overactive thyroids would do well to eat something from the cabbage family, raw, every day. Cooking and culturing the cabbage disarms the goitrogens, so those with underactive thyroids need to keep away from the raw cabbage family and only eat it cooked or cultured (see my recipe for sauerkraut on page 309).

**MODERATION:** To protect the thyroid gland from exhaustion, work and play need to be done in moderation. This is true for the underactive thyroid, where the tendency is to lie around all day, and the overactive thyroid, where the tendency is to work non-stop all day.

**EXERCISE:** The thyroid controls metabolism, which is why those with an underactive thyroid have no energy and struggle with weight gain, hair loss, and poor digestion, including constipation.

An overactive thyroid can cause weight loss, agitation, exhaustion, and even diarrhea.

Both can benefit greatly from HIIT, which is the best metabolic booster and stabilizer. While the exercise can wake up the underactive thyroid gland, it can bring normality to the overactive one.

---

9. Ramirez-Yanez German O. (2023) "Mouth Breathing: Understanding the Pathophysiology of an oral habit and its consequences." *Medical Research Archives*, Vol 11, issue 1, <https://esmed.org/MRA/mra/article/view/3478>. Accessed January 2024.

This should be done daily and only need take 15 minutes. Dr Michael Mosley's book, *Fast Exercise*, explains this well.

# OTHER HELPERS

**> For UNDERACTIVE Thyroid Gland** *(Hypothyroidism)*
Hot and cold alternating applications of water can be applied to the thyroid gland once or twice daily. See page 292 for information on the power of water treatments and how to administer them.

The underactive thyroid may respond to cayenne pepper compresses.

A little oil is sprinkled on double-layer paper towel, and half a teaspoon of cayenne pepper is then sprinkled on the oil. This is applied to the thyroid gland (located on the front of the neck), covered with plastic, then bandaged on to secure it. This can be worn for two hours a day, in the morning, every second day.

One lady applied it in the evening and stated the following morning: "The good news is it worked; the bad news is I hardly slept all night!" Her underactive thyroid had been given a boost! So, it is best applied in the morning.

**> For OVERACTIVE Thyroid Gland** *(Hyperthyroidism)*
Ice has the effect of inhibiting or slowing down, so it can be applied to an overactive thyroid gland to slow it down. To apply ice to the thyroid, place an ice pack over the thyroid for one minute, then take it off for one minute, and repeat until the area is numb. This can be done once or twice a day.

**> For NODULES, CYSTS, or an ENLARGED THYROID**
Overactive thyroid nodules, or lumps in your thyroid, are common and usually not cancerous. Hot and cold water applications can be applied to the thyroid gland to reduce the swelling.

Castor oil compresses placed over the thyroid can gradually reduce these growths, as castor oil penetrates deeper than any other oil and can break up unnatural formations and growths. This is not a quick process, but if applied consistently, there will be a result. The castor oil compress can be worn for at least eight hours a day, or overnight, to obtain results. Every two or three days a little more castor oil may need to be applied. See page 311 for instructions on how to make and use a castor oil compress.

CHAPTER 15

# WOMEN'S
## HEALTH

Men and women are alike in many ways, however, there are important biological and behavioral differences between the two genders. The truth is, your biological makeup impacts your predisposition to certain health concerns.

Many women today are experiencing compromised health. They are not enjoying life as God meant them to because of various ailments. In this chapter I want to focus on some of the more common problems that women face and show how the SUSTAIN ME principles can assist in the healing process.

# PART 1
# HORMONAL IMBALANCE

Hormones are chemical substances that act like messengers to coordinate different functions in your body by traveling through your blood to your organs, skin, muscles and other tissues. These signals tell your body what to do and when to do it. Hormones are essential for life.

A hormonal imbalance occurs when there is too much or too little of a hormone in the blood. It's a broad term that can represent many different hormone-related conditions that plague women today.

**THE SYMPTOMS CAN INCLUDE:**

- Early menstruation
- Dysmenorrhea (period pain)
- Premenstrual tension (PMS)
- Migraines
- Acne
- Cysts on the ovaries
- Polycystic ovary syndrome
- Abnormal cervical cells/cancer
- Uterine cancer
- Fibroids in the uterus
- Cysts in the breasts
- Breast cancer
- Depression
- Anxiety
- Heart disease
- Postnatal depression
- Insomnia
- Hot flashes, night sweats
- Thyroid problems
- Weight changes

There are several factors that can influence the disruption of a correct hormone balance in the body. Our body runs according to a precise balance, and even slight disruptions can have an effect.

Several hormones are involved in the menstrual cycle. Let us consider how God designed the female reproductive system to work.

## STAGES OF THE MENSTRUAL CYCLE

A woman's body goes through a monthly menstrual cycle from puberty to menopause. This is usually a 28 day cycle with four phases: menstruation, the follicular phase, ovulation, and the luteal phase. The menstrual cycle is complex and controlled by many different glands and the hormones that these glands produce.

**FIRST WEEK:** This begins when a woman menstruates, commonly known as a period. When you menstruate, your uterus lining sheds and flows out of your vagina. The average length of a period is three to seven days.

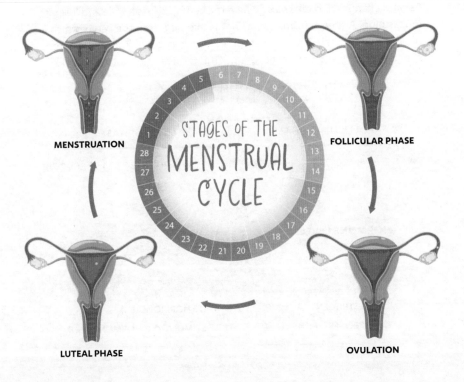

MENSTRUATION

FOLLICULAR PHASE

LUTEAL PHASE

OVULATION

**SECOND WEEK:** In the second week, estrogen levels rise to allow the rebuilding of the blood nest in the uterus. Estrogen, as a 'cell proliferator' causes massive cell growth, not only in the uterus but also in the development of the eggs in the ovaries.

The third main function of estrogen at this time, is to cause a form of lubricant to be released in the birth canal. By the end of the second week the egg is released from the ovaries and taken up in the Fallopian tubes. These two weeks, starting from the first day of your period, make up the follicular phase.

Females tend to feel more sexual arousal toward the end of the follicular phase which is their most fertile window as there is a surge of the luteinising hormone which triggers ovulation.[1]

**THIRD WEEK:** Entering the third week, we see a drop in estrogen levels and a rise in progesterone levels. This causes the lining of the uterus to thicken in preparation for pregnancy. Progesterone is often called the 'happy hormone' as it has a calming effect on the brain. It helps you to sleep well and prevents anxiety, irritability, and mood swings.

Cervical changes also take place where the cervix shrinks a little and loses its mucus plug. A special form of lubricant is released from the cervix which is designed to facilitate the entry of sperm into the uterus. This progesterone stimulated lubricant is clear and stringy. This is called the ovulation week.

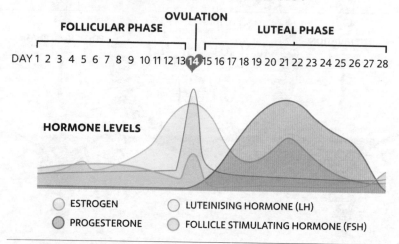

## THE CYCLE OF HORMONE LEVELS

**OVULATION**

**FOLLICULAR PHASE** | **LUTEAL PHASE**

DAY 1 2 3 4 5 6 7 8 9 10 11 12 13 14 15 16 17 18 19 20 21 22 23 24 25 26 27 28

**HORMONE LEVELS**

- ESTROGEN
- PROGESTERONE
- LUTEINISING HORMONE (LH)
- FOLLICLE STIMULATING HORMONE (FSH)

1. Roney JR, Simmons ZL. (2013). "Hormonal predictors of sexual motivation in natural menstrual cycles" *Hormones and Behavior*, Vol 63, Issue 4, April 2013, Pages 636-645

**FOURTH WEEK:** By day 26, if an egg has been fertilized it will implant in the lining of the uterus, progesterone will continue to be produced, which maintains the thickened lining of the uterus. Low progesterone levels are often a culprit in repeated miscarriages.

If pregnancy does not occur, estrogen and progesterone levels drop, which causes the blood supply to the uterus to be cut, this begins the blood loss which marks menstruation and takes us back to the first week of the menstrual cycle.

These two weeks make up the luteal phase.

An imbalance in any hormone can cause irregular periods, or absence of menstrual periods, excessive menstrual bleeding, premenstrual syndrome (PMS), and dysmenorrhea (period pain).

# THE SOLUTIONS
## STEP ONE: IDENTIFY THE DISRUPTERS

A hormonal imbalance happens when you have too much or too little of one or more hormones — your body's chemical messengers. Let us consider some of the main disrupters to this natural cycle.

### ❯ The Birth Control Pill
In 1957, the first birth control pill was given to women.

The 1960s was the time of sexual revolution, as women wanted to have sex without having a baby, but in the process, women's hormonal balance was disrupted.

A pharmaceutical company grows acres and acres of wild yam, which contains a plant chemical called diosgenin. In the laboratory, diosgenin can be converted to progesterone. It is called progesterone because it has an identical molecular structure to the progesterone our body makes. As the pharmaceutical company cannot patent this, it adds a few more atoms to one area to create a synthetic estrogen and in another area to produce a synthetic progesterone, called progestin or progestone.

These synthetic hormones in the pill are fed into the biochemical pathway that our body uses to make its own hormones. This causes the disruption necessary to prevent a pregnancy.

As the disruption inhibits the release of the egg, no corpus luteum develops. The corpus luteum is a short-lived but vital organ that appears in one of the ovaries during every menstrual cycle of a woman. The corpus luteum's job is to make the uterus a healthy place for a fetus to grow. It releases a hormone called progesterone that prepares the uterus for pregnancy. When fertilization does not occur, the corpus luteum will begin to break down. This causes a decline in estrogen and progesterone levels, leading to the start of another menstrual period.

The ramification of no corpus luteum is that progesterone is no longer produced in the corpus luteum.

Week after week and month after month on the pill, inhibiting egg release has an effect that causes a rise in artificial estrogen and a drop in progesterone. The result is a condition that is sadly too common today: estrogen dominance and progesterone deficiency.

One of estrogen's roles in the body is that of a cell proliferator causing massive cell growth. The estrogen dominance is one of the main causes for growths seen in the reproductive organs. Too much estrogen in males can lead to infertility and cause erectile dysfunction, cause breast tissue to develop, and produce more effeminate characteristics.[2] Excess estrogen in females can lead to decreased sex drive, feelings of depression or anxiety, weight gain, worsening of premenstrual syndrome (PMS), fibrocystic lumps in your breasts, or fibroids (noncancerous tumors) in the uterus.

High estrogen levels also oppose thyroid function with women being three-times more likely to get thyroid cancers than men, which suggests a role of estrogen in the development of thyroid diseases.[3]

> Chemicals

In the molecular structure of estrogen, there is a phenyl ring. This is the key that unlocks the door to allow the estrogen entry into the cell.

Nonylphenol and bisphenol A (BPA) are two synthetic estrogen-mimicking chemicals (xenoestrogens) that are added to plastics today. BPA is one of the most commonly exposed environmental chemicals in humans, with over 90 per cent of adults in the USA having detectable BPA levels in their urine.[4] This is another contributing factor to estrogen dominance, as both chemicals contain the phenyl ring allowing entry into the estrogen receptor sites on the cell.

2. "What to know about estrogen in men", *Medical News Today*, 9 Nov 2020, accessed December 2023. <www.medicalnewstoday.com/articles/estrogen-in-men>.

3. Santin AP, Furlanetto TW. (2011), "Role of estrogen in thyroid function and growth regulation." *Journal of Thyroid Research*; 2011:875125. doi: 10.4061/2011/875125. Accessed December 2023.

4. Shankar A, Teppala S. (2012) "Urinary Bisphenol A and Hypertension in a Multiethnic Sample of US Adults", *Journal of Environmental and Public Health*, vol. 2012, Article ID 481641.

Xenoestrogens can also be found in pesticides, household cleaning products, and some soap and hair products.

Roundup is a herbicide widely used in farming, its active ingredient, glyphosate, is currently under investigation because of its link with cancers of the endocrine or hormonal systems in the body. This chemical is another hormone disrupter.

## 〉 Growth Stimulants

For over 40 years, farmers have been giving growth stimulants to cattle and chickens. Government regulations have endeavored to regulate this practice, but it is still done.

If the growth stimulants are in the chickens, they are in the eggs. If they are in the cattle, they are in the meat and dairy products that come from their milk.

These growth stimulants are mainly estrogen-based, so the hormones of those that eat these foods can be affected. Almost, all foodstuff of animal origin contains estrogen steroid hormones, although the levels of hormone and its metabolites vary with the kind of food, gender, animal species, age and condition of the animals. Thus, estrogens are unavoidable hormones in non-vegetarian human nutrition.[5]

## 〉 Mold

One of the many mold wastes, zearalenone, has an estrogen effect. In Puerto Rico from 1978 to 1984, a growth stimulant derived from zearalenone called Zeranol, was being used to improve fattening rates in cattle. Children began going through puberty at the age of five, and boys started to grow breasts. They traced the source of this problem to the meat the pregnant mothers were eating. The meat source had been given Zeranol.[6]

Mold can be commonly found in grains. Most countries today test grain, particularly wheat, for traces of zearalenone. Eating a high-carbohydrate diet, particularly wheat and its products (bread, pasta, cereal, cakes, cookies, etc.) may cause a rise in the presence of zearalenone in the body with its corresponding estrogen effect.

This subject is covered in detail in my book, *Self Heal by Design.*[7]

5. Malekinejad H, Rezabakhsh A. (2015), "Hormones in Dairy Foods and Their Impact on Public Health - A Narrative Review Article." *Iranian Journal of Public Health* Vol 44, Issue 6 pages 742-758.
6. Sáenz de Rodríguez CA, Bongiovanni AM, Conde de Borrego L (1985). "An epidemic of precocious development in Puerto Rican children." *The Journal of Pediatrics.* Vol 107, issue 3, pages 393-396.
7. See my book *Self Heal By Design*, available from www.barbaraoneill.com or Amazon.com or in Australia at https://shop.mmh.com.au/collections/books-and-dvds

> **Stress**

Your body produces the hormone cortisol in response to stress. Producing high amounts of cortisol in response to stress can deplete your body's ability to produce progesterone. The estrogen in your body is left unchecked by progesterone causing an imbalance of the hormone.

# STEP TWO: REBALANCE THE HORMONES THROUGH THE 'SUSTAIN ME' PRINCIPLES

**SUNSHINE:** Vitamin D is one of the best vitamins to take to correct hormonal imbalance. Daily sunshine on bare skin actually makes vitamin D on its own when exposed to even small amounts of direct sunlight. Sunshine also sends a 'wake-up' call to our brain's pituitary gland, which aids in hormone balance.

**USE OF WATER:** Without adequate water, the body cannot make our hormones effectively. Water and water alone is the only liquid that the body can use to fulfill the production of hormones. A 2021 study found that increased water intake can have a positive role in reducing menstrual bleeding duration, the need of pain relievers, and pain intensity during menstrual period. It also claimed drinking water reduced acne and gave a brighter appearance.[8] At least eight glasses (1800ml) of water a day are needed for this process.

**SLEEP:** Sleep and hormone balance are closely connected. If you're having problems with one, you're almost certainly having problems with the other. Early nights allow rest and restoration. A compromise in the hours of sleep or sleeping at the wrong time (see page 183 for more on sleeping times) can inhibit the production of our hormones. Our endocrine system needs eight hours a night, particularly the hours before midnight, to ensure a correct hormone balance.

**TRUST IN DIVINE POWER:** Physical, emotional, social, mental, and spiritual health are all connected. Peace of mind affects all body functions to bring optimum performance. A vicious cycle begins with stress. Worry, anxiety and guilt can all affect our hormones, but at the same time a hormonal imbalance can increase anxiety. Just trying harder to be nicer and more appreciative to win our health battles is not easy (although it can help). These are spiritual

---

8. Torkan, B., et al. (2021) "The role of water intake in the severity of pain and menstrual distress among females suffering from primary dysmenorrhea." *BMC Women's Health* Vol 21, issue 40 <https://doi.org/10.1186/s12905-021-01184-w> accessed December 2023.

battles so we need spiritual tools, and thankfully God offers these tools through His Spirit that He longs to give us.

*"But the fruit of the Spirit is love, joy, peace, longsuffering, kindness, goodness, faithfulness, gentleness, self-control. Against such there is no law."*
Galatians 5:22-23

Give your battles to God and accept the working of His Spirit in your life to bring the healing you need.

**ABSTAIN:** Eliminating all known causative estrogen disrupters is the first step. The contraceptive pill, chemicals, and mold exposure disrupt the hormones. In addition to this, if you are suffering from hormone imbalances, all stimulants, such as refined sugar, caffeine, alcohol, and drugs, need to be ceased to allow the body to restore balance.

Drinking alcohol can increase your estrogen levels and reduce your liver's ability to break down estrogen and eliminate it from your body. If your liver's not functioning correctly, too much estrogen can accumulate.

### Healthy Cleaners

Organic and biodegradable cleaning products and laundry detergents reduce chemical exposure in the home and the environment.

Soap nuts are a popular natural chemical free substitute to normal detergents. They are highly-effective at washing clothes, dishes, windows, hair, treating head lice, dandruff, or even used as a natural pest controller in your garden. Soap nuts are available as a powder, liquid, or in the raw shell.

White vinegar and bicarb soda are healthy and cheap alternative cleaners. The best mold killer is white vinegar, and don't forget the sun. Clove essential oil can be added for extra power.

**INHALE:** It is important to breathe the purest air available, and breathe exclusively through the nostrils, using our diaphragm. This will guarantee delivery of the oxygen required to make our hormones and reduce pain.

When we are under stress or experience pain, such as menstrual cramps, our breathing pattern tends to become very shallow, causing us to breathe using our shoulders rather than our diaphragm to move air in and out of our lungs.

This style of breathing can cause muscles to tighten increasing the pain. When we breathe deeply into our abdomen, the muscles in the pelvis begin to relax, which helps reduce lower abdominal pain and cramping.

To relax the pelvis and bring relief from period pain, place one hand on your upper chest and the other just below your rib cage. This will allow you to feel your diaphragm move as you breathe. Breathe in slowly through your nose so that your stomach moves out, causing your hand to rise. The hand on your chest should remain as still as possible.

Slowly release the breath over five seconds by tightening your stomach muscles, so that your stomach moves in. This uses your diaphragm to empty out your lungs. Hold your breath after you have completely exhaled for 5 seconds. Repeat this process, concentrating on your breathing as you gently breathe in and out through your nose. Practice this exercise for two to five minutes about three to four times per day.

**NUTRITION:** Food provides the nutrients we need to maintain a healthy body, if we don't get enough of the right nutritious foods, our hormone balance can suffer. Eating foods that decrease inflammation in the body will help to reduce menstrual cramps. These foods include fruits (such as blueberries, blackberries, strawberries, and cherries), vegetables (including kale, spinach, and broccoli), whole grains, legumes, nuts, and seeds.

Research has shown that both a vegetarian and plant-based eating pattern work to decrease inflammation in the body.[9] This decrease is due to the high number of antioxidants and plant chemicals found in plant foods that help the body to function optimally. Additionally a plant-based diet eliminates the growth hormones found in animal products. If one chooses to eat animal products, they must be organic.

Organic food protects us from contamination by glyphosate, which is a major hormone disrupter. An abundance of fruit and vegetables, generous plant proteins and healthy fats will supply the raw ingredients for our hormones.

**MODERATION:** To keep happy hormones, an important part is moderation in sex. Moderation means not overdoing or underdoing. Multiple partners can be damaging not only physically and mentally but also can cause disruption to the hormones. The mixing of microbiomes, from having new or multiple

---

9. Craddock JC, Neale EP, Peoples GE, Probst YC. (2019) "Vegetarian-Based Dietary Patterns and their Relation with Inflammatory and Immune Biomarkers: A Systematic Review and Meta-Analysis." *Advances in Nutrition.* 2019 May 1;10(3):433-451. doi: 10.1093/advances/nmy103.

sexual partners, introduces new pathogens into your vaginal microbiome, and this is also one of the biggest risk factors for vaginal bacterial infections.[10]

**EXERCISE:** Regular exercise ensures a balance of blood and lymph flow, which contributes to body and hormone balance. Studies have shown that exercise may provide a large reduction in the intensity of period pain compared with not exercising.[11] Exercise not only strengthens muscle and bone but also boosts mood. Endorphins are released during exercise that has a direct effect on hormones.

# NATURAL CONTRACEPTION TIPS

Sex is two parts, in that it involves two people, and contraception should be two parts, as well.

THE WOMAN'S ROLE is to know when she is ovulating, which is her most fertile time. Her body will give her three signs:

▶ **Temperature change.** Her temperature will vary slightly each day, but as ovulation begins, her temperature will drop and then rise to a higher plane. This is the sign that ovulation has begun.

▶ **Lubricant change.** When not ovulating, the vaginal lubricant is thick and white in colour. During ovulation, the lubricant changes and becomes clear, stringy, and more profuse. This is often the first indication of the fertile days in a menstrual cycle, preceding ovulation.

▶ **Cervical change.** As a rule, the cervix is plump with a mucus plug, but as ovulation begins, the cervix shrinks a little, and the mucus plug is released.

▶ It is a good idea to document the changes. On the following page is an example of a symptothermal chart that can record a cycle.

The symptothermal method is used in natural family planning as a way for women to monitor their fertility to prevent or encourage pregnancy by recording different fertility awareness-based methods. The three signs mentioned above can be recorded in such a chart.

The woman starts recording her Basal Body Temperature on Day 1 of her cycle, which is the first day of the period when there is a flow of blood. She takes her temperature before she gets out of bed every morning (before

10. Fethers KA, et al (2008). "Sexual risk factors and bacterial vaginosis: a systematic review and meta-analysis." *Clinical Infectious Diseases.* Vol 47 Issue 11, pages 1426-1435. doi: 10.1086/592974.

11. Armour M, et al (2023). "Exercise for dysmenorrhea." *Cochrane Database of Systematic Reviews 2019*, Issue 9, Article No.: CD004142. doi: 10.1002/14651858.CD004142.pub4. Accessed December 2023.

drinking, eating or doing anything else) preferably at the same time each morning. To take her temperature the woman should remain lying down, with minimal movement.

The woman's hormones cause her body temperature to rise around ovulation. By analyzing this we can pinpoint where she is in her cycle.

The thermometer needs to be digital and show tenths of a degree. At first, you will have nothing to compare it to, but as the weeks go by you will begin to observe changes in your body. When the three signs, mentioned on the previous page, come together you will know you are ovulating and have the highest chance of getting pregnant.

After ovulation, due to the rise of heat-inducing progesterone, your body temperature should increase by 1.0 to 1.5 degrees (Fahrenheit) or higher. This rise should occur within one to two days of ovulation and then stay raised. If you became pregnant, your body temperature would remain high beyond when you would next expect to have a period. If you are not pregnant, a day or so before your next period, your body temperature will drop due to the drop in progesterone that signals the womb lining to shed.

Most women ovulate from day 14 to day 21 of their cycle. The signs allow them to define the beginning and end of ovulation.

The 'fertile window' can start as early as five days before ovulation due to the potential life span of sperm. An egg can also survive and be fertilized for 12-24 hours after ovulation.

It can take up to six months of monitoring your periods before you see patterns in your menstrual cycle. Once you begin to identify and understand your own natural cyclical rhythms, you will know how to best support yourself throughout your cycle and use this method to achieve or avoid pregnancy. Once you start charting fertility awareness it's almost impossible to not notice the influence of your cycle on your entire body.

THE MAN'S ROLE is to choose to either abstain from sex, use a condom, or master the art of withdrawal when his wife is most fertile.

Italian men prided themselves on not getting their women pregnant by mastering the art of withdrawal.

SCAN THE QR CODE to download your own printable Symptothermal Chart or visit www.barbaraoneill.com/downloads. Available in either Fahrenheit or Celsius.

# ONE CYCLE SYMPTOTHERMAL CHART

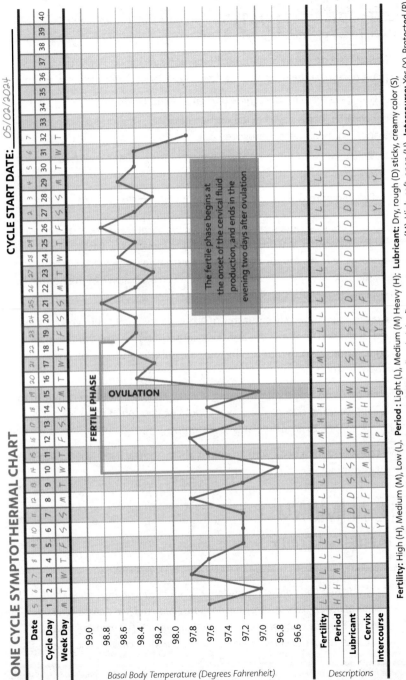

| Date | 5 | 6 | 7 | 8 | 9 | 10 | 11 | 12 | 13 | 14 | 15 | 16 | 17 | 18 | 19 | 20 | 21 | 22 | 23 | 24 | 25 | 26 | 27 | 28 | 29 | 1 | 2 | 3 | 4 | 5 | 6 | 7 |
|---|---|---|---|---|---|---|---|---|---|---|---|---|---|---|---|---|---|---|---|---|---|---|---|---|---|---|---|---|---|---|---|---|
| Cycle Day | 1 | 2 | 3 | 4 | 5 | 6 | 7 | 8 | 9 | 10 | 11 | 12 | 13 | 14 | 15 | 16 | 17 | 18 | 19 | 20 | 21 | 22 | 23 | 24 | 25 | 26 | 27 | 28 | 29 | 30 | 31 | 32 |
| Week Day | M | T | W | T | F | S | S | M | T | W | T | F | S | S | M | T | W | T | F | S | S | M | T | W | T | F | S | S | M | T | W | T |

Basal Body Temperature (Degrees Fahrenheit)

FERTILE PHASE

OVULATION

The fertile phase begins at the onset of the cervical fluid production, and ends in the evening two days after ovulation

| Descriptions | | | | | | | | | | | | | | | | | | | | | | | | | | | | | | | | |
|---|---|---|---|---|---|---|---|---|---|---|---|---|---|---|---|---|---|---|---|---|---|---|---|---|---|---|---|---|---|---|---|---|
| Fertility | L | L | L | L | L | L | L | L | L | L | L | L | M | H | H | H | H | M | L | L | L | L | L | L | L | L | L | L | L | L | L | L |
| Period | H | H | M | L | L | | | | | | | | | | | | | | | | | | | | | | | | | | | |
| Lubricant | | | | | | D | D | D | D | S | S | S | W | W | W | S | S | S | S | D | D | D | D | D | D | D | D | D | | | | |
| Cervix | | | | | | F | F | F | F | M | M | H | H | H | H | F | F | F | F | | | | | | | | | | | | | |
| Intercourse | | | Y | | | Y | | | | | P | P | | | | | | Y | | | | | | | | Y | | | | | | |

**Fertility:** High (H), Medium (M), Low (L).  **Period :** Light (L), Medium (M), Heavy (H);  **Lubricant:** Dry, rough (D) sticky, creamy color (S),
Slippery, watery, looks like raw egg whites (W).**Cervix:** Low, Firm closed (F), Medium height, firmness, openness (M). High, soft, open (H).  **Intercourse:** Yes (Y), Protected (P).

# OTHER HELPERS

Natural treatments through food, herbs, and specific nutrients can help decrease or resolve the discomfort women experience from menstrual cramps.

God gave *"herb for the service of man"* Psalm 104:14 KJV

For centuries, herbs have helped women ease the symptoms of hormone imbalance. Some of theses herbs are:

- Wild yam
- Maca
- Evening primrose oil
- Black cohosh
- Red clover
- Dong quai
- Chaste tree

**Wild Yam Creams** contain extracts of wild yam and vitex (chaste tree). The plant contains diosgenin, a natural chemical that stimulates the pathways that the body uses to make progesterone. As progesterone is the precursor to estrogen and testosterone, it is able to restore a correct balance in the hormones by boosting the body's production of progesterone.

**Dosage:** Approximately a quarter of a teaspoon of wild yam cream is applied to the skin (inside of the arms or thighs, chest, neck, or abdomen) twice daily for three weeks a month. The fourth week when it is ceased, is the week of menstruation.

If a woman is no longer menstruating, she can choose a week every month to stop applying the cream. The cream should be continued for at least a year, or maybe more, to ensure balance is restored.

We thank God for a body with an inbuilt ability to heal itself when given the right conditions.

# TESTIMONY
## DANIEL'S STORY

We recently received a message from a man with five children.

*"My wife and I had one child, but after several years and spending thousands of dollars, [there were] still no more children. Then, I came across a lady on YouTube who spoke of a cream that can help [women] conceive. It cost $40. Thanks to Barbara, we now have four more children, the youngest being 18 months"*—Daniel Hudgens.

# PART 2

# BEAUTIFUL BREASTS

B reasts are part of the female and male sexual anatomy. For females, breasts are functional (for breastfeeding), can be a symbol of femininity and, as the bible quote below points out, sexual (bringing pleasure).

> *"Rejoice with the wife of your youth. As a loving deer and a graceful doe, let her breasts satisfy you at all times; And always be enraptured with her love."* Proverbs 5:18–19

This makes breasts an indispensable part of the female body and helps a women feel whole. Hence, their loss can be extremely distressing. It does not matter the shape or size of your breasts, they are a part of you and who you are as a person.

Breast cancer is the most commonly diagnosed cancer and the second most common cause of death amongst women in Australia. The current figure is that one in seven women are diagnosed with breast cancer in their lifetime. This is an increase of 21 per cent over the last 10 years.[1] With that in mind, the health of the breasts needs serious attention.

Let us consider some of the contributing factors to breast damage.

---

1. "Breast Cancer Stats" *National Breast Cancer Foundation.* <https://nbcf.org.au/about-breast-cancer/breast-cancer-stats> accessed December 2023.

# THE SOLUTIONS

## STEP ONE: IDENTIFY THE DISRUPTERS

### > Dress

Bras, especially if underwire, can contribute to breast problems, including cancer, by inhibiting blood and lymph flow in and out of the breast. Premenopausal women who do not wear bras had half the risk of breast cancer compared with bra users.[2]

The lymphatic system is our bodies natural vacuum cleaner system, as its role is to clear waste away from the tissues. To do this the lymphatic tissue in the breast flows waste into the lymph nodes under the arm to be excreted. These lymphatic vessels are extremely thin and small, and have no pump, such as the heart, to propel contents forward. As a result, lymphatic vessels are easily constricted by external pressure, such as are applied by underwire bras, which can result in the breast tissue retaining and building up waste products. This can contribute to disease in the breasts.

This topic is researched extensively in the book *Dressed To Kill: The Link between Breast Cancer and Bras* by Sydney Ross Singer and Soma Grismaijer.

Breast tissue is very sensitive, and most bras are made from chemical fabrics. Nylon, polyester, and acrylic fibres are the most common. This is particularly dangerous in hot weather or during intense exercise, as the pores of the skin open, which increases the absorption of the chemicals from these fabrics.

The healthiest bra has no underwire and is made of natural fibres, such as cotton, silk, modal, bamboo, hemp, wool, and viscose.

### > Electromagnetic Fields (EMFs)

The effect of EMFs on human health has long been debated. A study in 2013 of four young women, aged from 21 to 39, showed a possible association of breast cancer in relation to EMF exposure from mobile phones. The breast imaging showed a clustering of multiple tumor foci in the breast directly under the area of phone contact.[3]

Phones should never be placed in the bra or top pocket and prolonged skin contact with mobile devices should be avoided. Ideally, do not put phones in

---

2. Hsieh C., Trichopoulos D. (1991), "Breast size, handedness and breast cancer risk" European Journal of Cancer and Clinical Oncology, Vol 27, Issue 2, Pages 131-135.

3. West JG, et al (2013). "Multifocal Breast Cancer in Young Women with Prolonged Contact between Their Breasts and Their Cellular Phones." *Case reports in medicine* 354682. doi:10.1155/2013/354682.

any clothing pockets. Some sports bras now contain a pocket for phones. Do not use it.

Breast surgeons are beginning to speak out about the high incidence of breast cancer in young women who carry their phones in their bras.

Sitting for long hours in front of a computer results in the breasts having a dangerously high level of exposure to EMFs. This is partially because the computer usually sits directly in front of the breasts.

Donna Fisher writes about these issues in her book *Dirty Electricity and Electromagnetic Radiation*, showing the dangers of EMF exposure and the clear proven link to disease in the body.

### ❭ Hormones

As a young girl enters puberty, her estrogen levels increase. Estrogen stimulates rapid cell growth, and in puberty, it is the main hormone responsible for skinny, young girls developing breasts and hips, giving them a womanly shape.

A common practice since the 1960s is for young women to take the birth control pill to prevent pregnancy. Unfortunately, in the process of preventing conception, the pill causes a rise in estrogen and a drop in progesterone. Contraceptive pills increase hormone levels more than four times what a woman would get from her own ovaries if not on the pill.[4]

Progesterone is the precursor of estrogen and testosterone. In other words, progesterone keeps estrogen under control. With the displacement of progesterone and rise in estrogen levels, breast tissue can develop cysts, fibrous or calcified lumps, and even breast cancer.

Hormone disrupting compounds are all through our environment. The feminization of male fish in rivers downstream of sewage discharges is being caused by estrogenic compounds in the effluent.[5] This is also affecting the quality of drinking water.

Other factors contributing to this rise in estrogen are mentioned in the section on Hormones, on page 158. Remember: if it causes massive cell growth, it is a cell proliferator.

---

4.  Lovett JL, et al (2017), "Oral contraceptives cause evolutionarily novel increases in hormone exposure: A risk factor for breast cancer." *Evolution, medicine, and public health*. Jun 5;2017(1) pages 97–108. doi: 10.1093/emph/eox009.

5.  Falconer IR. (2006). "Are endocrine disrupting compounds a health risk in drinking water?" *International journal of environmental research and public health*. June 3(2) pages 180–184. doi: 10.3390/ijerph2006030020. Accessed December 2023.

## ❯ Excess Weight

Women mainly make estrogen in the ovaries, in obese and post-menopausal women, adipose tissue, commonly known as body fat, is the main source of estrogen production in the body. While adipose tissue is crucial for health, too much fat mass increases estrogen levels giving rise to hormone imbalances and a higher risks of breast cancer as many breast tumors are dependent on estrogen for growth.[6]

## ❯ The Estrogen and Soy Connection

There has been much media coverage in the last few years warning us of the dangers of eating soy. It has been linked specifically with hormonal cancers such as breast cancer, uterine cancer, prostate cancer, and the like. There seems to be a great discrepancy between the soybean of the Orient and the soybean in developed countries. This is because the soybean in America has been genetically modified to resist Roundup. The field is often sprayed five times before harvest. This is five doses of glyphosate creating the soybean that will cause hormone disruptions.

> **The soybean has some of the most potent anticancer properties of any plant on planet earth.**

It is a fact that the soybean has some of the most potent anticancer properties of any plant on planet earth.[7] It is twice as high in protein as any other legume. It contains some of the finest oils to be found in plants. The natural estrogens found in the soybean have a balancing effect on our hormones. May I suggest then, that the problem is not the soybean; the problem rather is the way it has been grown and prepared. Considering the issues we have just discussed, it is essential that the soy products you buy are made from soybeans that have not been genetically modified, have been organically grown and the whole soybean used.

---

6.  Cleary MP, Grossmann ME. (2009). "Obesity and breast cancer: the estrogen connection." *Endocrinology.* Vol 150, issue 6, pages 2537-2542. <https://doi.org/10.1210/en.2009-0070>.

7.  Nurkolis F, et al (2022). "Anticancer properties of soy-based tempe: A proposed opinion for future meal." *Frontiers in Oncology,* Oct 24;12:1054399. doi: 10.3389/fonc.2022.1054399.

# STEP TWO: PROTECT YOUR BREASTS THROUGH THE 'SUSTAIN ME' PRINCIPLES

Eliminating any known causes is the first step. If you don't eliminate the cause, you will not have a cure. All known contributing factors must cease.

**SUNSHINE:** Daily sunshine, especially received through the eyes, stimulates the pituitary gland, which aids in hormone balance. Studies have found a lower risk of breast cancer associated with greater sun exposure in a population living with high, continuous sun exposure.[8] Breasts need sun, let them be touched by the sun. Most people have a secluded part in their house or yard where they can sunbathe in privacy.

For breasts that have never known sun, start with a short time. Begin with only ten minutes at a time and slowly increase as able.

The darker the skin, the more sun it can bear.

**USE OF WATER:** The breast tissue needs full hydration in order to function. Breastfeeding mothers need more water to meet the additional demand during pregnancy and lactation. A woman with insufficient milk production should be encouraged to drink a glass of water every time she breastfeeds and when thirsty.

Alternating hot and cold applications of water to the breast for any problems such as mastitis or breast cancer.

**SLEEP:** Allow the breasts to have their beauty sleep. Let them relax and rest between those night time hours of power. Whilst sleeping, breasts need to be free of any tight or restrictive night clothes. Remove your bra and wear very loose, comfortable, natural fibres as night attire, if anything.

Aim for the best for your breasts, which is eight hours a night.

**TRUST IN DIVINE POWER:** Love your breasts. No matter the size and shape, love them, and they will love you.

I love that passage in Psalm 139:13–14 that says:

*"You formed my inward parts; You covered me in my mother's womb.*
*I will praise You, for I am fearfully and wonderfully made;*
*Marvelous are Your works, and that my soul knows very well."*

Your whole body is a custom made masterpiece designed by God Himself and

---

8. Nazario CM, et al (2022). "Sun Exposure Is Associated with Reduced Breast Cancer Risk among Women Living in the Caribbean". *Cancer Epidemiology Biomarkers & Prevention*. Vol 31, Issue 2, pages 430–435. <https://doi.org/10.1158/1055-9965.EPI-21-0932>. Accessed December 2023.

it's a beautiful thing. When we love our breasts; blood, lymph, and nerve flow to them is enhanced. This contributes to the health and well being of the breasts.

Thank God every day for the body you have and the knowledge of how to give it the conditions for optimum performance.

**ABSTAIN:** Eliminate all exposure to anything known to cause hormone disruptions. This includes chemicals (check your personal care products), plastics, and stimulants, including alcohol, caffeine, and refined sugar. Meat and dairy products from conventionally grown cattle should also be avoided.

Fruit and vegetables grown with chemicals must be avoided as much as possible.

Discard restrictive and underwire bras. The tighter and longer the bra is worn the higher the health risk rises. Tight bras also cause breast pain and cysts, and are the leading cause of breast disease in bra-wearing cultures.

Explore natural methods of birth control to enable the ceasing of the contraceptive pill, IUD, Mirena, and any other artificial contraceptive devices.

**INHALE:** Oxygen is as necessary for breast cell function as in any other part of the body. When we breathe low, slow, and deep with shoulders back it allow the breasts to stretch which increases blood supply and brings more oxygen to the area. Inhaling in and out through the nose ensures we have enough oxygen.

**NUTRITION:** Eat only the highest quality plant-based food. Organic food prepared in the healthiest way is essential to provide the breast with the necessary nourishment to not only function at peak performance but also resist and overcome disease. This includes high fibre, and all unrefined plant foods containing fibre, especially fruit and vegetables.

Eat generous amounts of plant protein, which is found in legumes, nuts and seeds. The legumes need to be well soaked, rinsed, and pressure cooked.

Fats that are found in the plant kingdom, predominantly in nuts and seeds are healthy and can be eaten daily. Olive and coconut oils can be taken with plant foods, not only as taste enhancers but also to ensure that the cell membrane is kept supple.

**MODERATION:** Breasts need to have times of freedom, so moderation in wearing bras. Allow the breasts to breathe by covering them with natural fabric. It is important that a woman chooses the right type of bra in order to protect the general health of her breasts. A bra that doesn't fit well and offers little support can stretch and displace breast tissue and affect lymph flow. Ideally, choose a sports bra made with natural fibres. These include cotton, bamboo, and modal.

Keep your electronic devices in a bag, not on your body. Turn WiFi off at night. Do not sleep with technology in your bedroom.

Women working in healthcare who are regularly exposed to radiation from x-rays and other imaging procedures need extra radiation protection to help minimize their risk of developing breast cancer. Ionizing radiation is a known human carcinogen and breast tissue is highly sensitive to radiation. General personal protective equipment (PPE) such as lead gowns are inadequate protection for breast tissue as it leaves the area close to the armpit exposed.[9]

**EXERCISE:** It is the pectoral muscle that holds the breast tissue, and unfortunately, wearing a bra weakens the muscles that hold up the breasts, resulting in greater breast sagging.[10] To strengthen this muscle, women can do daily push-ups, begin small, implement them daily, and increase as able. If a standard push-up is too challenging, try dropping to your knees. As the pectoral muscles develop strength, this will hold the breast tissue more effectively and often allows women with smaller breasts to need very little, if any, support.

If you stay committed to your routine, you'll begin to notice increased strength and a perkier chest within a few months. To get the maximum benefit from chest exercises, make sure you're eating a well-balanced diet to keep body fat at a healthy level.

If a woman has large breasts, she needs to find a sports bra that will hold them comfortably but not be too restrictive. Especially when exercising and walking, as this excess movement in large breasts can be painful and can damage the tissues.

Swimming is excellent for breast health, as the arms receive an intense workout,

9. Pilkington I, Sevenoaks H, James E, Eastwood D. (2023), "Protecting female healthworkers from ionizing radiation at work" *BMJ*, 2023;381:e075406. Published 12 April 2023.
10. "Bras Make Breasts Sag, 15-Year Study Concludes," *Medical News Today*, <https://www.medicalnewstoday.com/articles/259073>. Accessed November 2023.

which increases blood and lymph flow to the breasts.

Rebounding is the best stimulator of the lymphatic system, and the breast is predominantly lymphatic tissue.

Choose a type of exercise that will not damage the breast tissue but builds up the pectoral muscle to help support and stimulate blood and lymph flow in and out of the breasts.

# OTHER HELPERS

Compresses and poultices applied directly to the breast can have a healing effect on the problem areas. I write more on how to make these compresses and poultices on page 305. Some specific remedies that can help the breasts include:

> **Castor Oil Compresses**
Castor oil compresses can be applied to blocked ducts in the breast, calcified deposits, cyst, tumors, or breast cancer.

Any lumps that appear in the breast can respond to the castor oil. Consistency is the key. The compress can be easily slipped into a sports bra and worn for at least five hours a day.

> **Potato Poultice**
This poultice is best for any tissue inflammation in the breast.

> **Charcoal and Flaxseed Poultice**
This can be used for infections and also breast cancer.

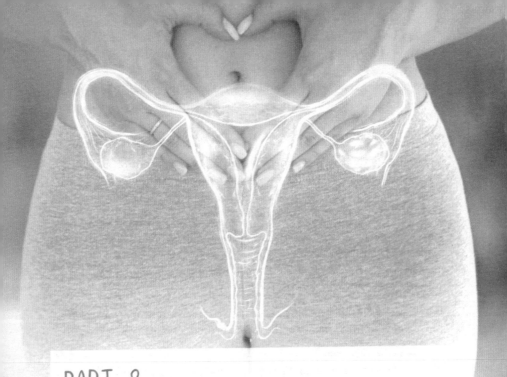

# PART 3
## CERTAIN HELP FOR THE CERVIX

The cervix is a barrel-shaped structure with a central canal and measures approximately two centimeters long. It is made of soft tissue and is like a small cushion forming the entry way from the vagina into the uterus.

This passage allows fluids to flow inside and out of a woman's uterus. It is also a powerful gatekeeper that can open and close in ways that make pregnancy and childbirth possible. It is the cervix (through labor) that is, little by little, thinned and then gradually opens, allowing the baby to emerge from the uterus into the birth canal.

As the gateway into the uterus, it also plays a protective role in preventing unwanted pathogens from entering the uterus. The small opening in the very center of the cushion-type form of the cervix contains a mucus plug. This plug is a protection for the small opening.

When a woman has a pap smear, a small scrape is taken from the surface of the cervix to test for abnormal cells.

What could be the cause of abnormal cells in the cervix? There can be several, as follows:

## > Hormones

A major contributing factor is hormonal imbalance. The body naturally makes two hormones: estrogen and progesterone. As estrogen is a cell proliferator, it can cause massive cell growth in the reproductive organs, contributing to abnormal cells in the cervix.

The causes of this rise in estrogen can include the birth control pill, with its synthetic (lab-made) versions of these hormones. Research suggests people who have used oral contraceptives for five or more years have a higher risk of cervical cancer than those who never used them.[1]

Also, environmental poisons, particularly glyphosate (Roundup) directly affect the hormones. Nonylphenol and bisphenol A are two chemicals that are added to plastics to soften them. These phenols mimic estrogen and can raise the estrogen levels in the body.

Growth stimulants that are often given to chickens and cattle for rapid growth can also affect the hormones of those who consume these items as foods.

## > Disease and Damage

Another cause of damage to the cervix can be sexually transmitted diseases or simply having multiple sexual partners. HPV is a very common virus that is spread through skin-to-skin contact (which often occurs during sex). Nearly all cases of cervical cancer are associated with the HPV infection with multiple sexual partners being the dominant risk factor.[2]

The cervix contains cells that play a key role in the defense against infection by destroying microorganisms, bacteria, and viruses that could affect the uterus, causing a woman's body to see sperm as alien, and every time sperm enters her, her immune system rises to attack. To get around this defense system, a males seminal fluid (semen) interacts with the females reproductive tract and exerts a immune suppressant allowing sperm to survive and promote the chance of pregnancy.[3] Women's bodies have memory, and every time the husband's sperm enters his wife, the seminal fluid priming effects causes her body to recognize it and her immune system steps back as it sees the familiar sperm. This biological response explains why a monogamous sexual relationship progressively protects against pregnancy disorders.

1.  Smith JS, Green J, Berrington de Gonzalez A, et al. (2003), "Cervical cancer and use of hormonal contraceptives: A systematic review." *Lancet* 2003; 361(9364), pages 1159–1167.
2.  Huang Y, Wu X, Lin Y, Li W, Liu J, Song B. (2020), "Multiple sexual partners and vaginal microoecological disorder are associated with HPV infection and cervical carcinoma development." *Oncology letters.* Aug; 20(2):1915-1921. doi: 10.3892/ol.2020.11738.
3.  Robertson SA, Sharkey DJ. (2016), "Seminal fluid and fertility in women." *Fertility and Sterility.* Vol 106, Issue 3, page 511–519, September 2016. doi: 10.1016/j.fertnstert.2016.07.1101.

Multiple sexual partners has a damaging effect on the woman's immune system which impairs the cervix's immune response, impacts fertility, and is associated with HPV infection, a key factor in developing cervical cancer.

## 〉 Malnutrition

Globally, malnutrition in all its forms is the greatest cause of death and morbidity, even though people may be eating plenty, mineral micro-nutrition mal-nutrition is widespread!

Declines of between 49–52% of essential minerals in fruits and vegetables since the 1940s has been recorded in the UK and elsewhere. These reductions have followed widespread changes in farming.[4] If the soil is deficient, plants will be deficient in nutrients, and so the body will be deficient. Food grown with chemicals depletes the nutrients. Other contributing factors include the refining of foods, genetic modification and the hybridization of crops.

# THE SOLUTIONS

The SUSTAIN ME principles covered in Part 1 and 2 of this chapter will also help with cervix issues, in addition to these principles some natural remedies that can assist are listed below:

### ■ TREATMENT: Wild Yam Cream

Many diagnosed cancers connected to the female reproductive organs are associated with obesity, either due to an excess of estrogen or a lack of progesterone. The key for good health is to get the balance right.

Yam creams, made from Mexican wild yam, contain the plant chemical diosgenin that works with the biochemical pathway of the body to make progesterone. Progesterone has the effect of restoring and maintaining a proper hormonal balance in the body.

Applying wild yam cream is essential for healing any problem in the reproductive organs of the body, the cervix being part of that system.

### ■ TREATMENT: Contrasting Hot and Cold Sitz Baths

Hydrotherapy is a powerful tool for healing and has been used for centuries. These baths are described in detail in the hydrotherapy section on page 291.

---

4.   Berenice Mayer A, Trenchard L, & Rayns F, (2022) "Historical changes in the mineral content of fruit and vegetables in the UK from 1940 to 2019: a concern for human nutrition and agriculture," *International Journal of Food Sciences and Nutrition*, Vol 73, 2022, Issue 3. Pages 315-326.

The application of alternate hot and cold water in the form of sitz baths is a booster of blood flow to the abdominal area, which accelerates healing of the cervix. Ideally, this is done at least once daily (twice daily if possible) for at least one month.

■ **TREATMENT:** Pokeroot and Goldenseal

Pokeroot is known as a herbal dilation and curet (D&C) because of its ability to cleanse the uterus, adding this to goldenseal, a herb known as 'king of tonics to all mucous membranes' will produce a powerful tonic that can be taken orally and as a douche.

### RECIPE

Take half a teaspoon of pokeroot and half a teaspoon of goldenseal. Add one cup of water to these herbs and gently simmer for ten minutes. When cool, strain the tea.

**Dose**

One teaspoon of the above tea mix is taken orally twice daily.

Two teaspoons of this tea is added to half a cup of warm water and applied to the cervix via a douche. This needs to be done twice daily for six days a week, and for three weeks a month, for at least six months.

# TESTIMONY
## HALEY'S STORY

Haley had just received the news that her pap smear had revealed abnormal cells. She was not keen to have her cervix treated by medical methods and so sought natural treatments.

Haley chose to implement the SUSTAIN ME principles of health and began to take the herbs as explained above.

Six months later, Haley contacted us with the news that she had received the all clear and no longer showed abnormal cells.

Ten years on, Haley is in fine health. She remembers how the natural treatments helped her to heal and is thankful for the wake-up call she had. Though in her 50's now, she is careful to implement healthful living practices and enjoys a better quality of life than her peers.

# PART 4
## PROLAPSE OF THE UTERUS AND BLADDER

The pelvic floor muscles support the bladder, uterus, and bowel. When working correctly these muscles wrap quite firmly around these passages to help keep them shut. The pelvic floor muscles can be weakened by pregnancy, childbirth, prostate cancer treatment, obesity, and the straining of chronic constipation. If the pelvic floor muscles are not functioning well, the internal organs will lack full support leading to a prolapse of either the bladder, uterus, or colon.

Prolapses can also be triggered by an injury, such as a difficult birth. The most common injury is from lifting heavy weights incorrectly.

Many are sick through ignorance, and it is the aim of this section to show the main causes and remedies for prolapse.

### ⟩ Lifting
It is vital that women know how to lift weights and recognize which heavy weights should be left for the men.

The biggest bone in the body is the femur, and the biggest muscles are the quads or thigh muscles. God designed the body so that the most strength to lift weights comes from the thighs and core (abdominal) muscles. When the back is straight, and core muscles are engaged, the thighs take most of the weight when lifting. If the back is bent, the weight is taken by the back and, in ladies, by the pelvic floor. This has an effect of weakening the back and pelvic floor.

### ⟩ Pelvic Muscles
Some other factors causing weak muscle tone are the lack of use, which comes from little or no exercise.

Our pelvic floor muscles also need oxygen, hydration, rest, and nourishing food to supply the cells with the basic ingredients to be able to function optimally, just like every other cell in our body.

A diet that includes more fruit, vegetables, fibre, and water will help in preventing straining from constipation.

# THE SOLUTIONS

## STEP ONE: STRENGTHEN YOUR PELVIC FLOOR

Strengthening your pelvic floor muscles is the key component to healing prolapses, urinary incontinence, and make sex better. The following are a few suggestions to assist with healing and preventing pelvic floor problems.

### ■ TREATMENT: Exercise Options

It is recommended that all women, at all stages of life, exercise their pelvic floor muscles everyday. Exercises that cause the muscles to defy gravity are the very process that strengthens them, thus keeping our organs in place will prevent the need for corrective surgery.

The best gravity-defying exercises are rebounding or trampolining. The constant leaping against gravity causes every single cell in the body to contribute to adapting to defying this force. This is also the reason why rebounding is the most effective exercise that the body can do.

Another pelvic floor exercise is core strengthening moves. Joseph Pilates is probably one of the most famous creators of a core workout. The core (abdominal) muscles, makes up part of the pelvic girdle, and exercises that target the strengthening of the core will help strengthen all the muscles that make up the pelvic girdle.

### Squatting

Squatting is a position that is very natural for the human body. Children are often seen squatting. In many Asian countries, this position can be observed in several workplaces, especially the garden.

It is the best position to be in for the daily evacuation of the colon. Different muscles automatically relax to allow for an easier release of body waste.

There is no better position to prepare for and successfully achieve childbirth. Daily squatting also helps regain strong pelvic floor tone after childbirth. This position stretches and strengthens the pelvic girdle.

If not used to the squatting position, try squatting with your back against the wall for five to ten minutes a day.

## The Slant Board

This simple board has been used for centuries to heal a prolapse. The point of the exercise is to cause the body to be in a slanted position, with the hips higher than the shoulders, causing the internal organs to fall upwards. This relieves the body from the daily pattern of compression and pull, by allowing muscles and organs to reposition themselves. The recommendation is to use the slant board twice a day for about ten minutes for best results.

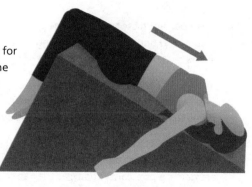

There are many companies that make slant boards, but you can easily make your own at home using a solid board elevated at one end by some type of support, such as a wood block, a couch or other skid-free support. For more comfort you can add padding over your board such as a blanket, padded mat, or thin cushion.

Begin slowly at a slight angle until you get used to the position then gradually increasing the angle over time. Necessity is the mother of invention here, so play with it to achieve the right angle for you.

## Knee-chest Position

An alternative is to take the knee-chest position in bed, with the hips in the air and hold that for one minute. Then roll onto your side to sleep for the night. This position also causes the prolapse to fall into place and allows the pelvis to stay in place all night, further contributing to the healing of the prolapse.

These methods will only bring temporarily relief to your prolapse as when you spend time upright again your pelvic organs will start to move back to the stretched position so it is important to do these exercise consistently and to follow them up with the other pelvic floor exercises that will strength your internal tissue supports. Gradually you may find that the prolapse stays in place a little longer. The key is consistency.

An important factor in healing the pelvic floor is keeping the muscles hydrated, rested, and nourished and believing that God gave us a body with an inbuilt ability to heal itself, when given the right conditions.

## ■ TREATMENT: Yoni Stones

The word *Yoni* means *sacred temple* in ancient Indian Sanskrit language and refers to a woman's vagina, vulva, cervix, ovaries, and uterus.

Yoni stones (sometimes called Yoni Eggs) are traditionally believed to be of Chinese origin and used in ancient Chinese sexual health practices. Yoni stones are gaining popularity today, as they are purported to strengthen the pelvic girdle and in the process, increase libido and natural lubrication, reduce PMS symptoms, and improve overall health and well being.

### 〉 The Pelvic Girdle

The stone is held in place by the pelvic girdle or the muscles that make up the pelvic girdle, sometimes called the pelvic floor muscles.

These muscles are called a girdle because that's exactly what they act like. This set of muscles begins at the belly button, continues between the legs, and ends up at the coccyx bone, which is the bottom tip of our spine.

These muscles include the anal sphincter and vaginal, cervical, and urethral muscles.

Many women have found wearing the stones strengthens their pelvic girdle muscles from the inside. As the muscles work to hold the stone, blood supply is enhanced to the area. The increased blood flow brings more nutrients, greater oxygen, and ensures that each cell is well hydrated.

As a result, all the muscles that make up the pelvic girdle are strengthened and toned.

Over-sensitive vaginal walls can be strengthened, and the glands that lubricate the vagina can once again release their oils. The increase in blood flow revives the cells that line the vagina, as well as the cells that make up the glands that supply the lubricant. This can also aid in the prevention or healing of urethral incontinence.

Yoni stones are usually made of a dense Nephrite Jade, however they can be made of Rose Quartz, Black Obsidian Rock, Silicone, Amethyst Quartz, or other materials. It is essential they contain no crevices or bumps to aid in comfort and cleanliness. Jade Yoni stones are usually considered the healthiest to use.

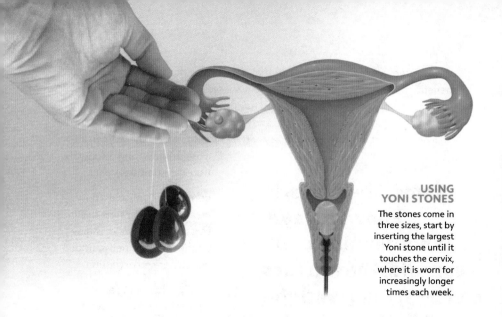

**USING YONI STONES**

The stones come in three sizes, start by inserting the largest Yoni stone until it touches the cervix, where it is worn for increasingly longer times each week.

The stones come in three sizes: large, medium, and small, the large being the size and shape of a small bantam hen egg.

Two small holes are situated near the pointed end of the stone, which dental floss can be threaded through to allow for easy extraction.

### ⟩ How to Wear the Stones

To begin, the larger end of the largest stone is inserted until it touches the cervix, where it is worn for one hour a day for the first week. For the second week, it is worn for two hours a day. In week three, the stone is worn for three hours a day, and in week four, it is worn for four hours a day until, in week five, the stone is worn for five hours a day.

Five hours a day is maintained for the next five months, and then the medium-sized stone is worn for five to six hours a day.

The stone continues to be worn for the next six months, and then the smallest stone can be worn for five to six hours a day. This can also be worn for several months. By now, the pelvic girdle will be strong, and a maintenance dose may be the wearing of the small stone for several hours for a few days a week.

Daily, after extraction, the stone needs to be washed with soap and warm water, dried, and returned to the little velvet bag it came in.

Women are being liberated by the use of these small stones with prolapses healing, preventing surgery, and the embarrassing effect of incontinence is being reversed.

While some gynecologists espouse that Yoni stones don't have any medical benefit, many women are reporting great success from using them. Women in their 50's and 60's who had stopped having sex because of pain caused by sensitivity in the lining of the vagina and a lack of lubricant, are also reporting healing, once again enjoying intimacy with their husbands. Some women are even experiencing a reduction in chronic back pain.

# Remember, muscle knows no age. Whether nine or 90 years old, the muscles can be strong, and the pelvic floor muscles are no exception.

Remember, muscle knows no age. Whether nine or 90 years old, the muscles can be strong, and the pelvic floor muscles are no exception.

Ideally, rebounding and core strengthening exercises are also included in a woman's daily program to help maintain and strengthen the pelvic girdle.

The stones can be ordered on the internet. Look for Yoni stones in Nephrite Jade.

## STEP TWO: THE 'SUSTAIN ME' PRINCIPLES

Ensuring the cells that make up the muscles are receiving optimum conditions is critical to the success of any treatment. The principles covered in SUSTAIN ME will sustain the cells that make up the pelvic girdle. These cells require full hydration, nourishment, and strength to defy gravity.

# TESTIMONIES
## SUE'S STORY

Sue and Tom had been married for 25 years and were both in their mid–50's. Their sex life had sadly deteriorated, as Tom was struggling to achieve an erection, and when he could, which was sometimes once or twice a month, Sue found that sex was painful. It was no longer enjoyable. It seemed that she had no lubricant, and the cells lining her vagina had become ultra sensitive.

They attended a lecture on how to balance the hormones and use the Yoni stones to restore strength and integrity to the cells lining the vagina. It was also explained how the corresponding blood flow increase to the pelvic girdle from wearing the Yoni stone revives the glands that supply lubricant to the vagina.

Tom began to apply wild yam cream daily. Sue also implemented daily use of the cream. When the Yoni stones arrived in the mail, Sue began to wear the biggest stone daily as per instructions.

After approximately two months, Tom noticed that he would often wake with an erection as he had done years ago. Sue found that penetration was no longer painful, the vagina wall was not so sensitive, and the lubrication had returned. Tom and Sue once again began to enjoy the intimacy in their marriage, as they had done ten years ago.

We live in a body that contains an inbuilt ability to heal itself, when given the right conditions.

## EMILY'S STORY

It was a surprise when Emily discovered, at 35 weeks pregnant, that she was carrying twins. The births went smoothly with a 20-minute break between babies. Both girls were around six pounds in weight.

Even though it had been six months since the birth, Emily found that whenever she laughed or coughed, she would lose a little urine. Thinking it was a result of carrying such a heavy load through pregnancy, Emily resigned herself to the discomfort and embarrassment of the incontinence. After a particularly busy day, with several embarrassing moments, Emily decided to investigate some solutions to her problem. She discovered Yoni stones and began wearing one daily, as per instructions. To her delight, within three months, she could laugh, cough, and even jump on the trampoline with no leakage at all!

The twins are now teenagers, and after a few more births, there has been no recurrence of the problem.

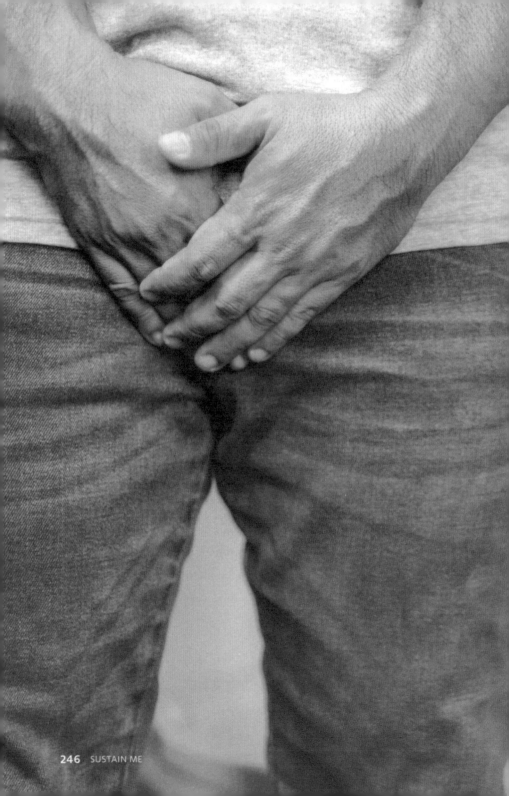

# CHAPTER 16

# MALE MATTERS

ust as there are a multitude of various hormone related problems affecting females, the same can be said for males. Penile dysfunction (the inability to hold an erection), low sperm count, prostate problems, depression, and heart disease are some of the of the main hormonal related complaints.

Pivotal to most of these problems is the prostate gland. The prostate is a part of the male reproductive system, it is a small gland about the size of a walnut that lives just below the bladder. It sits around the urethra, which is the tube that carries urine through the penis. It is important for reproduction, because it supplies part of the seminal fluid (semen), which mixes with sperm from the testes. Seminal fluid also contains an immune suppressant that protects sperm from the woman's immune system, this is to increase the likelihood of pregnancy.

This gland continues to grow gradually in most adult men, if it becomes enlarged enough it can obstruct the bladder, causing symptoms like a weak urine stream, difficulty with completely emptying the bladder, frequent trips to the bathroom, especially at night, as well as some dribbling after urination has ceased and difficulty in beginning urination.

The three most common prostate problems are inflammation (prostatitis), enlarged prostate, and prostate cancer. These are each individual problems and having one prostate issue does not necessarily increase your risk of having one of the others.

# PROSTATE ISSUES

The three most common prostate problems are inflammation (prostatitis), enlarged prostate, and prostate cancer.

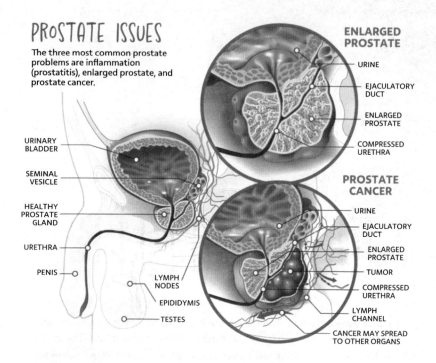

**ENLARGED PROSTATE**
- URINE
- EJACULATORY DUCT
- ENLARGED PROSTATE
- COMPRESSED URETHRA

**PROSTATE CANCER**
- URINE
- EJACULATORY DUCT
- ENLARGED PROSTATE
- TUMOR
- COMPRESSED URETHRA
- LYMPH CHANNEL
- CANCER MAY SPREAD TO OTHER ORGANS

- URINARY BLADDER
- SEMINAL VESICLE
- HEALTHY PROSTATE GLAND
- URETHRA
- PENIS
- LYMPH NODES
- EPIDIDYMIS
- TESTES

## CAUSES OF PROSTATE PROBLEMS

The prostate is the male equivalent to the uterus since they both develop from the same embryonic cells, thus men have all of the same hormones as women, most are just in much different doses and operate in a much more consistent nature.

Estrogen, or estradiol (the predominant form of estrogen), is usually associated with the female body, but this hormone also plays an important role for the health of males. Men should have more testosterone than estrogen, and the correct balance is what makes up their manly personality and traits.

When estrogen level rises, either endogenously (from within) or exogenously (from without), testosterone levels dips down. Some of the possible side effects of imbalance include enlarged breast tissues (sometimes referred to as man boobs or moobs), infertility, type 2 diabetes, erectile dysfunction, heart diseases, enlarged prostate, and some cancers.

As men age, progesterone levels can decrease. When progesterone levels decrease, an enzyme called 5-alpha reductase converts testosterone into a type of testosterone called dihydrotestosterone (DHT). This is an essential hormone in males for sexual development until puberty, after which it is considered the cause of inflammation of the prostate and conditions like diabetes, prostate diseases, some forms of cancer, and male pattern hair loss.[1]

It is known that growth promoting hormones in cattle causes an increase of estrogen residues in milk and other dairy foods. This has led to 60–80% of estrogens in western diets coming from milk and dairy products. Recent studies are revealing a very strong relation between milk and dairy products consumption and high incidence of testicular and prostate cancers.[2]

Other causes of high estrogen levels include medications, stress, liver problems, excess body fat, alcohol consumption, and synthetic xenoestrogens. Many of these items are explored in other chapters of this book.

Testosterone, like progesterone, counteracts high estrogen levels, preventing estrogen from causing prostate cancer by destroying the prostate cancer cells which estrogen stimulates.

Prostate cancer happens when cancer cells form in the prostate. Prostate cancer tends to grow slowly compared with most other cancers. Worldwide, it is the most commonly diagnosed male cancer and the fifth leading cause of cancer death in men.[3] While the usual risk factors include age, ethnicity, obesity, and family history, recent research has discovered that multiple lifetime sexual partners or starting sexual activity early in life can also increase the risk of prostate cancer.[4]

My first book *Self Heal By Design*[5] outlines the dietary requirements to help the body conquer cancer. When the principles in that book are combined with the points explained in this chapter, many have found how to manage, and even heal from prostate cancer.

To remedy inflammation of the prostate, there are a few specific things that can be done. These simple home remedies can also help in all problems related to the prostate.

1. Kinter KJ, Amraei R, Anekar AA. (2023) "Biochemistry, Dihydrotestosterone." *StatPearls* [Internet], StatPearls Publishing; 2023 Jan-. <https://www.ncbi.nlm.nih.gov/books/NBK557634>.
2. Malekinejad H, Rezabakhsh A. (2015), "Hormones in Dairy Foods and Their Impact on Public Health – A Narrative Review Article." *Iranian Journal of Public Health* Vol 44, Issue 6 pages 742-758.
3. Leslie SW, et al (2023). *Prostate Cancer*. StatPearls Publishing; 2023 PMID: 29261872. Accessed December 2023.
4. Leslie SW, Soon-Sutton TL, R I A, et al. (2023), "Prostate Cancer." *StatPearls* (internet article). <https://www.ncbi.nlm.nih.gov/books/NBK470550/0> accessed December 2023
5. *Self Heal By Design* by Barbara O'Neill, is available from Amazon or www.barbaraoneill.com

# THE SOLUTIONS

## STEP ONE: BRING RELIEF

In discussing the following simple home remedies that can help to alleviate prostate problems, we will also be touching on some of the causes.

### ■ TREATMENT: Balancing Hormones

**ZINC** reduces heightened estrogen levels in men, preventing the conversion of testosterone into dihydrotestosterone. The body loses zinc through perspiration, and when a man ejaculates he totally exhausts his zinc stores. When the diet is well supplied, this is not a problem. If ejaculation is over stimulated and the diet deficient, zinc depletion can arise. Alcohol, diuretics, and certain antibiotics can also contribute to depleting zinc stores. As a result zinc deficiency can be a contributing factor in male hormone related problems, such as previously listed. Being mindful of this can help to prevent prostate issues.

Zinc is not created in the body, to maintain adequate levels we need to receive it from external sources. It can be found naturally in abundance in pumpkin and sesame seeds; nuts, such as pine nuts, cashews, and almonds; and in grains like wheat, quinoa, rice, and oats. To get the zinc out of grains it is better to culture the grain, such as in sourdough bread, to make the zinc more available.

Initially, if you are suffering from severe zinc deficiency a supplement of up to 50mg may be needed.[6]

**WILD YAM CREAMS** contain the plant chemical, diosgenin. Diosgenin works with the body's hormone pathways to cause a boost in progesterone.

Men also need progesterone to counteract the effects of estrogen. Not only is progesterone naturally found in males, but men rely on it to preserve their masculinity as it is a building block for many hormones including testosterone—the male sex hormone.

Progesterone is the precursor to other hormones, and when it is stimulated, has an effect to reduce estrogen and balance testosterone.

Wild yam cream can be applied twice daily to the soft tissue parts of the body, inside of arms, thighs or use like an aftershave. These soft tissue areas take up the actives from the cream into the fat cells. It may take at least six months or a year to achieve a complete balance, though symptoms can ease within weeks.

---

6.   Maxfield L, Shukla S, Crane JS. (2023) "Zinc Deficiency." *StatPearls* [Internet], StatPearls Publishing; June 28, 2023. <https://www.ncbi.nlm.nih.gov/books/NBK493231>. Accessed January 2024.

By balancing the hormones, wild yam creams can also increase the sperm count and remedy penile dysfunction, and so assist with infertility problems. Optimal male fertility is just as important as female fertility in order to conceive.

## ■ TREATMENT: Herbs to Help

**SAW PALMETTO** is a herb that contains plant chemicals that directly reduce the swelling of the prostate and has traditionally been used to increase testicular function.[7] This can be taken in a supplement form, available at health food stores.

**SMALL WILLOW LEAF,** also known as Small Flowered Willow Herb, is a herbal tea useful for inflammation. It has been used successfully around the world for problems of the urinary tract and to treat prostate problems, bladder problems, and bed-wetting.

**STINGING NETTLE** is one of the most commonly used herbal remedies, it has anti-inflammatory, anti-tumor, and antiviral effects. In a clinical trial, patients who had nettle (*Urtica dioica*) showed a significant reduction in prostate size.[8] You can take these herbs as a tea or you may be able to buy a supplement that has a combination of these herbs.

## ■ TREATMENT: Poultices

Poultices are applied between the scrotum and the anus, as this is the area where the skin is closest to the prostate gland. These can be alternated and worn at night. Try a castor oil compress one night and a flaxseed and charcoal poultice on the next.

See my chapter on Poultices on page 305 for more information on how to use this treatment.

## ■ TREATMENT: Suppositories

**CASTOR OIL** is an anti-inflammatory agent. Inserting a castor oil suppository just before bed can be helpful, as this area is very close to the prostate gland. Castor oil penetrates deep and can help to reduce the inflammation of the prostate gland. The suppository is inserted just before retiring at night and expelled with the morning evacuation.

See page 312 for instructions on how to make suppositories.

---

7.  Suzuki M, et al (2019), "Pharmacological effects of saw palmetto extract in the lower urinary tract" *Acta pharmacologica Sinica*, Vol 30, Issue 3, pages 271–281.
8.  Safarinejad MR. (2005), "Urtica dioica for treatment of benign prostatic hyperplasia: a prospective, randomized, double-blind, placebo-controlled, crossover study." *Journal of Herbal pPharmacotherapyr.* Vol 5, issue 4, pages 1–11. PMID: 16635963.

# STEP TWO: PROTECT YOUR PROSTATE THROUGH THE 'SUSTAIN ME' PRINCIPLES

Adhering to the SUSTAIN ME principles is the basic foundation for long term healing of the prostate.

**SUNSHINE:** Frequent recreational sun exposure, without going overboard and burning, can significantly reduced the risk of fatal prostate cancer. Vitamin D is made from sunlight acting on the skin and has a great effect on sufficient progesterone production that protects against prostate cancer.

A 2017 study involving 102 men with a vitamin D deficiency found that taking a vitamin D supplement increased testosterone levels and improved erectile dysfunction.[9]

Don't wait until you are an adult though, young boys need sunshine also as it has a protective effect against prostate cancer in adulthood.[10]

**USE OF WATER:** Drinking plenty of water is essential for the prostate as it reduces the concentration of urine in the bladder thus easing irritation in the area. Drink at least eight glasses of water through the day, this will supply the water the body needs.

Water has a powerful effect when used inside and outside of the body. Contrasting hot and cold sitz baths can reduce the inflammation of the prostate gland and also boost healing from prostate cancer, and erectile dysfunction. See page 295 for details on this water treatment.

**SLEEP:** Melatonin is a hormone produced in the brain in response to darkness. A man that enjoys uninterrupted sleep between the hours of 9pm and 2am can get an increased level of this sleep hormone which will make him 75% less likely to develop advanced prostate cancer than those with less melatonin.[11]

**TRUST IN DIVINE POWER:** Religious and spiritual beliefs including forgiveness are an important aspect of cancer survival. Chronic stress, fear and worry can lead to hormonal imbalances and inflammation, affecting

---

9. Canguven O, (2017) "Vitamin D treatment improves levels of sexual hormones, metabolic parameters and erectile function in middle-aged vitamin D deficient men." *The Aging Male*, Vol 20, 2017 - Issue 1. doi: 10.1080/13685538.2016.1271783

10. John EM, Koo J, Schwartz GG. (2007). "Sun exposure and prostate cancer risk: evidence for a protective effect of early-life exposure." *Cancer Epidemiology, Biomarkers & Prevention*. Vol 16, Issue 6, 2007. pages 1283–1286. doi: 10.1158/1055-9965.EPI-06-1053.

11. Sigurdardottir LG, et al (2015). "Urinary melatonin levels, sleep disruption, and risk of prostate cancer in elderly men." *European Urology*. Vol 67, Issue 2, pages 191-194. doi: 10.1016/j.eururo.2014.07.008.

prostate health and make you more susceptible to disease. Let go of stress and put your trust in God.

*"Fear not, for I am with you; Be not dismayed, for I am your God. I will strengthen you, Yes, I will help you, I will uphold you with My righteous right hand."* Isaiah 41:10

Getting to a place where you are ready to let go of your stresses and forgive yourself or others takes a lot of work. God wants to strengthen you, guide you, and help you, all you need to do to call out to Him for help.

**ABSTAIN:** If you are a smoker, quit! The carbon monoxide in tobacco attaches to red blood cells until the cell dies, which can cause prostate cancer and other diseases to thrive.

Avoid caffeine and alcohol. The bladder is made up of layers of muscles, drinking alcohol weakens these muscles making it harder to control your bladder. This can contribute to an increase in urinary urgency and frequency, as well as an increase in urinary leakage. In addition to this, alcohol worsens the inflammation that is already present in prostate cells, thus interrupting the healthy flow of urine further and increasing your risk of developing an overactive bladder.

Caffeine is a diuretic and stimulates the bladder. For people with an enlarged prostate their bladders are already overactive, so it makes sense to avoid, or at least limit, caffeine.

Steer clear of pornography and overstimulating the sexual organs, such actions can result in excess ejaculation which depletes zinc levels, contributing to problems in the prostate.

Don't use plastic containers. Highly toxic chemicals used to increase the flexibility of plastic can leach out of these products into food, especially when heated. Known health effects from these chemicals include decreased testosterone production, increased BMI, and damage to the health of sperm.[12]

**INHALE:** Breathe. Deep breathing exercises involve taking slow, deep breaths using the diaphragm to inhale in and out through the nose. These techniques promote relaxation and reduce stress, helping to alleviate the impact of stress on the prostate, and improve the of quality of life for older adults with prostate cancer.[13]

---

12. Rowdhwal SSS, Chen J. (2018), "Toxic Effects of Di-2-ethylhexyl Phthalate: An Overview." *BioMed Research International.* 2018 Feb 22;2018:1750368. doi: 10.1155/2018/1750368.

13. Shahriari M, et al (2017) "Effects of progressive muscle relaxation, guided imagery and deep diaphragmatic breathing on quality of life in elderly with breast or prostate cancer." *Journal of Education and Health Promotion.* 2017 Apr 19;6:1. doi: 10.4103/jehp.jehp_147_14.

**NUTRITION:** A diet rich in green, leafy vegetables is important for a healthy prostate. Vitamins and antioxidants found in vegetables keep you and your prostate healthy. Try adding spinach, kale, and broccoli to your meals each day.

Cooking tomato with an oil (try olive) on a low heat causes a release of lycopene, a potent antioxidant from the vitamin A family, which is a fat soluble vitamin. Lycopene is known to reduce the inflammation of the prostate gland. Men make sure you have three to four olive oil and tomato dishes a week, having them with lentils tastes nice.

**MODERATION:** Obesity is linked to several prostate health issues, including prostate cancer. Enjoying a balanced diet and regular exercise are important for a healthy prostate and maintaining a healthy weight. Avoid having too much red meat. Eating red and processed meat increases the risk of advanced prostate cancer, especially when grilled or well done.[14] For this reason a vegetarian diet is the best.

**EXERCISE:** Participate in moderate to vigorous physical activity most days of the week. A lack of exercise actually increases the likelihood of developing an enlarged prostate.[15] Even 30 minutes of moderate activity each day, like a brisk walk, rebounding or a jog, can have far-reaching health benefits.

# TESTIMONIES
## THOMAS' STORY

Thomas had a rather traumatic experience, imprisoned in Vietnam during the war in the 1970s, he watched his best friend be slowly killed in front of him.

Now in his late 60s, he had developed prostate cancer. Coming to the health retreat was his wife's idea, as she was unsure about what to do next. Thomas carried a lot of bitterness and resentment over his experience, which added to his health problems.

Thomas was having a hormone injection every three months in an attempt to lower his testosterone levels. The side effects of this drug were most

---

14. John EM, Stern MC, Sinha R, Koo J. (2011) "Meat consumption, cooking practices, meat mutagens, and risk of prostate cancer." *Nutrition and Cancer*. Vol 63 Issue 4, pages 525-537. doi: 10.1080/01635581.2011.539311.

15. Platz EA, Kawachi I, Rimm EB, et al. (1998) "Physical activity and benign prostatic hyperplasia." *Archives of Internal Medicine* 1998;158:2349–56. PMID: 9827786.

uncomfortable, including hot flashes almost hourly, and the development of breasts. He was carrying about 40kg of excess weight.

What was of most concern to his wife was his almost daily recounting of his war experience from 40 years ago. She said, "I don't want to hear it anymore, but I do feel sorry for him. What do I do?"

Hearing the lectures on the right physical habits to promote health, Thomas decided to implement what he had heard: he engaged in daily exercise and cut out caffeine, sugar, and meat from his diet. He began to apply wild yam cream and chose to discontinue his hormone injection.

Upon learning of the power of forgiveness on our mental and physical health, Thomas made the momentous decision to forgive the Viet Cong soldiers who were responsible for his friend's death.

Six months later, we received an email from Thomas' wife. Thomas had just returned from a routine doctor's visit. He'd had no more hot flashes, his breasts had gone down, and his testosterone levels were the best they had been in years. With the lifestyle and dietary changes, he had lost weight, but she said the best thing was that he no longer related the story of his war trauma every day.

On request, Thomas will tell his story in church, but his main focus now is on how forgiveness freed him from the chains that had bound him to his painful past. He also believes that this played a part in how he healed from prostate cancer.

Thomas' story reveals the importance of adhering to every one of the SUSTAIN ME principles.

Trust in Divine Power freed him from the chains of unforgiveness that bound him. The physical healing was a nice side effect.

CHAPTER 17

# WEIGHING UP WEIGHT LOSS

The impact of COVID–19 on diet has revealed 35% of Australians gained weight during the pandemic.[1] Many factors can contribute to unintentional weight gain. Poor sleep, sedentary activities, consuming more alcohol, and eating too many processed or sugary foods are just some of the problems. Weight gain and obesity is a concerning epidemic worldwide that has been rising over the years since people began eating a high carbohydrate diet.

We are a fast society today, and everything happens quickly. People do not have the time to spend preparing and cooking food. So, the faster the food can be available, the more popular it is. Enter carbohydrates.

---

1. Ipsos Survey Press Release, https://www.ipsos.com/en-au/more-third-australians-have-gained-weight-during-pandemic-ipsos-survey> accessed December 2023.

Cereal, bread, pasta, pizza, doughnuts, pastries, pies, chips/fries, pretzels—they are everywhere and instantly available to eat. No preparation is necessary at all.

After you eat, your body breaks down carbohydrates into glucose (sugar). High carbohydrate intake equals high glucose released in the bloodstream. Glucose travels through the blood providing the required energy for all body cells, this process causes your blood sugar level rises. As it does, the pancreas releases the hormone insulin.

Insulin's role is to increase the uptake or delivery of glucose into the cell. If there is excess glucose beyond what the body needs for immediate energy, it is converted into glycogen and stored like a little bunch of grapes in the cell for future use.

The muscle cells are the biggest reservoir of glycogen stores, as they are the workhorses of the body and have the greatest requirements for glycogen.

After the energy cycle and filling of glycogen stores, the leftover or remaining glucose (which is common on a high carbohydrate diet) is stored as fat. If you are taking in more calories than your body needs, or is burning regularly over time, weight gain will likely result.

This brief overview of the journey of glucose shows fats don't make you fat!

# THE SOLUTIONS

## STEP ONE: DISCOVER THE CAUSE

There can be many reasons behind weight gain, understanding the causes of your weight gain is the first step to working on a plan to reduce that weight.

### What fat makes you fat?

**Carbohydrates:** One of the most damaging fats are those produced from high carbohydrate intake, and the most dangerous carbohydrate is modern wheat. In the 1950's wheat was hybridized to produce a higher yield of grain from each plant. In this process a starch was created that raises blood glucose levels quite dramatically. The response in the body to high carbohydrate intake influenced Dr William Davis to title his bestselling book, *Wheat Belly*. It is a very appropriate name for a book that clearly shows how this starch is converted quite quickly to a visceral type of fat that the body stores on the belly.

**Trans fats:** These altered fats are another type of fat that the body has difficulty using. Margarine and heated oils are among this group. Polyunsaturated fats such as vegetable oils, sunflower, and canola oil are the most common heated fats, and yet the most susceptible to damage because of their open molecular formation. When heated, the molecular structure of these fats change, increasing the formation of trans fats. Artificial trans fats also occur when vegetable oils are chemically altered to stay solid at room temperature, such as with margarines. Trans fats are well known in nutrition circles to be very damaging to the body.

The body's preferred fat for fuel is saturated fat as the body quickly burns it to create energy. In addition, recent studies are revealing that saturated fat has little effect on heart disease or death and in healthy adults may actually be linked to a lower risk of other conditions including obesity, type 2 diabetes, and high blood pressure.[2]

**Stress:** There is also a strong relationship between stress and weight gain. When stressed, our levels of cortisol (the stress hormone) increase. This may be tied to a higher risk of weight gain and obesity. Chronic stress is known to alter the pattern of food intake, dietary preference, and digestive issues.[3]

**Other issues:** Sugar intake from sweetened beverages; exposure to endocrine disrupting chemicals found in everyday household items like food containers, toys, cookware, personal care products, cleaning agents; medical supplies such as mercury; hormone imbalances; lack of exercise; and consuming over processed foods are also all of concern. Once a cause is identified, steps need to be put in place to eliminate or control the causative factor. This is where the SUSTAIN ME principles can help.

# STEP TWO: USE THE 'SUSTAIN ME' PRINCIPLES TO LOSE WEIGHT EASILY AND QUICKLY

**SUNSHINE:** A lack of regular exposure to sunshine has been shown to be the key to putting on weight. Vitamin D is created by our skin being exposed to sunshine, this is vital for the absorption of minerals, which help to nourish every cell. When our cells are well nourished, our body will not cry out for food.

It has also been discovered that white adipose tissue, which is known as the 'bad' type of fat that stores calories as fat, shrinks under the effect of sunshine. The sun penetrates our skin and reaches the white adipose tissue just beneath,

---

2. Gribbin S, Enticott J, Hodge AM, et al (2022). "Association of carbohydrate and saturated fat intake with cardiovascular disease and mortality in Australian women" *Heart* 2022; 108:932-939.

3. Scott KA, Melhorn SJ, Sakai RR. (2012). "Effects of Chronic Social Stress on Obesity." *Current Obesity Reports.* 1 March 2012, pages 16-25. doi: 10.1007/s13679-011-0006-3.

reducing it in size and releasing the fat cell so our cells don't store as much fat.[4]

When exposed to organic pollutants and heavy metals the body also uses fat cells to store these toxins in order to protects vital organs, increasing the amount of body fat. Ironically, these toxins may have contributed to weight gain in the first place. When a person starts to lose weight, this fat is broken down and these toxins are released into the blood stream increasing the risk that they will reach critical organs.[5] Arsenic, cadmium, lead, and mercury are all toxins known to be excreted through the skin, often at rates to match, or even exceed, urinary excretion.[6] Becoming hot in the sunshine or by saunas increases perspiration which can assist the body to expel these pollutants correctly.

**USE OF WATER:** Every cell, and therefore every function in the body, is dependent on water. Drought stricken land can be devastating, and so can drought-stricken bodies!

In his book, *Your Body's Many Cries for Water*, Dr Batmanghelidj shows how every part of the body is negatively affected by a lack of water. He even explains how it can cause weight gain through attempting to protect the tissues from the damaging effects of dehydration.

Our body loses an average of two and a half liters of water a day. This must be replaced by at least eight glasses of pure water. Herbal teas and fresh fruits and vegetables as part of our food plan do slightly contribute to our fluid intake.

As all caffeine and sugar drinks have a dehydrating effect on the body, they cannot be part of the daily fluid intake.

Ideally, cease drinking water half an hour before meals and resume one and a half to two hours after meals. This allows digestion to proceed without interruption, as watering down the digestive juices can compromise the digestive process.

Taking a small crystal of Celtic salt before each glass of water allows the water to be transported directly into the cells.

Often, the body cannot distinguish between hunger and thirst. Water, and water only, should be consumed between meals.

4.  Ondrusova, K., Fatehi, M., Barr, A. et al. (2017) "Subcutaneous white adipocytes express a light sensitive signaling pathway mediated via a melanopsin/TRPC channel axis." *Scientific Reports*, Vol 7, Article number: 16332.<https://doi.org/10.1038/s41598-017-16689-4>

5.  Lee YM, Kim KS, Jacobs DR Jr, Lee DH. (2017) "Persistent organic pollutants in adipose tissue should be considered in obesity research." *Obesity Reviews*. Vol 18, Issue 2, pages 129-139. PMID: 27911986.

6.  Sears ME, Kerr KJ, Bray RI. (2012). "Arsenic, cadmium, lead, and mercury in sweat: a systematic review." *Journal of Environmental and Public Health*. 2012:184745. doi: 10.1155/2012/184745.

**SLEEP:** The timing and amount of sleep is essential for maintaining healthy physical, mental, and emotional functioning. In his fascinating book, *Why We Sleep*, Dr Matthew Walker explains in detail how even having six hours of sleep a night instead of eight can cause weight gain.

Disturbed sleeping patterns, in terms of both quantity and quality, interferes with the part of our brain where we make decisions, thus affecting the choices we make on when and what we eat. This also interferes with leptin production, the hormone which controls appetite, which can lead to increased energy intake, mainly from snacking, especially on foods rich in fat and carbohydrates.

Dr Walker found that when people have eight hours of sleep a night, they are able to make better decisions on what food they eat and when they eat it.

Studies are also showing how the release of weight-controlling hormones are closely related to the body's circadian rhythm. This is recognized as a risk factor for weight gain in the constantly changing sleep patterns of shift workers.[7]

In addition, a full night's sleep increases the effectiveness of digestion; thus, we are more likely to burn our fuel instead of storing it.

The most effective sleeping patterns for optimal hormonal and metabolic function is a duration of eight hours of sleep a night that includes several hours before midnight. For example, 9pm to 5am or 10pm to 6am. For the very diligent, it may be 8pm to 4am. These times allow for all the sleep cycles that we go through every night to be fully accomplished and will help with weight loss.

When we sleep, our stomach needs to sleep, too. We sleep more peacefully when we have an empty stomach. A well rested stomach digests more efficiently which contributes to weight loss by better distribution of the glucose. Sleeping with a stomach full of food gives the body no choice but to store the glucose, thus increasing weight gain and can also cause acid reflux.

Retiring early also prevents evening hunger.

**TRUST IN DIVINE POWER:** In his book, *The Gabriel Method*, Jon Gabriel explains how he successfully went from 183kg down to 80kg. That is a loss of 103kg in two and a half years!

He discusses the power of High Intensity Interval Training (HIIT) and how it flips our metabolism to burning fat. He also claims a major part of his weight loss success was picturing a slender body in his mind. The cells in the body are very obedient to the mind, more so than most realize.

---

7.   Suwazono Y, et al (2008). "A longitudinal study on the effect of shift work on weight gain in male Japanese workers. *Obesity* (Silver Spring). Vol 16, pages 1887-93. doi: 10.1038/oby.2008.298.

When we imagine a trim shape to our body, the cells begin to work toward fulfilling the dream. Sorry to disappoint you, but this alone is not enough! All the pieces come together in the jigsaw of our body, and the mind plays a part.

*"For as he thinks in his heart, so is he."* Proverbs 23:7

It is a principle that God placed in our body; our thoughts affect our body just as much as the health of the body has an influence on the functioning of our mind.

You can also call this faith; faith in an amazing body that God created with an inbuilt ability to heal. Believing that you will heal and that everything you are doing will help with weight loss gives added power to be able to achieve this result.

Dr Norman Doidge is a neurologist who wrote *The Brain That Changes Itself* a book full of the science and stories that illustrate this principle.

 **ABSTAIN:** If your aim is to lose weight then there are some items to abstain from or greatly reduce, these include carbohydrates, especially wheat.

Eliminate refined sugars.

Eliminate caffeine and alcohol.

Abstain from a sedentary lifestyle.

## Endocrine Disrupters

Avoid endocrine disrupters. These are chemicals, such as the contraceptive pill, that interfere with our natural hormones, especially estrogen. These chemicals are also often used to make plastic containers, cans, or BPA water bottles. If you do keep plastic containers, don't use them to store fatty foods, and never microwave them. When these containers are heated or used for storing food the endocrine disrupting chemicals leak out at an increased level into the food.[8]

**INHALE:** Pay closer attention to your breathing. Inhale low, slow and deep, breathing from your belly using your diaphragm, in and out through your

---

8.   Sáiz J, Gómara B. (2017). "Evaluation of Endocrine Disrupting Compounds Migration in Household Food Containers under Domestic Use Conditions." *Journal of Agricultural and Food Chemistry.* Vol 65 Issue 31, pages 6692-6700. doi: 10.1021/acs.jafc.7b02479.

nose. Controlled breathing reduces hunger and appetite and decreases stress levels by lowering the stress hormone, cortisol.[9]

Excess cortisol levels can cause food cravings, especially for sweet, fatty, and salty foods that stimulate glucose production. This excess glucose is then converted into fat, which gets stored in your body. When cortisol goes up, your body holds onto calories and when it goes down, your body lets go of them.

Deep breathing through your nose increases the supply of oxygen to your whole body which aids to improve digestion. When digestion improves, we are able to access the nutrients out of our food more effectively which increases nutrition at a cellular level.

Try taking ten deep breaths before your next meal and see if you notice a difference!

**NUTRITION:** A change in the food we eat can dramatically influence weight loss. Even though carbohydrates are an important part of our diet they are often overused and can contribute to weight gain and obesity.

### › Low Carbohydrates
On a vegetarian diet, it is impossible to totally eliminate all carbohydrates, but there is no need to do so. Carbohydrates are not bad; it is only when they are overeaten and refined that a problem arises.

The highest carbohydrate food group is grains, they are also a significant source of protein, a nutrient that is crucial for muscle and bone health, digestion and more. This makes grains an important addition to our diet but they are best kept to a small part of the menu and ideally gluten free, for example rice, corn, buckwheat, millet, and spelt.

Not all carbohydrates release energy at the same rate. Some foods such as quinoa, vegetables, and most legumes, are known as slow-release carbohydrates, or low GI. These foods provide a more sustained, slower release of energy avoiding the usual spike in blood sugar levels that carbohydrates usually cause, this will help you feel full longer.

### › High Fibre
All plant foods are high in fibre and are necessary to clean and sweep the colon, particularly fruit and vegetables. Fibre also contributes to the full feeling after a meal, causing your intestinal tract to send a signal to your brain to release more leptin, this hormone makes you less hungry,

---

9. Ma X, et al (2007). "The Effect of Diaphragmatic Breathing on Attention, Negative Affect and Stress in Healthy Adults." *Frontiers in Psychology.* 2017 Jun 6;8:874. doi: 10.3389/fpsyg.2017.00874.

# WHAT CARBOHYDRATES LOOK LIKE

*Grams of carbohydrates per 100 grams of food.*[10]

COCO POPS 87g

DATES 67g

CORN CHIPS 62g

FRUIT AND NUT MUESLI 51g

REFINED FOODS

JELLY BEANS 91g

CORNFLAKES 81g

WEET-BIX 67g

PRETZELS 64g

PEANUT M&Ms 57g

WHITE BREAD 45g

preventing overeating, promoting reduced food intake and increasing the use of stored fat.

As fruit is higher in sugar, if your aim is to lose weight it is best to keep to low-GI fruits and concentrate more on vegetables.

Whole carbohydrates are minimally processed and contain the fibre found naturally in the food, while refined carbohydrates have been processed more and have had the natural fibre removed or changed.

> **Generous protein**

The three food groups that keep food in the stomach longer are fibre, protein, and fat. They also give the feeling of satiation, or satisfaction, preventing overeating.

**Animal protein** it is not a clean-burning protein. Red meat and processed meat are the most common acidic foods in the Western diet. A high dietary acid load is associated with higher risks of obesity and excess belly fat.[11] The state of animals today is not a healthy one, animals are often subjected to many medications, antimicrobials, environmental poisons, and growth hormones. Growth hormones, by definition, promote growth. So it's not surprising that eating meat contaminated with high levels of hormones and growth-promoting agents have the potential to cause weight gain,[12] while the introduction of antimicrobials in animal feed is a major concern

10. Adapted from nutritional dated in "Calorie, Fat & Carbohydrate Counter" Colorieking.com

11. Fatahi S, et al (2021). "Associations between dietary acid load and obesity among Iranian women." *Journal of Cardiovascular and Thoracic Research.* Vol 13, issue 4:285-297. doi: 10.34172/jcvtr.2021.44.

12. Belachew B. et al, (2020). "Hormones and Hormonal Anabolics: Residues in Animal Source Food, Potential Public Health Impacts", *Journal of Food Quality,* vol 2020, Article ID 5065386.

FRESH FRUIT

RYE SOURDOUGH BREAD

WHITE PASTA

QUINOA

BAKED BEANS

3–9g

WHOLEMEAL BREAD

36g

21g

13g

14g

27g

BROWN LENTILS

WHOLE FOODS

40g

24g

33g

10g

36g

10g

PORRIDGE

CARROT CAKE

17g

MASHED POTATO

WHITE RICE

WHOLEMEAL PASTA

POTATO WEDGES

to the disruption of normal human intestinal flora.[13]

**Legumes** including lentils; chickpeas; kidney; navy; and soy beans, are all slow release carbohydrates which are high in protein and fibre. These traits help people to feel fuller for longer and are beneficial in aiding weight loss. Adults who regularly eat a variety of legumes have significantly lower body weights compared with those who do not consume legumes.[14]

In her book, *Nourishing Traditions*, Sally Fallon investigates the way legumes were traditionally prepared, such as being soaked overnight, well rinsed, and slow cooked with several more rinses. Then, they are added to a sauce and cooked for a little longer to flavor them. This method of cooking legumes ensures their digestibility.

**Nuts and seeds** are high in protein and low in carbohydrates.

Legumes, nuts, and seeds can be included in every meal.

> **Healthy fats**
As previously mentioned, fat doesn't make you fat. The only harmful fats are those that have been changed by heat or chemicals.

Traditionally, fats were eaten from healthy cows and goats or extracted in the kitchen from plants. Olive and coconut oils are the main two that were extracted from the flesh of a plant. The oils you ate depended on where you lived and what was available.

13. Jeong SH, et al (2010) "Risk assessment of growth hormones and antimicrobial residues in meat." *Toxicological Research*. Vol 26, issue 4, pages 301-313. doi: 10.5487/TR.2010.26.4.301.

14. Polak R, Phillips EM, Campbell A. (2015) "Legumes: Health Benefits and Culinary Approaches to Increase Intake." *Clinical Diabetes*. Vol 33, issue 4, pages 198-205. doi: 10.2337/diaclin.33.4.198.

Coconut oil, palm oil, lard, and butter are saturated fats and are the most stable oils as their chemical structure is not as susceptible to damage from light, heat, and oxygen.

Unlike the saturated fats in animal products, over 50% of the fats in coconut oil are medium chain fatty acids, such as lauric acid. Coconut oil is the highest natural source of lauric acid. This natural acid can prevent and treat obesity and lower the risk of developing type 2 diabetes. These medium chain fatty acids are absorbed in the small intestine, being directly used in the body as fuel to produce energy.[15]

The best sources of fats are avocados, olives, nuts, seeds, coconut, and extra virgin olive oils.

**MODERATION:** Spelt and Kamut are two varieties of wheat grain that have not been hybridized, so they do not contain the starch structure that forces dramatic rises in blood glucose levels, but as they are in the carbohydrate class they should play a very small part in our overall food plan.

The body loves routine and functions better in every aspect when we can keep to a timetable in our daily lives. This can also influence the way our body either burns or stores our food. Rising, exercise, eating, and sleeping at roughly the same times every day allows the body to anticipate and prepare for each function, so its machinery operates smoothly. This leans toward a burning rather than storing of our fuel.

Time Restrictive Eating (TRE), sometimes called intermittent fasting, can greatly aid in weight loss. This involves eating twice a day with a six-hour break in between. Such as breakfast at 7am and lunch at 2pm, or 9am and 3pm. In his book, *Fast Diet*, Dr Michael Mosley shows why this is very beneficial.

The research is proving that this form of eating reduces body weight and blood glucose and improves insulin sensitivity in overweight patients with type 2 diabetes.[16] This way of eating gives the stomach a big break between meals, allowing digestion to be more effective. When we are digesting our food effectively and efficiently, we are able to absorb more nutrients into our body. So, we burn our food rather than storing it.

*"The controlling power of appetite will prove the ruin of thousands, who,*

---

15. Boateng L, Ansong R, Owusu WB, Steiner-Asiedu M. (2016). "Coconut oil and palm oil's role in nutrition, health and national development: A review." *Ghana Medical Journal.* Vol 50, issue 3, pages 189-196. PMID: 27752194; PMCID: PMC5044790.

16. Tingting Che T, Yan C. et al (2021). "Time-restricted feeding improves blood glucose and insulin sensitivity in overweight patients with type 2 diabetes: a randomized controlled trial." *Nutrition & Metabolism* vol 18, Article number: 88. https://doi.org/10.1186/s12986-021-00613-9>.

*if they had conquered on this point, would have had the moral power to gain the victory over every other temptation."*[17]

Conquer appetite and you're empowered to overcome every temptation.

This brings to mind the age-old saying 'eat breakfast like a king, lunch like a queen, and dinner like a pauper.' Paupers often don't eat at all!

When we eat a large meal at the end of the day, our stomach is unable to digest the food as well as in the morning or middle of the day, as the setting sun messages the body to begin winding down to sleep. We are not able to burn the fuel as efficiently as we do in the morning or middle of the day, so the fuel consumed in the evening is often stored as fat.

**EXERCISE:** The most popular form of exercise today is High Intensity Interval Training (HIIT). There are a few reasons for this, and one is time. All you need is 12 minutes a day.

*Body by Science* by Dr Doug McGuff, *PACE* by Dr Al Sears, and *Fast Exercise* by Dr Michael Mosley are three books that show why this form of exercise is so effective for weight loss.

As the name implies, it involves periods of High Intensity (HI), usually 20–30 seconds, with a Recovery (RE) time of one to two minutes, done in six cycles.

The HI can be running, cycling, swimming, push-ups, walking fast up a steep hill, or jogging on the rebounder.

The RE is a drastic slowing down of the pace to allow recovery.

In his book, Doug McGuff takes us inside the cells and explains how HIIT sheds extra weight.

By the third HI session, our glycogen stores are depleted (these are the quick-release glucose stores in our muscle cells). In response to this, our pituitary gland releases the human growth hormone (HGH). This activates hormone-sensitive lipase, which unlocks our fat stores for use as fuel. The HGH causes the body to switch from burning glucose as fuel to burning fat as fuel. Glucose burns at four calories per gram, whereas fat burns at nine calories per gram. A calorie is a unit of energy, so fat is a high-energy fuel!

This explains why exercise is a key component in weight loss.

---

17. Ellen G White, *Christian Temperance and Bible Hygiene*, page 154.2.

# HORMONES TO HELP

Often the missing link for weight loss, as well as a causative factor in weight gain for both males and females, is hormone imbalance.

Hormones are chemicals that coordinate different functions in your body by carrying messages through your blood to your organs, skin, muscles, and other tissues. The sex hormones (testosterone, estrogen, and progesterone) are present in both men and women. While men have more testosterone and less of the other two hormones, in women, it's the other way round. A variation in these three sex hormones can cause weight gain in both men and women.

The birth control pill, plastics, chemicals, such as Roundup, and fish that have been contaminated with environmental poisons and have the ability to disrupt estrogen levels in the body. As a result, they are given the name xenoestrogens or estrogen mimics. The causes and effects of high estrogen is discussed more in The Birth Control Pill on page 217.

Estrogen causes cell proliferation, which can cause weight gain. High levels of estrogen can trigger the pancreas to secrete more insulin, which leads to sugar cravings and an unhealthy diet. Low levels such as during menopause, causes the body to looks for other sources of estrogen, one source is fat, so the body converts all energy sources into fat. Progesterone is required to help balance the effects of estrogen.

Estrogen causes fluid retention, while progesterone which has a diuretic effect reduces that extra fluid. So what can be done to balance these hormones?

**Wild Yam Creams** contain a plant chemical that stimulates the body to boost progesterone. This hormone is vital for the maintenance of a correct hormone balance and can reduce estrogen to its proper level. This limits estrogen's effect to increase weight, benefiting both males and females.

The cream is applied to the skin, particularly on the fatty parts of the body, twice daily for three weeks a month. The break is to coincide with the menstruation period. Post menopausal women choose a week every month to cease application. Men apply the cream twice daily continually, with no break.

As the weeks and months go by, little by little, the hormones begin to balance. It may take a year for the process to be fully completed, but many people see results within the first month or two.

# TESTIMONY
## HELEN'S STORY

Having reached a point of great frustration, Helen shared her history with me. She had suffered from excess weight since her teenage years. As she had heavy periods, her mother took her to the doctor, who put her on the birth control pill at the age of 15. This was when her weight really began to increase. As this caused her to feel bad about herself, especially when most of her friends were slim, she began to overeat sweet things.

In her 20's, Helen stopped this destructive habit. She was in a job she loved with a lot of support and also began to read the Bible, which showed her that her worth was not in her size but in the fact that she was loved by God. Happily, Helen lost about 20kg.

Now at the age of 45, Helen was still carrying an extra 40kg that she didn't seem to be able to shed. Visiting the doctor for advice was very discouraging. They told Helen that she ate too much and should be exercising. This frustrated her, as she was eating quite moderately and exercising daily.

In the initial consultation it was revealed that spending 20 years on the birth control pill had majorly disrupted Helen's hormones. Her symptoms of pre-menstrual tension, insomnia, and excess weight all indicated this was an issue.

The bloating Helen experienced whenever she ate wheat showed an intolerance to gluten, and her lack of appetite was a sign of low hydrochloric acid.

I said to Helen that balancing her hormones, eliminating wheat, and taking herbs to boost digestion would make a big difference. Helen told me later that it was the most encouraging news she had ever received regarding her health.

It was as if the day had dawned for Helen. With great excitement, she embraced the new lifestyle and herbs.

In the first six weeks, Helen lost 10kg. Her mood lifted consistently, she began to sleep better, and she had more energy. Helen's friends and family were noticing a difference.

Within three months, with another 10kg lost, Helen was a different woman and was now experiencing life as God designed.

*"Beloved, I pray that you may prosper in all things and be in health, just as your soul prospers."* 3 John 1:2

# CHAPTER 18

# ARRESTiNG ARTHRiTiS AND GOUT

The term arthritis is derived from the Greek words *artho* meaning joint and *itis* for inflammation, which describes this disorder well. Joints are where two bones meet and this chronic inflammation in one or more joints usually results in pain and is often disabling.

There are more than a hundred different forms of arthritis, the more common being osteoarthritis, rheumatoid arthritis, and gout. Reducing inflammation not only brings relief, if achieved without the use of drugs, also greatly contributes to healing.

Osteoarthritis is a degenerative joint disease, in which the tissues in the joint break down over time. This is the most common type of arthritis and is more prevalent in older people. Women are more likely than men to have osteoarthritis, especially after age 50. For many women, it develops after menopause which is not surprising considering there can be a hormonal cause to this condition that I will cover shortly.

Rheumatoid arthritis is a disease in which the immune system attacks the joints, beginning with the lining of joints, resulting in inflammation.

Gout is a type of inflammatory arthritis that causes pain and swelling in the joints. This occurs when high levels of uric acid in the blood cause crystals to form and accumulate, in and around the joint.

# THE DiFFERENT FORMS OF ARTHRiTiS

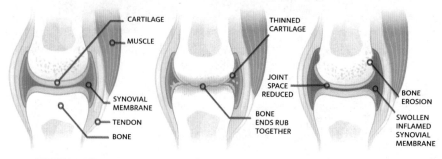

CARTILAGE

MUSCLE

SYNOVIAL
MEMBRANE

TENDON

BONE

THINNED
CARTILAGE

JOINT
SPACE
REDUCED

BONE
ENDS RUB
TOGETHER

BONE
EROSION

SWOLLEN
INFLAMED
SYNOVIAL
MEMBRANE

### HEALTHY JOINT

*Healthy joints move freely due to cartilage that acts like a cushion lubricating your joints.*

### OSTEOARTHRITIS

*With osteoarthritis the tissues in the joint break down over time, causing bones to rub together.*

### RHEUMATOID ARTHRITIS

*Rheumatoid arthritis occurs when the body's immune system attacks its own cells, mainly joints.*

# THE SOLUTIONS

## STEP ONE: BRING RELIEF

If you are suffering from gout you often know the signs that a flare-up is on the way. Most pain is due to inflammation, this is the natural response of the immune system, the body's inbuilt fighting mechanism designed to heal and protect us from injury or disease, and so the first step is to listen to our body's warning system and look at ways to relieve the problem.

The most common medications are anti-inflammatory drugs, however these drugs have serious adverse events in the gastrointestinal tract and cardiovascular system. Herbal and complementary therapies are safer to use and can be taken for longer periods to relieve symptoms of arthritis.[1]

> **Hydrotherapy**
> » **Alternating hot and cold baths**, as described in the Hydrotherapy section (page 291), can be administered once every two hours to the affected part when inflammation and pain are intense. As pain eases, the treatment can be brought back to two to three times a day.
>
> The process is three minutes hot and 30 seconds ice cold, three times in a row.

---

1.  Daily JW, Yang M, Park S. (2016), "Efficacy of Turmeric Extracts and Curcumin for Alleviating the Symptoms of Joint Arthritis: A Systematic Review and Meta-Analysis of Randomized Clinical Trials." *Journal of Medicinal Food.* Vol 9, issue 8, pages 717-729. doi: 10.1089/jmf.2016.3705.

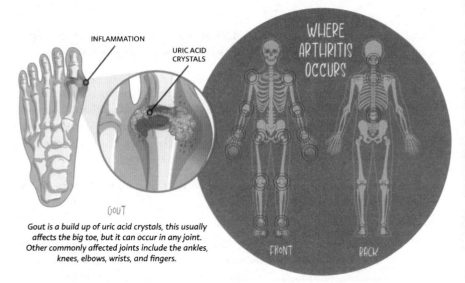

INFLAMMATION

URIC ACID CRYSTALS

GOUT

WHERE ARTHRITIS OCCURS

FRONT          BACK

*Gout is a build up of uric acid crystals, this usually affects the big toe, but it can occur in any joint. Other commonly affected joints include the ankles, knees, elbows, wrists, and fingers.*

> **Herbs**

▸ **Turmeric** is the most potent herb in reducing inflammation, especially from osteoarthritis.[2] It is very safe and can be taken in quite high amounts, even up to 6,000mg a day. The dose is reduced as pain subsides. **Cayenne pepper** can be added which increases the potency of the turmeric.

▸ **Lemongrass tea** is very alkalizing. Drink three or four glasses of hot tea every day.

> **Poultices**

▸ **Castor oil compresses** over painful joints overnight can soothe and help reduce inflammation.

▸ **Grated ginger poultices** applied to swollen joints reduces inflammation and pain quite dramatically by pulling the inflammation out to the skin. This explains why the skin can get very hot within half an hour of applying the poultice. It will not burn, but if it is too uncomfortable, the poultice can be removed. This poultice can be applied for two to three hours in the afternoon.

> **Balance the Hormones**

▸ **Wild Yam Cream** can be used as a natural alternative to estrogen therapy to balance estrogen and progesterone to a healthy level. Estrogen and progesterone are both equally important for the healthy functions of the body. If they're at proper levels, these two hormones can support your

2. *ibid*

optimal health and wellbeing. When women reach menopause, estrogen levels decrease which can lead to increased inflammation and joint pain for some women.

▶ Estrogen loss is also linked to decreased collagen production and affects bone density, potentially worsening osteoarthritic symptoms. Diosgenin, the active ingredient of wild yam, is a powerful plant steroid that can trigger the production of a range of hormones that can rebuild the bones and strengthen the joints.

Apply a small amount to the skin, particularly on the fatty parts of the body, twice daily.

⟩ **Alkalize the body**
Our body has a natural pH balance that is slightly alkaline. The standard Western diet is considered to be 'acidogenic' or 'acid-heavy' due to high consumption of animal protein and the lack of minerals typically found in fruit and vegetables. People with arthritis usually have high acid systems, and until this is corrected, their joints will keep deteriorating.

As a rough guide, the more processed something is, the more acid it makes in the body. Targeting a more alkaline food program will create an environment at the cellular level that can reduce inflammation. This is discussed more in the following SUSTAIN ME principles.

# STEP TWO: MANAGE AND EVEN CONQUER ARTHRITIS WITH 'SUSTAIN ME' PRINCIPLES

**SUNSHINE:** The blood supply to any area touched by the sun is increased. Allow the arthritic joints to be exposed to the sun every day. Vitamin D levels will rise, which increases the mineral availability to the bones and joints to allow healing. Sun exposure is the major source of vitamin D for children and adults of all ages. It is best to get this exposure early in the day or late afternoon to prevent the risk of sunburn during the hottest times.

Rheumatoid arthritis is often noted as being more severe in winter, when vitamin D levels tend to be naturally lower. An 11 year health study of older women noticed that a greater intake of vitamin D, either achieved by diet or with supplements, is associated with a lower risk of rheumatoid arthritis.[3]

---

3.  Merlino, L.A., et al. (2004), "Vitamin D intake is inversely associated with rheumatoid arthritis: Results from the Iowa Women's Health Study." *Arthritis & Rheumatism*, Vol 50, Issue 1, pages 72-77. <https://doi.org/10.1002/art.11434>

**USE OF WATER:** Staying hydrated is vital when you live with arthritis. Consuming alkaline water will allow your cells to flush toxins out of your body, which can help fight inflammation. In the process it alkalizes the tissues and helps to keep joints well lubricated. A lack of water robs the joints of the fluid needed to smooth movement. Drink eight to ten glasses daily, a sip at a time.

**SLEEP:** Many people notice that their symptoms get worse at night. While arthritis can make it difficult to sleep, sleep deprivation can also worsen arthritic pain. To conquer arthritis we need those hours of power sleep before midnight. These begin at 9pm in winter and 10pm in summer.

Establishing a bedtime ritual, such as going to bed at the same time each night, taking a bath, meditating on God's goodness, or doing another calming activity can help prepare your body to sleep. It is also essential to avoid stimulants such as caffeine, nicotine, watching television, doing work, or eating too close to bedtime. Allow your body and mind to naturally calm down and relax.

Eight hours of sleep each night are required for effective healing and regeneration of damaged joints.

**TRUST IN DIVINE POWER:** High levels of stress and negative thoughts can keep a person awake and increase inflammation, resulting in more joint pain. Trust in God to deal with your worries and fears. Living each moment to its fullest helps to fade past heartache and reduce future concerns. All we have is this moment. That is a gift from God.

*"A merry heart does good, like medicine, But a broken spirit dries the bones."* *(and joints!)* Proverbs 17:22

*"I have learned in whatever state I am, to be content"* Philippians 4:11

*"Casting all your care upon Him, for He cares for you."* 1 Peter 5:7

**ABSTAIN:** Eliminate any foods that have an acidic effect on the body. This includes some seafood, meat, especially organ meats like liver, caffeine, refined sugar, refined fats, drugs, and wheat. These foods are high in substances called purines, and can raise the uric acid in your blood inflaming pain from gout, as can fructose-sweetened drinks and alcohol, especially beer.

Some people report an increase in inflammation after eating nightshade vegetables. This family of vegetables includes potatoes, capsicums (bell peppers), eggplants, and tomatoes. These foods are high in lectins and can have an acidic effect, also increasing inflammation in the body. When arthritis is at its peak, you may find benefit in avoiding these foods until relief is achieved.

**INHALE:** When suffering chronic pain we often tense our muscles in reaction to the pain, but this tension actually aggravates the pain more. Deep, slow breathing in and out through the nose, using your diaphragm, activates a relaxation response. This automatically relaxes the muscles which usually tense up as a result of pain.

Nasal breathing (as opposed to mouth breathing) also makes your lungs more efficient which results in a 10-20% greater oxygen uptake in the blood. As the lungs fill with oxygen, the concentration of oxygen in the blood collected by the pulmonary veins is increased, creating an alkalizing effect on the whole body and encouraging inflamed joints to relax.

**NUTRITION:** Many people with rheumatoid arthritis have repeatedly reported positive effects of dietary changes on their disease and the big difference it has made in conquering arthritis and gout.

> **Alkalizing your diet**
> Alkalizing foods reduce inflammation. Incorporating 80% alkaline-forming foods and 20% acid-forming foods into your daily menu can help to prevent an acidic environment at the cellular level.

| > **Alkalizing Foods** | > **Acid-forming Foods** |
|---|---|
| · Lemons | · Meat |
| · Dark green leafy vegetables and juices, including products such as green barley, wheatgrass, and chlorophyll | · Refined sugar |
| | · Hybridized wheat |
| | · Aged cheese |
| · Vegetables | · Alcohol |
| · Lima beans, lentils, and non-genetically modified soy products | · Tobacco |
| | · Drugs |
| | · Caffeine |
| · Millet, quinoa, buckwheat, spelt, amaranth, and Kamut | · Rice, cornmeal, rye, oats, and barley |
| · Almonds and Brazil nuts | · Navy, kidney, black, turtle, cannelloni beans, and chickpeas |
| · All seeds | |
| · Fruit | · Peanuts, walnuts,pecans, hazelnuts, cashews, and macadamia nuts |
| · Cold pressed olive and flax oil | |
| · Herbal teas | |

Vegetarian and Mediterranean diets are naturally low acid diets due to the abundance of anti-inflammatory alkalizing fruits and vegetables. Such diets have been shown to reduce inflammation, increase physical function, and improve vitality.[4] In addition, the dietary fibre found in plant-based diets can also improve gut bacteria, which further reduces inflammation and joint pain.

## > Drinks to alkalize your body

Lemon is acidic and thus a great digestive aid, as it is broken down in the gut, and the minerals are absorbed into the blood; however, it has an alkalizing effect. Lemons are high in the alkaline minerals of sodium, potassium, calcium, magnesium, and iron.

Alkalizing juices can have a dramatic affect on counteracting an acid environment in the body. A mix of 80% carrot, 10% celery, and 10% apple juice is very alkalizing, and at least two 250ml glasses can be taken a day.

Green vegetables and grasses are an excellent way to alkalize the body. The greener the better! The green juice extracted from plants is not only one of the most alkalizing foods there is, it is also a potent tissue and blood cleanser. They can take the form of green barley, wheatgrass or spirulina, or you can add chlorophyll to the alkalizing juice described above.

Green drinks can also be made if you have an abundant supply of leafy green herbs and vegetables. Four cups of leafy greens blended with four cups of water can be strained and drunk through the day.

Ideally, green liquids or powders are taken several times daily.

4.  Sköldstam L, Hagfors L, Johansson G. (2003). "An experimental study of a Mediterranean diet intervention for patients with rheumatoid arthritis." *Annals of the Rheumatic Diseases.* Vol 62, issue 3, pages 208-214. doi: 10.1136/ard.62.3.208.

## ⟩ Reduce lectins

Lectins are a type of carbohydrate-binding protein that are found in all plants, but raw legumes (beans, lentils, peas, soybeans, peanuts), the nightshade family, and whole grains like wheat contain the highest amounts of lectins. Usually they bind to carbohydrates, forming glycoproteins where they strengthen our immune system. However if the digestive system is impaired by a bowel disorder, such as Crohn's, leaky gut syndrome or celiac disease, lectins sneak their way into the bloodstream resulting in inflammatory conditions like rheumatoid arthritis. For this reason gluten free diets have been shown to be effective in reducing arthritic symptoms especially in celiac patients.[5]

Eating foods with a high amount of active lectins is rare. One reason is that lectins are most potent in their raw state, and foods containing them are not typically eaten raw. Techniques that dramatically reduce the amount of lectins to a safe level include: cooking legumes, especially with wet high-heat methods like boiling or stewing, sprouting or soaking in water for several hours; deskinning and deseeding tomatoes and capsicums (bell peppers); or culturing grains, such as in the sourdough method of bread making.

**MODERATION:** Keeping yourself active is vitally important but be mindful of aching joints, pain is given as a warning sign and you should listen to it and not irritate or overdo activity in these joints, remember to balance activity with periods of rest. When starting or increasing physical activity, start slow and pay attention to how your body tolerates it.

Keeping active has many benefits and the body will quickly let you know if you have pushed the joints too far. Start with a small amount of activity, for example, three to five minutes twice a day, as you start to move the joints you will find gradually you will be able to increase the amount of exercise you can do.

You may find a few days are better than others as pain, stiffness, and fatigue, may come and go. Even on those bad days some physical activity is better than none.

**EXERCISE:** Severe joint pain, reduced muscle strength, and impaired physical function are common with rheumatoid arthritis, this by no means indicates you should cease exercising. Participating in joint-friendly physical activity can improve your arthritis pain, function, mood, and quality of life.

---

5.   Cordain L, et al, (2000). "Modulation of immune function by dietary lectins in Rheumatoid Arthritis." *British Journal of Nutrition.* Vol 83, issue 3, pages 207-217. doi:10.1017/S0007114500000271

Exercise delivers high doses of oxygen as the lungs expand. Exercise also increases the life-giving blood in and out of the joints, which is vital for joint maintenance and recovery.

Low impact or low intensity exercise is the most effective at increasing aerobic capacity, muscle strength, joint mobility, and physical function.[6] Those with arthritis should aim to do at least 150 minutes a week of physical exercise, this is a must to prevent the seizing up of joints and to encourage the healing blood to these areas. Suitable activities include water aerobics, swimming, walking, rebounding, and working out on an exercise bike.

Being physically active can also delay the onset of arthritis-related disability and help manage other possible chronic lifestyle conditions such as diabetes, heart disease, and obesity.

As simple natural remedies are implemented, and the SUSTAIN ME principles followed, the body's inbuilt ability to heal itself is supported, relief is experienced, and little by little, the body is restored to health.

# TESTIMONY
## KATE'S STORY

Kate had suffered with rheumatoid arthritis for many years and had been told it was incurable. Her finger joints, knees, and feet were all swollen, making walking slow and difficult.

Medication brought minor relief at first, but Kate had been taking it for 20 years, and she felt it was no longer making enough of a difference. The cortisone had caused weight gain, putting even more pressure on her knees and feet. Kate was now 65 years of age, weighed 90kg, at only five foot two inches.

Her mother had also suffered from rheumatoid arthritis and spent her last five years in a wheelchair in tremendous pain. Kate was terrified when the doctors told her that it was in her genes and that she would end her days as her mother did.

It was with great excitement that Kate received the news that this condition could be managed, and even cured, by natural remedies.

---

6.  Cooney JK, et al. (2011), "Benefits of exercise in rheumatoid arthritis." *Journal of Aging Research*. 2011 Feb 13;2011:681640. doi: 10.4061/2011/681640.

She had been told by her doctor that diet had nothing to do with arthritis. In her first interview at the health retreat, it was discovered that Kate's diet was high in meat, dairy, refined wheat, and sugar, with two coffees and three cups of tea a day. Kate didn't like water and had believed she was receiving enough fluid in her hot drinks.

The first two days were juicing days, predominantly drinking fresh juice made with 80% carrot, 10% celery, and 10% apple. These are highly alkaline, compared with the highly acidic diet that Kate had previously consumed.

**As Kate heard the health presentations, her eyes were opened, and she began to see that her food and lifestyle habits had fed her condition.**

As Kate heard the health presentations, her eyes were opened, and she began to see that her food and lifestyle habits had fed her condition.

Our fresh mountain water tasted far better than town water, and Kate began to enjoy water for the first time in a very long time.

Though her knees prevented her from taking part in the morning walks, Kate found she could gently rebound and also use the exercise bike. These activities were encouraged several times a day. Kate was like a person whose prison doors had been opened. Though still suffering pain and discomfort, she felt hope for the first time in many years.

As the days went by, Kate's pain lessened. The turmeric capsules that she took three times a day and the poultices were having an effect. The grated ginger poultices on her knees for two hours every morning seemed to reduce her inflammation a little more each day. After five days, the staff applied castor oil compresses, as her skin was getting tender from the ginger poultices. By the seventh day, Kate declared that the pain in her knees had reduced by 60%. She hadn't taken a painkiller for two days.

This prompted Kate to begin reducing her anti-inflammatory medication and cortisone little by little.

By the middle of the second week, Kate had ceased her anti-inflammatory medications and was down to 15mg prednisone (cortisone) from 20mg.

An excited Kate went home, armed with a program to continue what she had experienced at the health retreat. She had already ordered her rebounder and was looking forward to a new life where she would be conqueror, and not victim.

Six months later, Kate made a return visit to the health retreat. The staff did not recognize her, as she had lost 30kg and was looking great.

Kate was keen to stop the last of her prednisone as she was now down to 5mg a day. She wanted to do this last drop in dose under the care of our staff.

It was exciting to hear of Kate's journey since her first visit. Kate was now basically pain free, her finger joints were less swollen, and she had taken up crochet again. Walking was so much easier, as her knees and feet were almost back to normal.

To achieve these results was remarkable, and they were not by chance. Kate diligently kept to the program, which was a plant-based diet that excluded all meat, refined sugar, and wheat products. After her first two weeks at the retreat, Kate had no desire to return to her tea and coffee and now enjoyed her water. When meeting friends at the coffee shop, she now orders peppermint tea.

Nothing can deter Kate from her new lifestyle and eating regime. She said that coffee and cake no longer appeal to her, as she knows they were part of her downfall into the pain and suffering she had experienced for too long.

Kate's body is still recovering and regenerating, but she said even if no more regeneration happens, she is happy, for life is so good for her now.

Her doctors scratch their heads because she has defied their expectations and proves that though genetics may load the gun, lifestyle pulls the trigger. Her experience has also shown them that there is an effective alternative to medication.

CHAPTER 19

# ANALYSiNG
# AUTOiMMUNE DiSEASES

The definition of an autoimmune disease is when the body's own immune system mistakenly attacks healthy cells. These disorders may attack multiple organs or may be localised to one specific organ, such as the skin. Medicine defines the following diseases as being autoimmune:

- Rheumatoid arthritis and osteoarthritis, affecting the joints

- Lupus, affects connective tissue and can strike any organ of the body

- Celiac disease, affects the small intestine

- Inflammatory bowel disease (IBD), this includes Crohn's disease and ulcerative colitis, both of which affect the bowel

- Diabetes (type 1), affects the pancreas

- Multiple sclerosis, affects the nervous system

- Graves' disease, affects the thyroid gland

- Psoriasis, affecting the skin

There are over 100 types of autoimmune diseases that predominantly affect women. Approximately 80% of all patients diagnosed with autoimmune diseases are women.[1]

---

1.  Angum F, Khan T, Kaler J, Siddiqui L, Hussain A. (2020). "The Prevalence of Autoimmune Disorders in Women: A Narrative Review." *Cureus.* 12(5). Published online 13 May 2020. doi: 10.7759/cureus.8094.

Sir Isaac Newton's third law of motion states 'To every action there is an equal and opposite reaction'.

*"Like a fluttering sparrow or a darting swallow, an undeserved curse will not land on its intended victim."* Proverbs 26:2 NLT

The body was not designed to attack itself. Something triggers this response, and an investigation needs to be undertaken to find the cause. Every single case is different, and history and lifestyle need to be considered as to what may be the cause.

It is not uncommon for there to be multiple causes. We have found that people respond positively, and the body begins to heal, when given the right conditions.

*"The spirit of a man will sustain him in sickness, but who can bear a broken spirit?"* Proverbs 18:14

Our mind, and what we choose to focus on, plays a major part in the healing process from any disease.

Often, exposure to chemicals, heavy metals, vaccines, mold, artificial EMFs, side effects of drugs, food allergens, or an emotional crisis can trigger an inflammatory response in the body. This response can produce symptoms that are classified as an autoimmune disease.

Genetics may be a factor. Remember though, genetics may load the gun, but lifestyle pulls the trigger.

Some researchers are finding a link between damage from childhood vaccinations and autoimmune disease later in life. Although vaccines are generally advertised as 'safe and effective', numerous reports highlight the occurrence of neurological (Guillain-Barré syndrome, multiple sclerosis, autism), articular (arthritis, rheumatoid arthritis), and autoimmune effects (systemic lupus erythematosus, diabetes mellitus) after single or combined multi-vaccine procedures.[2]

---

2. Vadalà M, et al. (2017). "Vaccination and autoimmune diseases: is prevention of adverse health effects on the horizon?" EPMA Journal. Vol 8(3), pages 295-311. doi: 10.1007/s13167-017-0101-y.

# AN ILLUSTRATION

Here is a simple story that shows how autoimmune diseases can originate, the compounding of the trigger, and the possible side effects.

The situation may begin with a genetic weakness, then the child is bombarded with the various neurotoxins in childhood vaccines. The child is often exposed to dirty electricity from the baby monitors in his bedroom, the family computer, and his parents' phones, which they often use when holding him.

Food is introduced before his teeth appear, which disrupts gut function. The appearance of teeth in a child brings the enzymes required to digest food.

The child is given cow's milk formula, and asthma develops because of an allergy to the milk. Drugs are administered to ease the symptoms of the asthma. Despite this onslaught, the child grows and somehow survives.

Ventolin is now used daily, and corticosteroids are taken when an asthma attack is acute. The parents and the teenager do not realize that one of the side effects of Ventolin is reduced lung capacity.[3] Plus, the corticosteroids slowly wear away at the adrenal glands and his gut flora.[4]

Colds appear throughout the winter, and the drugs and antibiotics taken disrupt the gut flora. Many do not realize that healthy gut flora is essential for an effective immune system.

Neither he nor his parents are aware of the debilitating effect of glyphosate, the non-organic herbicide used to grow most vegetables today, on gut flora. They continue to encourage him to eat his vegetables.

As he grows into a young man, he likes to eat fast food.

The young man's teeth are deteriorating and filled with amalgam fillings, which can be up to 59% mercury. Now, the neurotoxin mercury is added to the chemical load in his body.

Parents and son are not aware that the EMFs that surround his bed while he sleeps every night and the computer, iPhone, and iPad exposure in many of his waking hours are triggering oxidative stress, disrupting the electrons in the

---

3.   Lai CH, Liao XM. (2021). "Paradoxical bronchospasm: a rare adverse effect of fenoterol use." *Respirology case reports.* 2021 March 17;9(4):e00698. doi: 10.1002/rcr2.698.

4.   Hansen RA, et al (2008). "Risk of adverse gastrointestinal events from inhaled corticosteroids." *Pharmacotherapy.* Vol 28, issue 11, pages 1325-34. doi: 10.1592/phco.28.11.1325.

atoms that his body is made up of.[5]

In his late teens, the young man is diagnosed with celiac and Crohn's disease. His family is told these are autoimmune diseases, and more cortisone is prescribed.

This sad story is, unfortunately, too common. It didn't develop overnight, and the situation won't be conquered overnight. There is no quick cure for an autoimmune disease.

*"In case of sickness, the cause should be ascertained, unhealthful conditions changed, wrong habits corrected, then nature is to be assisted in her efforts to expel impurities and re-establish right conditions back-in the system"* page 127, Ministry of Healing by Ellen White.

# THE FORMULA FOR HEALING:

1. Through investigation, the cause should be ascertained. There are often several causes.

2. After investigation, unhealthful conditions must be changed and wrong habits corrected.

3. Then, nature is to be assisted through simple natural remedies to expel impurities and re-establish the right conditions in the body.

We have found that when people are taught proper lifestyle habits and the correct way to eat, they are able to make the changes necessary to bring about a shift in illness, including autoimmune diseases.

**Let us end with a happy story**
We will call the young man just described Tom. Tom has an aunt who has been observing his gradual deterioration over the years. Tom's parents view Aunt Kate as a bit of a fanatic, as she doesn't drink alcohol or coffee, nor does she smoke, and she is a vegan.

Upon learning of Tom's diagnosis, Aunt Kate offers Tom a vacation for two weeks at a health retreat. His parents are concerned, but Tom is keen. He is 20 now and does not want to be sick. He is putting on weight from the drugs and does not feel good. He wants to look and feel like his friends.

Aunt Kate joins Tom at the retreat for support.

In the initial consultation, the naturopath discovers that Tom is still eating

5.  Kivrak EG, (2017). "Effects of electromagnetic fields exposure on the antioxidant defense system." *Journal of Microscopy and Ultrastructure*. Vol 5, issue 4, pages 167-176. doi: 10.1016/j.jmau.2017.07.003.

foods that have an extremely irritating effect on the lining of the gut. Refined sugar, wheat, peanuts, dairy, and caffeine are some of the main culprits. Tom is totally unaware these foods could be contributing to his problem.

Lunch at the retreat is a surprise to Tom, as the food is delicious and contains nothing that would inflame his gut.

Four times a day, Tom is given a mix of mostly slippery elm, with a small amount of goldenseal and myrrh.

As is his tendency, Tom has five bouts of diarrhea through the night, but as the day progresses, this begins to slow down. It is not unusual for Tom to have ten bowel movements a day.

The second night, Tom only has one bowel movement. He is pleasantly surprised, as he had only taken two-hourly juices the day before, on Monday. Tuesday is also a juice day. Tom continues the herbs, four times a day, with just four bowel movements in 24 hours. He is very surprised that his body is responding so quickly.

Tom is advised to eat slowly and be careful not to overeat when food is introduced on Wednesday. As his gut has ceased cramping, there is no longer blood in his stools, and as his stools are beginning to take form, Tom decides to reduce his cortisone from 20mg to 15mg a day.

Being able to sleep eight hours a night from 9pm is a blessing that Tom has not experienced for a long time. His eyes are opened as he learns about the healing power of sleep, especially during the hours before midnight. The damaging effects of artificial EMFs are new to Tom. It is rightly called the silent killer. Tom begins to read of the research of Donna Fisher, exposing the dangers of dirty electricity. He realizes that this has played a part in his illness.

It all sounds too good to be true to Tom's parents. They are very hesitant to believe the reports that Tom gives them every evening, but they are happy that he is experiencing relief from the debilitating symptoms that have plagued him for years.

**Tom is inspired by three main areas:**

1. What he hears in the lectures explaining how the body works.

2. What he confirms with the medical research from the books in the retreat's library.

3. What he is experiencing in his body.

Though his body is responding quickly, Tom is not yet healed. He is inspired to realize that he is now on the path to recovery. At the retreat, he tries different foods and sees what agrees with his gut more than others.

In the first week, his food program consists of mostly thick vegetable soup, avocados, sometimes organic tofu, and a little white rice. After the second week's two-day fast, with protein drinks and juice, Tom begins to try some legumes, baked vegetables, and millet. There are no reactions, and Tom continues to have three bowel movements in 24 hours.

Herbs are continued and are an important part of Tom's healing.

A program is formulated for Tom as he considers how to implement all that he has learned into his daily life at home.

Tom is so excited about the advances he has made in just two weeks that nothing can deter him from the guidelines he has discovered that have brought him lasting relief when nothing else had. Within two months, Tom ceases the cortisone medication with no flare-ups.

His doctor is impressed but cautious. He is not sure that this will last.

Six months later, Tom has eased off the herbs as he no longer needs them and is feeling great, putting on muscle, and losing the fat that he had gained from the drugs.

Tom has successfully conquered the 'autoimmune disease' that he was told was incurable.

Not only does Tom heal from Crohn's disease but he also teaches his family a better way of living and eating. The change in Tom has been a testimony for everyone who knows him, of the amazing body we live in, with its inbuilt ability to heal, when given the right conditions.

Tom is now considering changing his studies to become a nutritionist.

# THE SOLUTIONS

In illness, the place to begin is treating the symptoms. These are the voices or signs that the body uses to alert us that there is a problem.

With allopathic treatments using drugs, the medications are really only masking the problem. They do alleviate the symptoms, but they are not helping the body to heal.

Using healthy herbs, foods, water therapies, and poultices, we are all able to relieve symptoms and help the body to heal.

> *"Drugs never cure disease; they only change the form and location. Nature alone is the effectual healer, and how much better could she perform her task if left to herself. But that privilege is seldom allowed her."* Ellen G. White

With each autoimmune disease, treatment depends on symptoms, and the first step is to relieve them.

Cause is often revealed when history and lifestyle are assessed. The SUSTAIN ME principles of health are implemented, and any known irritant or contaminant is removed.

Time is now needed to allow for healing.

We have seen many heal by implementing these simple principles.

# CHAPTER 20

# HYDROTHERAPY
## (WATER THERAPY)

Water therapy, or hydrotherapy, has been used for centuries to relieve and treat pain, and to boost healing. As the name implies this is a system of using water as therapy, either externally or internally. It is the purpose of this chapter to explain how water can be used at home to stimulate a healing response in different parts of the body.

Hydrotherapy increases the circulation of blood through the body carrying with it oxygen, nutrients, water, and white blood cells to every cell. These commodities are essential for the life and healing of every cell. The movement of white blood cells also helps the lymphatic system to do its job of sweeping waste away from the tissues, effectively 'cleansing' us. This waste eventually gets expelled from the body via the lungs, skin, kidneys,and colon.

*"The life of the flesh is in the blood"* Leviticus 17:11

The application of hot and cold water moves the blood in specific areas more powerfully than anything else known.

Water can be used in its liquid form, its solid form as ice, or its gaseous form as steam. This can take many forms, from aquatic physical therapy, sitz baths, wet saunas/steam rooms, foot baths, and contrasting water temperatures. Each style of hydrotherapy works on specific issues and areas of the body.

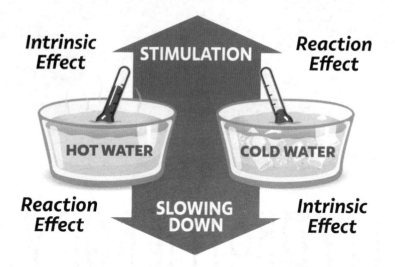

# CONTRAST BATH THERAPY

This is a series of brief, repeated immersions in water, alternating between hot and cold temperatures. This contrast between hot and cold water has been shown to help athletes reduce pain from injury through vasodilation and vasoconstriction, thereby stimulating blood flow and reducing swelling.[1]

Vasoconstriction is the contracting of your capillaries which happens during cold water immersion therapy. On the contrary, when your body is exposed to hot water, your capillaries open up and become larger, which is called vasodilation. When you quickly switch between these two therapies, your blood vessels contract and then dilate, which creates a pulsing, pump-like motion. This explains why this process can improve your circulation significantly. Your heart also reacts to different water temperatures, cold water causes your heart rate to speed up, while hot water slows it down.

## HOW HEAT HELPS

The initial effect of hot water on the body is stimulating, called the *intrinsic*. We know that when a cool body lays in a hot bath there is a tingling feeling and a stimulation of blood flow. It only takes three minutes until a feeling of relaxation is experienced. This is called the *reaction* stage, which has a depressive or slowing effect on blood movement.

---

1. Cochrane DJ, (2004), "Alternating hot and cold water immersion for athlete recovery: a review" *Physical Therapy in Sport*, Vol 5, Issue 1, Page 26

# COLD'S CONTRAST

The initial effect of cold on the body is called the *reaction*, which is stimulating. This is why we might scream when plunging into very cold water! We are warm-blooded creatures, and when cold water touches our skin, our body reacts.

If we stay in that cold water, it only takes 30 seconds to have a depressing or slowing down effect on blood flow, to the point where body functions eventually shut down if the water is ice cold and if the body remains there for an extended period of time. This is what is called the *intrinsic* effect of cold on the body.

Ending your daily shower with cold water, even just briefly, is a convenient way to get some of the benefits of cold therapy, but the true power comes when it is alternated with heat.

In hydrotherapy, regarding the alternating application of hot and cold water, we use the stimulating (intrinsic) effect of HOT and the stimulating (reaction) effect of COLD to significantly move blood into the area of concern. The reason why the increase of blood flow to an area is important lies in what blood carries: **red blood cells** and **white blood cells**.

The **red blood cells** carry oxygen, nutrients, water, and white blood cells. These elements are everything that the cell requires for healing. As this is delivered to the cells, the blood also carries away the waste. These processes are vital for healing when there has been an injury.

The **white blood cells** are your internal army. They sound an alarm when infectious agents invade your blood and create antibodies to fight against bacteria, viruses, and other potentially harmful invaders. When your body is in distress and a particular area is under attack, white blood cells rush in to help destroy the harmful substance and prevent illness.

# HOW TO USE CONTRAST BATHING

**REQUIRED EQUIPMENT:** Two tubs, bowls, or mugs, large enough to immerse the part of the body that needs help, and a towel for drying off.

One tub is filled with hot water, how hot to make the water will vary depending on the age, health and fitness of the recipient (see note on the next page). The second tub is filled with cold water, adding ice gives an even better reaction, but again keep in mind the health of the recipient.

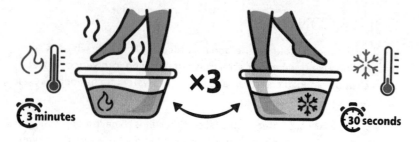

**3 minutes** ×3 **30 seconds**

1. Immerse the injured part of the body into the hot water for three minutes.

2. After accessing the stimulating effect of hot for three minutes, before the slowing down (intrinsic) effect kicks in, the part of the body being treated is then placed into the cold tub. The cold section is now maintained for 30 seconds to utilize the stimulating (reactive) effect of cold.

   While the part of the body is in the cold, a little boiling water can be added to the hot to maintain the heat.

3. Before the intrinsic, or slowing down, effects of the cold kick in we move back into the hot for three minutes.

All in all, there will be **three HOT dips** and **three COLD**. Always begin with hot and end in cold. Ending with cold equalizes the circulation and prevents chilling.

It is a good idea to dip a healthy hand, finger, or foot into the hot water to gauge the temperature before you begin. Different people can handle different temperatures.

Sometimes, in cases of severe inflammation, such as gout, one minute of HOT and one minute of COLD may be more effective. Do this three times as before.

The body's response is your best guide.

After three sessions of these alternating hot and cold applications, the body can be exhausted, as the blood has been moved dramatically, and three sessions are enough.

Problems in the hands, fingers, elbows, feet, toes,and ankles can all be helped by the alternating hot and cold baths.

In a crisis, this treatment can even be administered two-hourly. As the condition improves, the frequency can be reduced to two or three times a day until the desired healing is achieved.

# SITZ BATHS

The word sitz comes from the German word *sitzen*; which means *to sit*; and clearly describes this health treatment.

Traditionally a sitz bath is a single warm, shallow bath people sit in to cleanse the perineum, which is the space between the rectum and the vulva or scrotum. Soaking this area in warm water relaxes your anal sphincter, which helps increase blood flow through your anal tissues. This promotes healing and reduces the pain, itching, and irritation felt due to various health conditions.

By combining the contrast bathing technique with the traditional sitz bath posture, greater success can be achieved for any complaint in the abdominal area, this includes:

- **BOWELS:** Crohn's disease, constipation, irritable bowel syndrome, gastritis, colitis, hemorrhoids, anal fissures, anal strictures, and prolapse of the colon

- **UTERUS:** Fibroids, cysts on the ovaries, endometriosis, period pain, and prolapse of the uterus

- **PROSTATE:** Inflammation of the prostate, prostate cancer, and erectile dysfunction

- **KIDNEYS AND BLADDER:** Cystitis, Urinary Tract Infections (UTIs), incontinence, and bladder prolapse

## HOW TO HAVE A CONTRASTING SITZ BATH

**REQUIRED EQUIPMENT:** Two tubs big enough for the hips to be immersed in; soft towel for drying off.

1. Just like with the contrasting baths, fill one tub with cold water and the other with warm to hot water, deep enough to cover from the waist to mid-thigh. Don't add shower gel, bubble bath, or any type of soap.

2. Soak in the hot tub for three minutes, then the cold tub for 30 seconds. Make sure your private area is covered with water, and add more cold or hot water as needed to keep the temperature contrast high. If possible, dangle your legs over the side of the tubs to keep them out of the water. Repeat this process three times.

3. Afterward, gently pat yourself dry using a soft towel.

4. The most effective way to implement this treatment is to have the sitz baths each evening for 30 days. Depending on your condition you may find having a sitz bath three times a day is beneficial. Each treatment extends the effectiveness of the previous bath.

Depending on the severity of the problem and how chronic it is, this treatment can be done on a month-on/month-off basis until healing is achieved.

# COMPRESSES

For an area that cannot be immersed in water, hot and cold compresses can be used. These can be used on the chest, back, upper arms, thighs, and abdomen.

The same times apply as in the baths, but a compress is used instead.

**REQUIRED EQUIPMENT:** Two tubs, one with boiling water, the other with icy cold water. Rubber gloves to protect your hands from the boiling water, several towels or cloths for wetting that are large enough to cover the area requiring treatment; a small dry towel, and a small woolen blanket to retain the heat.

**HOT:** Dip one towel into the boiling water, then with rubber gloves on, hold each end of the towel, take it out of the water and twist, allowing the excess water to be squeezed out. This hot towel is untwisted and folded into the size of the area requiring the application. Apply the small dry towel over the injured area to protect the skin from the hot compress, then lay the hot wet towel on top of the dry one and cover both with the small woolen blanket. This is lightly placed over the hot pack to ensure the compress keeps its heat.

COVER HOT TOWEL WITH WOOLEN BLANKET TO KEEP HEAT IN

HOT WET TOWEL

DRY TOWEL TO PROTECT SKIN

If the compress is too hot, the pack and small towel can be lifted by one corner, and the excess moisture can be wiped off the skin, then reapply the compress. This might be done several times on the initial application until the person is comfortable with the temperature. Three minutes are timed, and the compress is removed.

**COLD:** Wet the second towel or cloth with the cold water, then gently wipe over the area. This is done for 30 seconds dipping frequently into the bowl of ice water if needed, as it will warm quickly. The skin is then dried well with a dry towel.

**HOT:** The second hot compress is applied as before, but a fresh, dry towel must be used to ensure peak heat, along with a small, fresh, dry towel on the skin under the compress. Often, it is found that the heat can be tolerated a little better on the second application.

**COLD:** As before.

**HOT:** As before.

**COLD:** This is the final cold compress, and the skin is to be dried well after this application.

Alternatively some have found that a wet wrung-out towel can be folded, then rolled and heated in a microwave to supply the compress or heat pack. To achieve optimal results, the hot towel must be as hot as can be borne, and the cold is to be ice cold. Placing the small, dry towel on the skin before the hot compress will protect the skin from burning.

Nurses were trained in hydrotherapy more than 100 years ago. It is a very effective and powerful treatment and is well worth the effort involved. Unfortunately, that is one of the reasons that it is no longer used. The manpower and equipment involved were not considered efficient use of time. It is much easier today just to give a pain relieving pill that will mask the pain but do very little to actually heal the body.

# TESTIMONY
## CALEB'S IRRITABLE BOWEL

Caleb was only 15 and yet had a very embarrassing health problem.

His anal sphincter was not strong, and sometimes he had accidents at school. This had been happening for a few years. In an attempt to remedy the problem, the doctor had tried to tighten the sphincter by surgery, but this had not helped, and the recovery had been very painful.

At times, Caleb suffered from constipation, and he didn't have accidents, at other times, he suffered from diarrhea, and he feared this, as this was when the accidents happened.

Caleb's aunt had heard of our retreat, and she felt that this was the last resort, as the doctor said he could not operate again on such a tender area.

The colon habits indicated irritable bowel syndrome, and the fasting and foods at the retreat would help heal that issue. Caleb's eyes were opened as he listened to the lectures and learned of the foods that irritate the colon and those that can heal it. Twice a day, Caleb took contrasting hot and cold sitz baths. It didn't take long before he quite enjoyed them, especially how the rush of blood to his anal sphincter could tone and strengthen that muscle.

Caleb went a whole week without any accidents, which was unusual in itself. His bowel habits became more normal, and without the diarrhea, he seemed to have more control.

On discussing his program at home, Caleb committed to changing his dietary habits and doing sitz baths every evening for the next 30 days.

We didn't hear again from Caleb, but one year later, his aunt attended our retreat and reported that Caleb was fully healed. He functions now as a happy, healthy 16 year old, though he eats much better than most his age. He has good reason.

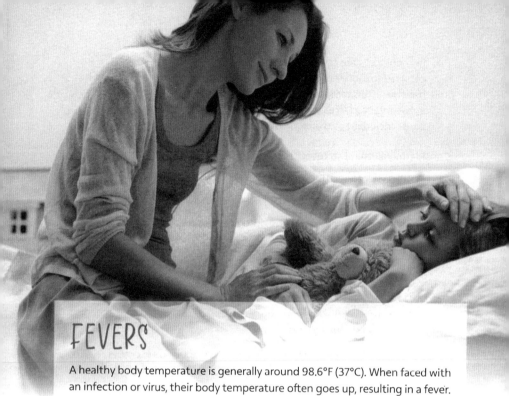

# FEVERS

A healthy body temperature is generally around 98.6°F (37°C). When faced with an infection or virus, their body temperature often goes up, resulting in a fever.

A fever is not an illness.

Fevers have a purpose.

Fevers are a process created by God to help fight and recover from disease.

In health centers and sanitariums all over the world, for hundreds of years, fever treatments have been used to treat disease.

These are most commonly in the form of fever baths, steam saunas or allowing the fever to run its course. All these methods will raise body temperature temporarily by two to three degrees centigrade.

This rise in temperature has several effects:

1.  Circulation of the blood increases quite dramatically, causing a boost of oxygen, water, nutrients, and white blood cell delivery to every part of the body, and more waste is taken away.

2.  The rise in temperature causes the skin's pores to open and increase the elimination of waste products through perspiration.

3.  Bone marrow begins to produce more red and white blood cells.

4. Immune cells are recruited to the site of an infection where they are exposed to high temperatures, these cells also generate extra heat of their own. This temperature boost is crucial to locally warm the tissues at the infected sites to a level that can burn and kill harmful pathogens,[2] including bacteria, viruses, and fungi.

Considering all this, the three things to remember during a fever are:

1. Fever is your friend (it has a purpose).

2. Water puts the fire out, internally and externally.

3. When all the waste is burned up, the fire goes out.

Interestingly, evidence from randomized controlled trials on critically ill patients suggests that intervening to reduce fever does not improve a patients' survival. On the contrary, aspirin and paracetamol, often used to reduce soreness and fever, will suppress antibody responses to infections. Forced reduction in body temperature, to levels lower than normal by using intravenous or mechanical cooling, has been shown to cause harm.[3]

While these studies do not cover artificially raising a person's temperature to fight a virus, they do clearly show the benefits of fevers and allowing them to run their course.

## SHOULD YOU ALLOW A FEVER?

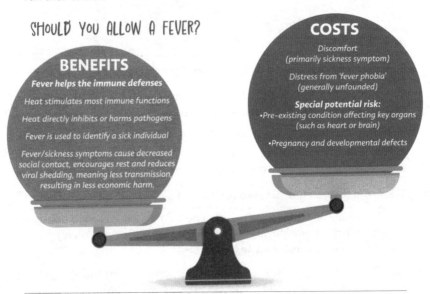

**BENEFITS**

*Fever helps the immune defenses*

Heat stimulates most immune functions

Heat directly inhibits or harms pathogens

Fever is used to identify a sick individual

Fever/sickness symptoms cause decreased social contact, encourages rest and reduces viral shedding, meaning less transmission, resulting in less economic harm.

**COSTS**

Discomfort
(primarily sickness symptom)

Distress from 'fever phobia'
(generally unfounded)

*Special potential risk:*
•Pre-existing condition affecting key organs
(such as heart or brain)

•Pregnancy and developmental defects

2. Wrotek S, et al. (2020). "Let fever do its job: The meaning of fever in the pandemic era." Evolution, Medicine, and Public Health. Nov 23;9(1):26-35. doi: 10.1093/emph/eoaa044.

3. ibid

# HOW TO USE FEVERS CORRECTLY

Clearly a fever is considered a good thing, however it is vitally important to keep the body well hydrated and to assist the fever by giving it a way to pull the heat out of the body. Wet fever is a good fever, dry fever is a bad fever.

**INTERNAL:** Keep the person well hydrated, even sipping water or sucking on ice every few minutes. The only part of the body that can not handle high heat is the brain, but if the body is well hydrated, that will protect the brain cells.

If no water can be given by mouth, a simple enema of one and a half cups of water for an adult is a quick way to hydrate them. Use a little less water for a child. Enema kits, also known as douche kits, are an easy-to-use unit, convenient for cleansing the bowel in the privacy of your own home and can be purchased at most chemists.

**EXTERNAL:** Often, the problem with a fever is that the body cannot dispel the heat quickly enough. Water is the best conductor of heat and cold, so it can be used to pull the heat out of the body, thus reducing the heat or fever in the body.

Let us consider the different ways water can be used externally to reduce fevers.

**A)** A hot foot bath, with a cool cloth on the head, can often bring a fever down to a reasonable temperature so it is more comfortable. Feet are often cool when a person has a fever. Begin with a warm foot bath and slowly increase the temperature, the hot foot bath is usually continued for about 20 minutes.

**B)** Laying in a tepid or lukewarm bath will often bring the temperature down a little. This water will feel cool to the person with a fever, but that tepid water can draw the heat out of the body. This is usually continued for at least 20 minutes.

**C)** The sponging technique is very simple and can be helpful for a child.

Lay the child in their underwear on a dry towel, and cover them with another towel. Take a bowl of lukewarm water and a small cloth or washer. Lightly squeeze the cloth, and sponge an arm. Then, dry it and place it back under the towel. Step by step, do this to each body part, keeping the rest of the body covered while sponging.

Continue until the whole body has been sponged.

After the front of the body has been completed, lay the child on their stomach and repeat the process for their back parts.

# WET SHEET PACK

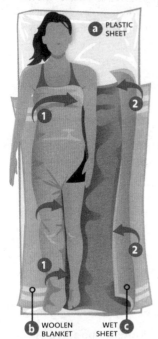

a PLASTIC SHEET

1

2

2

1

b WOOLEN BLANKET

WET SHEET c

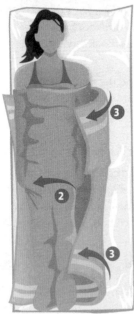

3

2

3

This sponging technique can often reduce the temperature and allow the child to sleep. Sometimes, this may need to be repeated a few times a day until the fever passes.

**D)** The Wet Sheet Pack is more work but very effective.

a Cover a single bed with a shower curtain or plastic sheet. b Lay a woolen blanket over this (only wool works). c Wring out a wet cotton sheet and lay it over the blanket.

1 Lay the person in their underwear, on the wet sheet with their arms in the air and pull the right side of the wet sheet around their torso and between their legs. Ask them to lay their arms down. 2 Now, pull the left side of the sheet over and around both arms and legs so their whole body is wrapped. This is uncomfortable for the person, but only briefly so. 3 Now very quickly bring up one side then the other of the woolen blanket to cover the wet sheet, the discomfort will soon eases, and the person will quickly relax.

In only 5–10 minutes, the cold, wet sheet becomes quite hot as it draws the heat out of the body. While this happens, the fever reduces. Sometimes, the person can be taken out in 20–30 minutes, after which a tepid shower is taken, and often, the person is ready to sleep. They may even fall asleep in the sheet pack, having experienced relief from the fever. If they are asleep, then they are comfortable and they can safety be left there.

Many mothers have found that the wet sheet technique is the easiest for a small baby. The little one is quickly encircled in a small, wet sheet, then wrapped in a woolen blanket. If this is done speedily, there is not too much discomfort, and the baby soon relaxes as they are held close in their mother's arms. The baby usually falls asleep as their fever drops and they become more comfortable. The mother can lay the little one down in the sheet and blanket when they are asleep.

When the sheet and blanket are removed, the baby can have a warm bath. The wet sheet pack can be kept on for 20 or 30 minutes, maybe longer if the baby falls asleep.

As the body has been designed to heal itself, it makes sense to work with the fever which is a powerful way to stimulate this process.

# TESTIMONY
## FIGHTING THE FEVER

Arthur contacted me most distressed, as his six month old daughter had developed a fever following her vaccination. He was perplexed that this should happen, considering the baby was breastfed.

Unfortunately, Arthur lived in a country where the vaccine was mandatory. I reassured him that his baby's body was fighting the poisons in the vaccine by developing a fever.

He had taken the nurse's advice and given the baby an infant painkiller drug, which did reduce the fever, but within a couple of hours, it returned. This had now happened several times, and Arthur was so challenged, as he was not happy about medicating his small baby. Arthur was experiencing sleepless nights over concern for his small daughter.

As I dialogued with Arthur, I explained the role that fevers play in helping fight disease and boosting immunity.

Arthur chose to try some simple water treatments and ceased administering the drugs. He found a tepid bath effectively reduced the fever enough for his baby to sleep well. Being breastfed, the baby was feeding a little more comfortably and so was well hydrated.

Within 24 hours, the fever had passed. A very happy dad emailed me, as he was so grateful that his baby had recovered and pleasantly surprised at how simple the remedy was, while also an effective healing agent.

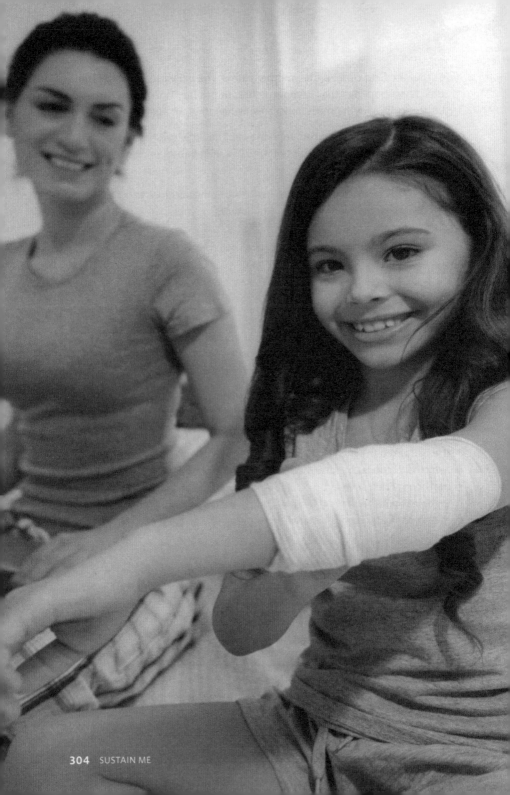

CHAPTER 21

# HEALTHY HEALERS

The use of plants to treat disease and enhance general health and well-being is one of the oldest forms of health treatment. These powerful plants can be administered in various ways, from taking herbal tonics, tinctures, poultices, compresses, or suppositories. Each of these methods work with the body to bring about healing through reacting to the natural stimulants.

A **poultice** is usually a direct application of the raw, fresh herb to the skin, applied to treat infection by killing bacteria and drawing out the infection. A **compress** is an application of a cloth that has been soaked or covered in a blend of aromatic and therapeutic herbs and oils that will penetrate into the body to break up congestion. Compresses help relax muscles, stimulate nerves, improve circulation, and increase blood flow.

**Suppositories** are similar to a compresses in that the same herbal arrangements can be used, however instead of being infused onto a cloth for external use, the herbs are mixed with a base that can remain solid at room temperature, and melt at normal body temperature. This mixture gets inserted in various body cavities such as the rectum or vagina, where it dissolves to release the herb once inside the body.

Different herbal tinctures, poultices, compresses, and suppositories are used for different situations and sometimes they can be alternated for greater effect. In this chapter I look at the benefits of some of the more common

**305**

natural household ingredients that can assist in the healing process and how to best use them.

# ALOE VERA

The aloe vera plant has been known and used for centuries for its health, beauty, medicinal, and skin care properties. Thousands of years ago, Greek scientists regarded aloe vera as the universal solution for all ailments, while the Egyptians referred to it as the plant of immortality. The gel from the aloe vera plant contains growth stimulants, these are very similar to those found in comfrey and slippery elm. The growth stimulating effect can be observed in action when a leaf is cut: within one hour a thin skin covers the cut.

The high mucilage (gel) content of aloe vera also contains antibacterial and antifungal properties, a feature that makes the gel well suited to bring relief to certain skin conditions and wound healing. This feature is the reason aloe vera is readily found in hundreds of skin products, including lotions and sun blocks.

More than 75 active ingredients from the plant's inner gel have been identified including a very impressive line-up of minerals and vitamins: vitamins B1, B2, B3, B6, B9 (folic acid), A, C, and even vitamin B12. Minerals include calcium, zinc, chromium, magnesium, potassium, sodium, manganese, chlorine, copper, phosphorous, sulphur, silicon, iron, cobolt, and boron.[1]

Aloe vera, when taken internally, can also assist in promoting the growth of natural probiotics, *Lactobacillis acidophilus* and *Bifidobacterium*, which aid in the digestion of food.

Herbal mouthwash containing aloe vera has been shown to be comparable in anti-plaque efficacy to the gold standard 0.2% chlorhexidine gluconate mouth wash, but with fewer side effects.[2]

Glyconutrients are a group of plant sugars that are found in many plants, especially in aloe vera. Glyconutrients can promote the growth of certain beneficial bacteria in the colon, stimulate the immune system, and encourage

1.  Surjushe A, Vasani R, Saple DG. (2008), "Aloe vera: a short review." *Indian Journal of Dermatology.* Vol 53, Issue 4, page 164. doi: 10.4103/0019-5154.44785.

2.  Chhina S, et al. (2016), "A randomized clinical study for comparative evaluation of Aloe Vera and 0.2% chlorhexidine gluconate mouthwash efficacy." *Journal of International Society of Preventive & Community Dentistry* 2016 May-Jun;6(3), pages 51-55. doi: 10.4103/2231-0762.183109.

cell-to-cell communication in the body, which is why these sugars are often used to make medicine.

There are many different species of aloe and when choosing fresh aloe vera for medicinal purposes the variety *Aloe Barbadensis*, has been shown to be the best option, and can be used internally and externally.

## INTERNALLY

▶ **STOMACH AILMENTS:** For issues such as stomach ulcers, colitis, Crohn's disease, gastritis, and irritable bowel syndrome, the aloe vera gel is soothing and healing to the cells that line the gastrointestinal tract.

▶ **CANCER:** For cancer and other chronic diseases, cell-to-cell communication is usually inhibited, and the glyconutrients in aloe vera have the possibility to help restore this communication.

### HOW TO USE ALOE VERA

When using the inside gel, it is best to peel the skin and only use the clear gel inside the leaf. This clear gel can be put through a fruit and vegetable juicer, mashed with a fork, or even added to a smoothie.

Avoid using the yellow sap just under the skin of the aloe leaf. This yellow sap is very bitter and slightly toxic and can cause diarrhea which is why we remove this section.

**Dosage:** Two teaspoons up to three times a day.

**ALOE WATER:** Alternately, a few leaves of aloe vera can be freshly cut at the base and sat in a glass with the cut area facing down. Within an hour, the bitter yellow liquid lining the leaf will drain out. The leaves are then rinsed and sliced across in half-centimeter sections. These aloe slices are added to a jar of water overnight (usually one foot long leaf to one litre of water), in summer, refrigerate overnight.

In the morning, the aloe water, including the slices, is poured into jugs, with mint leaves or lemon slices are added to improve the flavor. This can be strained into cups as required through the day. This makes for a very refreshing drink, which can be drunk as part of your daily water intake. As the water in the jug is depleted, fresh water can be added. Begin a fresh mix every day.

▶ Only cut as much aloe vera leaf as you need at a time, as the healing properties quickly deteriorate when exposed to air.

▶ **SKIN ISSUES:** Aloe vera has excellent properties for all skin problems, including eczema, psoriasis, skin rashes, grazes, or nappy/diaper rash. Scoop out the clear gel and apply it straight to the skin.

▶ **ALL BURNS:** Aloe vera has long been used to treat burns as it accelerates the healing process of wounds. The leaf needs to have the sharp edges or barbs removed then cut in two lengths through the middle and apply straight to the burn with the aloe vera skin intact and the gel side touching the burn. Keeping the aloe vera skin on prevents the burn from drying out.

The aloe vera leaf can be bandaged on and left for 24 hours. Replace with fresh leaves every day.

This not only brings relief but also stimulates healing so rapidly that improvement can be seen with each dressing change.

▶ **HEMORRHOIDS:** An aloe vera suppository can bring relief and healing to hemorrhoids, this is discussed in detail on page 102.

# CABBAGE

Cabbage is highly nutritious and rich in vitamins C and K, fibre, and while you may associate it commonly as a vegetable to eat, the leaves of this vegetable are one of the oldest methods for dealing with inflammation. When used as a poultice the chlorophyll in the cabbage encourages the skin to eliminate toxins while supplying nutrients to the affected area.

▶ **STOMACH ULCERS:** Raw cabbage juice can significantly decrease the healing time of peptic ulcers, including stomach ulcers. If used regularly cabbage juice will also prevent stomach ulcers. You can make cabbage juice simply by placing the raw leaves in a juicer or blender. Combining cabbage juice with fruits or other vegetables may help improve the flavor.

▶ **GUT HEALTH:** Sauerkraut is finely cut raw cabbage that has been fermented by various lactic acid bacteria. It is one of the most common and oldest forms of preserving cabbage and has a variety of beneficial effects on human health. Sauerkraut increases digestive flora and as most of our immune system is located in our gut, the good bacteria or probiotics, helps to keep the lining of your digestive system healthy.

▶ If you buy sauerkraut off-the-shelf you should be aware that many varieties are pasteurized to extend their shelf life, this kills the beneficial bacteria.

**TO MAKE SAUERKRAUT:** Shred a fresh raw cabbage thinly, reserving one outer leaf. Add Celtic salt (about three to four teaspoons per kilo of cabbage), and pound the mixture together until the cabbage has reduced in size and released quite a bit of liquid.

Tightly pack the cabbage into sterilized jars and ensure the liquid extracted from all that crushing rises up and covers the kraut for optimum fermentation. Use the reserved outer leaf to hold the cabbage below the surface of the liquid.

Screw a plastic lid onto the jar and place the jar in a bowl to catch any overflow. Store at room temperature out of direct sunlight for one to four weeks to let it naturally ferment.

## EXTERNALLY

▶ **SPRAINS:** Cabbage is particularly helpful with bruised and swollen tissue, as it aids in the elimination of stale blood and built-up fluids. Sprained ankles respond well to the cabbage poultice.

▶ **SWOLLEN BREASTS:** Many breastfeeding mothers apply the cabbage leaves in the first two weeks of lactation and testify to the relief that the cabbage poultices bring when the breasts are uncomfortable and swollen with milk.

**TO MAKE THE POULTICE:** remove the hard center stalk from the leaf and either dip the leaf in boiling water briefly to soften it or pound it with a mallet until limp. When the leaf is softened, it can easily be molded to the affected area. Cover with plastic wrap and bandage it.

# CASTOR OIL

Castor oil is naturally extracted from the castor oil plant, this is native to Africa and India and now naturalized throughout Australia. No oil can penetrate as deep in the human body as castor oil.

Wherever this oil penetrates, it cleanses, breaks up congestion, and disperses wastes and toxins. Castor oil is able to dissolve any unnatural formation in the body, such as a tumor or bone spur. These tasks are accomplished when castor oil is applied via the skin.

Only use this oil externally. While castor oil is considered safe in small doses, this plant is classified as poisonous to both humans and animals and larger amounts can cause abdominal cramping, nausea, vomiting, and diarrhea.

## EXTERNALLY ONLY

▶ **CONSTIPATION:** A castor oil compress can be applied to the abdominal area for at least four hours a day, four days a week. If convenient, it can be worn overnight. In cool weather, apply a hot water bottle over the compress, which will help to thin the oil to increase the speed of absorption. A castor oil suppository can also be used in conjunction with the compress on the abdomen for quicker results.

Constipation can occur at any age, however, the elderly are particularly susceptible. Research was done to examine the effect of a three day treatment of castor oil packs (compress) on the elderly suffering with long term constipation of ten years or more. This study found that the castor oil packs did not affect the number of bowel movements or amount of feces, but it did improved fecal consistency, decreased straining during defecation, and gave a feeling of complete evacuation after a bowel movement, thus decreasing symptoms of constipation.[3]

▶ **ARTHRITIS AND INFLAMMATION OF THE JOINTS:** Ricinoleic acid, the main fatty acid found in castor oil, has anti-inflammatory and pain-reducing properties and may assist in relieving arthritis pain by using a castor oil compress over the affected joints. This is a great compress to use overnight.

---

3. Arslan GG, Eşer I. (2011). "An examination of the effect of castor oil packs on constipation in the elderly." *Complementary Therapies in Clinical Practice.* 2011 Feb;17(1) pages 58–62. PMID: 21168117.

- **LUMPS, BUMPS, AND BONE SPURS:** Castor oil has the ability to break up and disperse these growths. Apply a castor oil compress nightly. If the bone spur has been there for three years, it may take three months to disappear. If it has been there for three months, it may take three weeks.

- **TOE NAIL FUNGUS:** The antifungal and antioxidant action of castor oil helps to reduce the inflammation that can come from a prolonged infection. Apply castor oil directly to your feet after showering and cover with a pair of cotton socks. This will allow the oil to penetrate deep into the nails and skin. This should help to eliminate the infection that causes the fungus. As toe nails grow slowly it may take several weeks to be fully rid of the effects from the fungus.

- **CYSTS, FIBROIDS, AND TUMORS:** Castor oil can penetrate and dissolve cysts and tumors. Consistent and regular action is necessary. Apply the compress nightly or for at least five hours.

- **BREAST CANCER:** Many have experienced reduced pain after using castor oil compresses. Castor oil compresses can also be effectively applied for breast cancer as it opens up lymphatic channels to increase lymphatic flow. The more chronic the problem the longer it may take.

Some ladies have found it is more convenient to use an organic panty liner as a compress since it is very absorbent, has a plastic backing and can be held in place quite easily with a sports bra.

## TO MAKE THE CASTOR OIL COMPRESS:

- Moisten three or four layers of a soft natural fibre cloth with castor oil.
- The thicker the compress, the more oil can be held, the more oil is available to penetrate into the body.
- Apply to the affected area and cover with plastic.

This compress can be secured in place by bandages or well-fitting underwear. As this compress does not draw but rather penetrates, it can be reused several times, even for a few weeks, with a little more oil applied as it dries out.

- **HEMORRHOIDS AND PROSTATE:** To get closer to the problem a suppository can be used. This is like an internal compress. It will not take long for the hemorrhoids to shrink and the pain to ease, especially when diet and lifestyle are also assessed.

This suppository is used for prostate issues also, as the last part of the colon is very close to the prostate gland so the castor oil can penetrate across to the prostate gland quite easily.

CASTOR OIL AND COCONUT OIL

DISPOSABLE GLOVE

FILL FINGERS OF GLOVES

**FREEZE**

INSERT THE SUPPOSITORY AT LEAST 6 CM

### HOW TO MAKE A CASTOR OIL SUPPOSITORY:

1. Mix equal amounts of melted coconut oil with castor oil.

2. This mixture is poured into the fingers of disposable gloves, the ends are tied to prevent the mixture from escaping, and placed in the freezer. This freezing action could take several days.

3. Once the mixture is frozen, remove it from the glove and insert the suppository through the anus into the rectum and leave overnight. The oil mixture will be released with the morning's first bowel movement.

4. It is important to ensure that the suppository is inserted at least 6cm into the rectum for comfort and best results.

# CHARCOAL

Charcoal's value lies in its ability to not only absorb poisons (up to 300× its own weight) but also neutralize them. This phenomenon of taking in and disarming the poison is called adsorption.

Activated charcoal (sometimes referred to as activated carbon) is not the same charcoal that you will find in a fireplace, it is a special type of fine black powder made by heating charcoal in the presence of a gas. This process causes the charcoal to develop lots of internal spaces or pores that can trap many toxins and chemical molecules. This explains why NASA uses charcoal to filter air and water in outer space. Dialysis clinics use charcoal to filter blood and many face masks and water filters contain charcoal.

There are several plants that draw poisons, but activated charcoal stands alone in its ability to not only absorb but also to neutralize the poisons. Since the activated charcoal is not absorbed by the human body when taken internally, when it is excreted from the body it takes with it all the adsorbed chemical molecules and toxins it has picked up. These adsorbing and neutralizing properties gives charcoal the ability to reduce inflammation quite dramatically.

The adsorbing and oxidizing qualities of charcoal makes it naturally antiseptic and unlike drugs, charcoal has no known poisonous side effects.

Activated charcoal is used internally or externally and exists in the form of carbon tablets, powder,or granules.

## INTERNALLY

▶ **UPSET STOMACHS**: For symptoms such as nausea, gas, fermentation, indigestion, heartburn, and diarrhea, activated charcoal taken internally is an excellent remedy to alleviate these conditions. One to two teaspoons can be mixed in half a glass of warm water, then drunk. To make this drink more palatable, especially for children, a teaspoon of carob powder can be added to the drink.

▶ **POISONING:** For food poisoning or chemical poisoning, one to two tablespoons can be mixed in half a glass of warm water, then drunk to adsorb the poison. For activated charcoal to be effective at eliminating poison, it must come into contact with the substance concerned. Therefore, it must be given promptly before the body absorbs the poison. Repeat doses may be required for intoxications that persist for a longer time in the stomach and for time-release drugs.

Medical Emergency Departments administer charcoal by mouth to overdose victims. In all cases of poisoning, charcoal can be effectively taken to prevent the poison from being absorbed from the stomach into the body.[4]

## EXTERNALLY

▶ **FOR POISONOUS BITES AND STINGS:** To bring relief from any creature that inflicts a poisonous bite, such as an ant, bee, snake, or spider, a charcoal poultice can be applied. The value of the charcoal poultice with poisoning lies in its ability to adsorb and thus neutralize the poison. Another quick poultice is to combine equal amounts of charcoal and Manuka honey to

---

4.  Silberman J, Galuska MA, Taylor A. (2023) "Activated Charcoal." In: StatPearls [Internet]. StatPearls Publishing. Available from: <https://www.ncbi.nlm.nih.gov/books/NBK482294/>

cover a bite then cover with a band-aid. In cases of severe poisoning, it is recommended to also take charcoal orally every half an hour as described for upset stomachs and to change the poultice every half hour.

Cases have been reported where the quick action of applying charcoal has saved a life. See the book or website, *Charcoalremedies.com*, by John Dinsley to discover more uses for charcoal.

▶ **INFECTIONS,** ulcers, boils, and bruises—a charcoal poultice can be applied. It is an excellent choice for an overnight poultice because the skin will not re-absorb the waste in the poultice, as the charcoal neutralizes it.

▶ **CONGESTED CHEST**—make sure the charcoal poultice is applied warm. This is a very effective poultice for breaking up congestion in the lungs, such as with bronchitis.

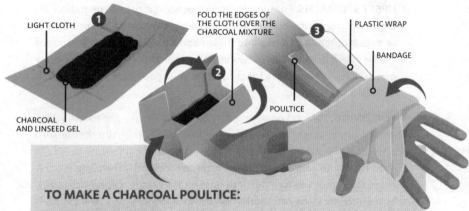

LIGHT CLOTH

FOLD THE EDGES OF THE CLOTH OVER THE CHARCOAL MIXTURE.

PLASTIC WRAP

BANDAGE

POULTICE

CHARCOAL AND LINSEED GEL

### TO MAKE A CHARCOAL POULTICE:

▶ Mix a tablespoon of linseed in a tablespoon of water; gently simmer it in a small saucepan until it thickens like a soft gel.

**①** Add a tablespoon of powdered charcoal. Place this soft, black jelly onto a cloth and spread out to the desired size. **②** Pull the edges of cloth over to make a package and apply the poultice to the affected area, with the thin side of the poultice touching the skin. Always check that the poultice is not hot enough to burn. **③** Cover it with plastic wrap and secure it with a bandage or skin tape.

▶ If unable to cook the linseed, powdered linseed, slippery elm, psyllium husk, or even flour could be used in equal quantities to bind the charcoal. Add enough water to make a soft paste and continue as above to apply the poultice. These binders will also keep the charcoal moist longer—when charcoal is wet it has more drawing power.

# CAYENNE PEPPER

Cayenne pepper comes from the paprika family and is used worldwide to treat a variety of health conditions, including poor circulation, weak digestion, heart disease, chronic pain, sore throats, headaches and toothache. Cayenne is the greatest herbal aid to circulation and can be used on a regular basis. Dr Richard Schulze, the medical herbalist, says, 'If you master only one herb in your life, master cayenne pepper. It is more powerful than any other.'[5]

Cayenne is a systemic stimulant, not a neurological or nervous system stimulant, its stimulating effect is on the bloodstream. As a result, it strengthens arteries and veins and yet thins the blood. Cayenne pepper never irritates; it stimulates blood flow and brings blood to the surface to allow toxins to be taken away. Cayenne pepper revitalizes everything it touches; it never harms. Cayenne pepper is high in potassium, which is an essential mineral that the body uses for healing. This mineral is especially depleted when a person is under stress.

Cayenne pepper, as the most potent circulatory herb, has the ability to intensify the action of every other herb. Cayenne pepper can be used in conjunction with various herbs to increase their effect on the body.

Cayenne pepper can be used internally and externally.

## INTERNALLY

- **FOR CHILLS, HEART FAILURE, AND SHOCK:** When quick action is required, a quarter of a teaspoon of the powder can be put directly on the tongue. This has the most dramatic effect. The small capillaries immediately dilate, and blood flow is increased to every part of the body. There is no known equal to this effect.

- **HEART AND CIRCULATORY SYSTEM:** The above treatment can be used for an acute or crisis situation, but cayenne pepper can be taken regularly to strengthen the arterial system and keep the blood thin, thus preventing heart attacks or strokes. Begin with adding a quarter of a teaspoon

---

5.   Mukul, C (2018). "Blood Circulation Stimulation Properties of Cayenne Pepper: A Review." *Journal of Applied Chemistry*, Vol 11, Issue 5, pages 78–83.

to a third of a cup of water, three times a day and build up to half a tea-spoon three times a day. An alternative can be to take a capsule of cayenne pepper three times a day.

▸ **DIGESTION:** Research shows that the production of digestive enzymes decreases by about 10% per decade after we reach 20 years of age. Cayenne pepper is very effective at waking up and reviving the gastric glands that produce these enzymes. Take a quarter to a half teaspoon of cayenne pepper in water minutes before a meal, or adding the dried powder to your meal is also effective.

▸ **SORE THROATS:** The cayenne pepper water solution can be gargled and taken every two hours if needed. When the initial tingle subsides, the sore throat is greatly relieved as the result of added blood being brought to the throat.

▸ **PAIN:** One of cayenne pepper's effects on the body is as an analgesic or painkiller. I have met several people on my travels who have taken a tea-spoon of cayenne pepper and experienced pain relief. If the stomach is sensitive to that amount, some can be taken with a meal or a soother, such as aloe vera or slippery elm.

The easiest and most effective way to take cayenne pepper is ¼ to ½ teaspoon of powder in a third of a cup of water. The reason this is the most effective way, is that as soon as the cayenne pepper touches the inside of the mouth, the circulation of the blood is influenced. The accompanying tingle on the mucous membranes of the mouth quickly subsides within five minutes.

## EXTERNALLY

▸ **TO STOP BLEEDING:** Cayenne pepper is a very adaptive herb. Internally, it dilates the blood vessels, but if sprinkled on a cut, it causes the broken vessels to constrict and seal.

▸ **ARTHRITIC JOINTS:** Cayenne pepper compress can be applied to painful, swollen arthritic joints.

▸ **CRAMPED MUSCLES:** The heat that cayenne produces relaxes the mus-cles when the compress is applied to the muscle. Many Deep Heat-style ointments contain cayenne pepper.

▸ **UNDERACTIVE THYROID GLAND:** The cayenne pepper increases blood supply which can wake up the underactive thyroid gland. The cayenne pepper compress can be placed over the thyroid for several hours in the early part of the day. This can be used every second day to be an effective part of the program to revive the thyroid gland.

▶ **POOR CIRCULATION, LACK OF FEELING IN THE FEET (PERIPHERAL NEUROPATHY), AND COLD FEET:** A cayenne pepper compress can be applied to the feet. Being a circulatory stimulant, the cayenne pepper in the compress on the feet draws the blood to the area, thus warming it. The compress can be left on all night. At about 4 or 5am, the feet will be feeling quite warm, the poultices can be taken off, and the foot can be wiped over with a warm wash cloth. For severe cases of cold feet, this poultice can be applied every three or four days until the feet remain warm. This compress can be used when the hydrotherapy can not, and can be worn every second night until feeling returns.

## HOW TO MAKE A CAYENNE PEPPER COMPRESS

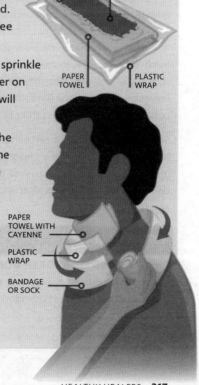

▶ Fold a paper towel to the size of the area where the compress is to be applied. Make sure the paper is at least three layers thick.

▶ Very lightly drizzle with olive oil, then sprinkle a half of a teaspoon of cayenne pepper on the olive oil on each paper towel, this will hold the powder in place.

▶ Place the cayenne pepper side of the compress directly against the part of the body needing attention, then cover the compress with a small piece of plastic wrap and secured with a bandage or sock.

Cayenne pepper will never harm the skin. This compress can relieve joint pain, cold feet, thyroid issues, a congested head and a tight, congested chest. It is effective when used in conjunction with an onion poultice on the chest.

OLIVE OIL   CAYENNE PEPPER

PAPER TOWEL   PLASTIC WRAP

PAPER TOWEL WITH CAYENNE

PLASTIC WRAP

BANDAGE OR SOCK

# COMFREY

Comfrey is small shrub with large hairy oblong leaves, a thick, hairy stem, and dull purple flowers that clump together. The plant contains a growth stimulant called allantoin, which causes massive cell growth. This growth-stimulating effect can act on every cell in the body, whether muscle, skin, nerve, or bone. This is particularly helpful wherever tissue or bone damage has occurred and explains its nickname, knitbone.

Comfrey contains a substance that depresses the secretion of prostaglandins, which are primary triggers for inflammation. This is why comfrey is considered an anti-inflammatory agent.

Comfrey has a high mucilage content, acting as a lubricant, making it extremely helpful in the lubrication of joints.

In addition to essential nutrients, comfrey also contains pyrrolizidine alkaloids (PAs) which are compounds believed to be damaging to the liver. For this reason some countries have restricted the use of comfrey, especially internally. The conclusion that comfrey is not safe for internal use in humans is primarily based on studies in which high levels of purified PAs were administered to rodents, and several documented cases of excessive use by either eating the leaves or drinking large amounts of comfrey tea over several months. The PAs content of comfrey is less than 1% and variably dependent on the plant part.[6]

Several recent randomized clinical trials have proved the efficacy of external use of comfrey in the treatment of pain, inflammation, and swelling of muscles and joints in the case of degenerative arthritis, acute myalgia in the back, bruises and strains after sports injuries and accidents, also in children aged 3 and over.[7]

## EXTERNALLY

▶ **DAMAGED OR BROKEN BONES:** Comfrey was used by Roman soldiers to treat bone fractures more than 2000 years ago, and many are finding today that ligaments, tendons, muscles, and skin respond quickly to the

---

6. Mei N, (2010) "Metabolism, genotoxicity, and carcinogenicity of comfrey." *Journal of Toxicology and Environmental Health.* Oct;13(7-8):509-26. doi: 10.1080/10937404.2010.509013.

7. Staiger C. (2012) "Comfrey: a clinical overview." *Phytotherapy Research.* 2012 Oct;26(10) pages 1441-8. doi: 10.1002/ptr.4612. Epub 2012 Feb 23.

application of comfrey. As soon as it is applied, cell regeneration begins at a rapid rate.

In the spring and summer, the leaves are used, but in the winter months, the healing properties are found in the root, so that is used in autumn and winter.

## TO MAKE THE POULTICE:

- **In summer**, the leaves are best pulverized with a mortar and pestle. The larger the leaf the less potency, the smaller the leaf the more concentrated the actives in the leaf. Add a small amount of boiling water to the leaves to bring out the mucilage, then spread it onto a cloth, fold the edges over, and apply to the area. Cover with plastic wrap and secure with a bandage or skin tape.

- **In winter**, dig the root, scrub it well to remove dirt, and grate it very finely. The comfrey in its grated state will resemble a thick, gooey mix. Spread this over the poultice cloth, dribble a teaspoon of boiling water over this to moisten it a little more, fold over the edges of cloth to make a package, and apply it to the affected area. Cover with plastic and secure with a bandage or skin tape.

- **CAUTION:** Comfrey cannot be used if there is a prosthesis in the body, for example, a pin and plate, screws, or hip ball and joint. Comfrey is such an effective healer that it will try to expel anything that is not natural to the human frame.

# EPSOM SALT

Epsom salt is magnesium sulphate. It occurs as a deposit left by evaporated mineral waters.

It has the ability to draw off poisons and replenish lost magnesium from the system, conveying it to the nerve endings.

Magnesium is essential for the regulation of muscular contraction, blood pressure, insulin metabolism, tone of blood vessels, and nerves. Unfortunately magnesium deficiency is not uncommon in the Western world.

The effectiveness of oral magnesium supplementation for the treatment of magnesium deficiency is well recognized. Epsom salt however is NOT an oral magnesium supplement and should not to be taken internally. Epsom salt is for exterior use only.

EXTERNALLY ONLY

▶ **FOR INSOMNIA AND MUSCLE CRAMPS:** Putting two cups of Epsom salts in a warm-to-hot bath relieves pain and muscle cramps. Add the Epsom salts while the water is running to help them dissolve. Soak in this mix for 20–30 minutes, adding more hot water if required.

If you don't have a bath to soak in, try just soaking your feet in a bucket of warm water with Epsom salt to ease muscle soreness. The crystallized structure of Epsom salt will also provide exfoliation of the dead skin on the feet decreasing roughness and leave the feet softer.

▶ **FOR BURNS:** Make a saturated solution of Epsom salt. The crystals of Epsom salt can also be mixed with grated potato and applied to burns. This combines two excellent treatments for burns.

**To make a saturated solution,** keep adding a teaspoon of Epsom salt to a small jar of water until it won't dissolve any more. Dip cloths in, keep them quite moist, and place them on the burns. This is covered with plastic to retain moisture and gently bandaged on. The Epsom salts replace the lost magnesium while cooling the area and encourages rapid healing in the damaged tissues. It is a very old and effective remedy.

# GARLIC

Garlic is not only used for enhancing the flavor of food, but is also useful for therapeutic purposes. Throughout history garlic has been well known for it's dietary and medicinal importance. It contains phytochemicals that act as antioxidant, antibiotic, antimicrobial, antibacterial, antifungal and antispasmodic agents,[8] making it a wonder herb!

Those with sensitive skin may find the high sulphur content of garlic to have an irritating effect, both internally and externally. This is why garlic can be effective at burning out a wart. If you have a stomach ulcer, raw garlic could be irritating.

The sulphur-containing component of garlic is known as allicin. This is the antibiotic and cholesterol-lowering compound that gives garlic it's medical power and prevents the growth of fungi and bacteria. This compound is destroyed at temperatures above 60°C (140°F), which is why raw garlic is recommended for all medicinal uses.

Garlic remedies include raw garlic and commercial preparations such as powders, oil and aged extracts.

## INTERNALLY

▸ **ANTIFUNGAL AGENT:** Garlic can be taken as an antifungal agent to help eradicate yeast and fungus from the body. One clove of raw garlic is taken three times daily, ideally with food.

▸ **ANTIBIOTIC:** Garlic is probably most famous for its antibiotic effect. The compound allicin is responsible for this and is released when raw cloves are crushed or chewed. If need be, you can take a week's course of one raw clove three times daily with food.

▸ **CHOLESTEROL LOWERING:** Garlic has been widely recognized for the prevention and treatment of cardiovascular diseases. One to two cloves of raw garlic per day may help lower cholesterol and can be a safer alternative to conventional cholesterol-lowering medications in patients with slightly elevated cholesterol.[9]

8. Ansary J, (2020). "Potential Health Benefit of Garlic Based on Human Intervention Studies: A Brief Overview." *Antioxidants* (Basel). 2020 Jul 15;9(7):619. doi: 10.3390/antiox9070619.
9. Ried K, Toben C, Fakler P. (2013). "Effect of garlic on serum lipids: an updated meta-analysis." *Nutrition Reviews*. Vol 71, issue 5 pages 282-299. doi: 10.1111/nure.12012.

- **COLDS AND FLUS:** Using the healing potency of garlic, the flu bomb recipe below can bring great relief.

**FLU BOMB**—this mixture taken three times a day will relieve symptoms and speedily bring recovery for head and chest colds. Children may have half the suggested dosage.

**The recipe:**

- Juice of one lemon
- Crushed garlic (one, or two cloves if you dare)
- ¼ teaspoon freshly crushed ginger (or ginger powder as a substitute)
- ¼ teaspoon freshly crushed turmeric (or turmeric powder as a substitute)
- One drop tea tree or eucalyptus oil
- One teaspoon honey (more can be added to taste)
- One teaspoon cayenne pepper powder (a pinch for the hesitant; ½ teaspoon for the brave, it will tingle but this subsides quickly)

Pour half a cup of boiling water over the ingredients and allow to steep for 5-10 minutes before drinking. You may strain the solids out if desired.

Ginger, garlic, lemon, and honey are all packed with natural components that help to improve respiratory health, when combined they become stronger to fight off infections.

## EXTERNALLY

- **FOR WARTS:** Place a slice of raw garlic over the wart while lightly oiling the surrounding skin. Apply a band-aid to keep it in place. Leave overnight and repeat if necessary.

- **FOR HEAD AND CHEST COLDS:** Finely slice garlic (don't crush or grate as this could burn the skin) and bind it to the soles of the feet with a cotton cloth, making sure the cloth is between the garlic and the skin. If the garlic touches the soles of the feet, it could blister them. After bandaging the feet, put socks on; this can be left overnight and is particularly good for babies and small children.

The garlic odor can be sensed on the breath of the person within half an hour of applying the garlic to the feet.

# GINGER

In addition to great taste, ginger provides a range of health benefits that you can enjoy in many forms, including fresh, dried, pickled, preserved, crystallized, candied, powdered, or ground. For thousands of years this spicy root of the ginger plant has been used to treat numerous sickness, such as colds, nausea, arthritis, migraines, and hypertension.

Ginger is wonderful for joints. Studies on ginger extract has revealed a significant reduction of osteoarthritis symptoms of the knee.[10]

Ginger is one of the most potent anti-inflammatory herbs on Earth. It is also a very warming herb.

Internally, ginger is a gastric stimulant.

## INTERNALLY

- **DIGESTION:** Eating ginger encourages efficient digestion. Low HCl, indigestion, nausea, and bloating can be relieved with ginger.

- **COLD AND CHILLED BODY:** Fresh ginger tea warms and revitalizes the body. It is a great drink in cold weather.

- **SORE THROAT:** Hot ginger tea can bring relief.

- **NAUSEA AND VOMITING:** Slowly sipping a cup of ginger tea is effective in helping to prevent nausea and vomiting especially during pregnancy, for chemotherapy-induced nausea, or motion sickness. Drinking it too quickly may increase nausea.

- **INFLAMMATION:** As it is an anti-inflammatory agent, ginger tea can help reduce inflammation anywhere in the body.

**TO MAKE GINGER TEA:** Finely grate a teaspoon of fresh ginger into the teapot and pour boiling water on top. Let it steep for ten minutes, strain it, and drink it. For extra flavor you can add some honey or lemon juice.

10. Altman RD, Marcussen KC. (2001). "Effects of a ginger extract on knee pain in patients with osteoarthritis." *Arthritis and Rheumatism.* Vol 44, issue 11, pages 2531-8. PMID: 11710709.

- **INFLAMED JOINTS:** A ginger poultice may relieve issues such as gout, arthritis, tennis elbow, or bursitis. The ginger appears to pull the inflammation out of the joint to the skin, so don't be surprised if the skin becomes quite hot half an hour after applying the poultice.

  Many have testified to relief from painful joints after a ginger poultice.

**TO MAKE THE POULTICE:** Finely grate fresh ginger, place it onto a cloth, fold the edges in to make a parcel, and place the thin side on the affected area. Cover it with a square of plastic or woolen material and bandage it in place. If uncomfortable, the poultice can be removed, but it will not burn. The ginger poultice can be left on overnight if desired. Ginger can irritate the skin if overused. Wear poultice for an hour a day until you are sure your skin will not be irritated.

# MANUKA HONEY

Honey is an excellent natural sweetener with more health benefits than other forms of regular sugar, like granulated and cane. However, people with yeast problems, cancer, or diabetes need to drastically reduce the sweet content of their diet, which includes honey.

When using honey for medical purposes Manuka honey is the preferred option. This honey, native to New Zealand, contains antibacterial properties setting it apart from traditional honey. Honey is commonly used orally to treat coughs and sore throats such as in the Onion Cough Syrup on page 326.

## EXTERNALLY

- **WOUND HEALING AND BURNS:** Studies on chronic non-healing infected wounds observed rapid healing after Manuka honey was used as a wound dressing.[11] When used over a wound, honey creates a moist antibacterial environment containing enzymes to break down dead decaying tissue. Honey can also amplify tissue regeneration, and even decrease pain in people with burns, boils, or diabetic ulcers.

---

11. Kapoor N, Yadav R. (2021) "Manuka honey: A promising wound dressing material for the chronic nonhealing discharging wounds." *National Journal of Maxillofacial Surgery*. 2021 May-Aug; 12(2): 233–237. doi: 10.4103/njms.NJMS_154_20.

# ONION

Onions are part of the same family of plants as garlic and as such, share some of the same medicinal properties. They boast a wide range of healthy vitamins, minerals, and plant compounds, and the oils and essences in onion have a stimulating effect on human tissues.

Onions absorb morbid matter (dead or infected tissue).

Onions can be used for absorbing toxic fumes, for example paint fumes, or the strong odor in a new fridge or car. Please don't wrap half an onion in plastic, as it will absorb the chemicals from the plastic.

Onions can be used cooked or raw, depending on the condition.

## COOKED

> **FOR INFECTED WOUNDS, INCLUDING BOILS:** Roast an onion, when it is hot enough to feel comfortable to touch without burning, split it in half and apply it directly to the wound. Cover it with a cloth and bandage the area. Try and leave it on overnight.

> **FOR EARACHES:** Bake or steam a whole onion until soft. Cut the onion in half around the middle section. Wrap half the onion in a cloth, cover it with plastic to insulate, and when it reaches an acceptable temperature, bind it to the ear. Leave it on for as long as it stays warm.

Place two drops of the cooked onion juice onto a teaspoon and drop them into the ear for added help.

## RAW

> **FOR A CONGESTED HEAD:** Slice an onion onto a plate and leave it near the bed overnight. Breathing in onion fumes clears the airways.

> **FOR CALLUSES:** Cut an onion in half and steep it in strong vinegar for three hours. Bind the onion halves to the callus overnight. In the morning, the top layers of the callus can be removed. Repeat until it's gone.

> **FOR CHEST COMPLAINTS:** An onion compress is excellent for complaints such as bronchitis, colds, flu, and asthma. Grate a small amount of raw onion and spread it in the middle of a cloth. Fold the edges over like a

parcel. Apply the single layer to the chest and cover it with plastic wrap or a woolen square. Bind it with skin tape. The inhalations of the onion fumes from the poultice will also help to clear the respiratory system.

▸ **FOR NIGHT CONGESTION AND COUGHING:** An onion can be chopped into small pieces and placed into two plastic bags large enough for your feet. A foot is placed into each bag, ensuring the onion is under the sole of the foot. The bag is then twisted and secured around the ankle, and a sock is put on each foot over the plastic bag to keep it in place. This is worn overnight. Many have testified that the night coughing ceases while wearing the onion on the feet overnight.

## ONION COUGH SYRUP

In a jar, layer 2cm of chopped onion and a heaped teaspoon of honey. Continue in this way, layering the onion and honey until the jar is almost full. Over the next few hours, syrup will form. Leave the mix for 24 hours, then strain and keep the syrup in the fridge. This is excellent for sore or dry throats, coughs, colds, flu, bronchitis, and asthma. Take a teaspoonful three times a day; in a crisis, it can be taken every 15 minutes.

# POTATO

The potato is a versatile root vegetable and one of the most commonly consumed vegetables in the world. They are packed with a variety of nutrients and may also improve digestive health by feeding the *good* bacteria in your gut, which helps to maintain a healthy microbiome and support immune health. There are many ways to enjoy eating potatoes but the real healing ability of this plant appears when used raw externally on our body.

Consuming raw potato can lead to digestive issues and discomfort. However for external medical purposes always use potato raw, as heating it destroys the healing properties.

Potatoes are extremely alkaline and can effectively be used wherever there is swelling or inflammation in the tissues. The potato's rich mineral content of potassium and phosphorus are absorbed through the skin when the potato is applied as a poultice. This contributes to restoring intracellular fluid pressure and balance. These minerals also contribute to normal nerve and muscle response.

## EXTERNALLY

- **SPLINTERS:** Potatoes are quite famous for their drawing powers; many a splinter has been drawn out after a potato poultice has been applied for a few nights. Do not reuse a potato poultice but replace with a fresh potato each day.

- **INFECTIONS:** Place a raw potato poultice over the infected area, such as boils and abscesses, holding it in place with tape. It is best not to apply to open wounds.

- **TISSUE INFLAMMATIONS:** Potato poultices have been used for hundreds of years to relieve inflammation caused by strains, bruises, or ingrown toenails. Let it stay there for about 15 to 20 minutes so that it can help to reduce inflammation in the case of sprains or leave it on overnight for more persistent injuries. Within one to three days the inflammation should be cleared.

- **EYE ISSUES:** Conjunctivitis and red, swollen eyes respond well to the cooling/soothing effect of potato poultices.

- **FOR INFLAMED EYES:** Dip a cotton ball into potato juice and apply it to the eye. Cover with a folded dry wash cloth and leave for half an hour, or longer if it feels nice. Potato has a soothing, cooling effect.

**TO MAKE THE POULTICE:** Finely grate a small amount of potato (one teaspoon for a 5×5cm area)*, place it in the middle of a cloth, and spread it out thinly. Fold the edges of the cloth inwards to make a parcel; place this parcel over the affected area with the single side facing the skin. Cover with a plastic or wool square, and either bandage or secure with skin tape.

In general, this poultice can be used wherever the tissues are congested, inflamed, swollen, or hot.

**\*A WORD OF CAUTION:** Don't make the poultice too big as leaking potato juice can stain the sheets.

# SLIPPERY ELM

Slippery elm is the powdered bark from the slippery elm tree. It contains strong drawing properties and a growth stimulant that enhances rapid healing anywhere it is applied.

Slippery elm soothes the mouth, throat, stomach, the lining of the intestines, and also causes the stools to have more form. Stomach ulcers can also be soothed and healed with slippery elm.

Slippery elm can be used alone or in combination with other herbs.

## INTERNALLY

▸ **COLIC:** Slippery elm is an excellent remedy for babies with colic. For a three-month-old baby, a quarter of a teaspoon mixed with a little breast milk and given on a spoon can bring great relief. Slippery elm is very safe and can even be given to a newborn.

▸ **INTESTINAL TRACT PROBLEMS:** For ailments such as stomach and duodenal ulcers, irritable bowel syndrome, colitis, Crohn's disease, gastritis, and diarrhea, taking slippery elm can assist as it is high in mucilage. This feature makes it excellent for coating and soothing the gastrointestinal tract. Not only does slippery elm coat and soothe but it also lubricates, provides nutrients, and stimulates healing in the mucous membranes.

### SLIPPERY ELM DRINK RECIPE

▸ Mix one teaspoon of slippery elm powder in half a cup of warm water or juice before breakfast every morning. Stir just before taking, as the mixture can quickly thicken on sitting.

▸ In the case of a flare-up crisis where diarrhea is happening ten times a day, this drink can be taken every hour until the gut settles down.

▸ As a maintenance dose, such as for the intestinal tract problems listed above, this drink can be take prior to each meal or before retiring at night. When the gut is healed the frequency this drink is taken can be reduced. The body's response is your best guide.

In his bestselling book, *Back to Eden,* written in 1939, Jethro Kloss states that slippery elm is one of the best drawers we have, as a result it is a great additive to a poultice.

▶ **ABSCESSES, TUMORS, INFECTIONS, AND ANY INFLAMED AREAS:** Slippery elm can be used by itself or with equal quantities of charcoal. Add enough water until a jelly-like consistency is achieved. Make a sufficient amount to liberally cover the area being treated. Place the mixture on a cloth and follow the same directions for a poultice as described in the charcoal section.

▶ **BOILS:** The poultice for the boil needs to be twice as big as the boil itself.

Mix together one teaspoon of slippery elm, 1/8 teaspoon of cayenne pepper, and enough water to make a stiff dough.

Spread this over a small piece of cloth that is twice the size of the boil. Place directly onto the boil, where it should mold and stick quite well. After several hours, this will dry out. Remove the cloth after 24 hours. If this is too painful, the whole area can be washed or soaked with warm water until the poultice is softened, then it can be taken off with a little more ease. When this poultice is removed, the boil often opens, and all the contents are released. If needed the wound can then be covered with a light dressing.

## SLIPPERY ELM SCALP CLEANSER AND HAIR CONDITIONER

1. In a bowl, mix together four teaspoons of slippery elm with enough water to make a soft jelly. A few drops of rosemary oil can be added.

2. Section the hair as if applying hair dye and, section by section, paint the whole scalp. Tie a plastic bag around the head or wear a shower cap and leave for at least three hours.

3. Rinse out by shampooing hair as normal. This treatment can be very helpful for people with dandruff or eczema on their scalp.

# CHAPTER 22

# PAiN

Pain is an essential part of the body's defense system. The best illustration of pain, in my opinion, is explained by Dr Paul Brand in his enlightening book, *Pain: The Gift Nobody Wants*.

*"In the modern view pain is an enemy, a sinister invader that must be expelled. And if Product X removes pain 30 seconds faster, all the better.*

*This approach has a crucial, dangerous flaw: once regarded as an enemy, not a warning signal, pain loses its power to instruct. Silencing pain without considering its message is like disconnecting a ringing fire alarm to avoid receiving bad news . . .*

*Pain is no invading enemy, but a loyal messenger dispatched by my own body to alert me of some danger."* Dr. Paul Brand, *Pain: The Gift Nobody Wants*, page 188.

When someone is experiencing pain, the first step to take is to ascertain the cause. If the cause is not ascertained, there will be no remedy.

Some of the most common reasons for pain are as follows:

## CAUSES OF PAIN

- Present or past injuries
- Stress
- Dehydration
- Stimulant withdrawals
- Hormonal imbalance

Pain can often be due to inflammation, and inflammation with an injury can be the body's way of protecting and also boosting the presence of red and white blood cells.

In an injury, the blood can sit or pool in the area, adding to the pain. Upon investigation, many people who are experiencing pain today can source it back to a previous injury ten or more years ago.

When a serious injury is sustained, that person will be managing this for the rest of their life. As I commented to one lady, it is a miracle that you are alive, considering the injuries you sustained, but you will forever be managing this, and if you can, you will do well.

On my travels, I have met several people who are managing serious injuries and doing well. I am always impressed when I see this, but the true winner is the person who lives in that body. Everyone has stress, but it is constant distress that people struggle with the most.

Dehydration is often overlooked as a contributing factor to pain, this can reveal itself as muscle, joint pain, headaches, stomach pain, eyestrain, or constipation. Pain is often very common when someone is withdrawing from stimulants or drugs. Caffeine withdrawal is well known to cause severe headaches and muscle pain.

Monthly period pain and growth pains are usually a result of a hormonal imbalance.

How are these injuries managed?

# THE SOLUTIONS
## STEP ONE: BRING IMMEDIATE RELIEF

After you have ascertained the cause of the pain, the next step is to find a way to relieve the pain. Remember the pain is there for a reason so you don't want to silence it and continue with the activity that caused the pain, such actions will increase the problem. Give your body time to heal.

- **ICE:** a well-known inflammation reducer. The instructions on the application of ice include alternating the ice application in an on/off motion until the body can bear the cold and a numbing effect is felt. This is usually seven seconds on and seven seconds off repeatedly. This may take 10–15 minutes. This simple procedure can reduce the inflammation quite quickly.

- **COLD CLOTHS:** If ice is found to be too painful, the continual application of cold wet cloths can reduce the inflammation. A bowl of cold water is required (no ice), and a couple of face cloths. The wet, slightly wrung out cloth is placed over the inflamed area, as soon as it warms up it is replaced with a fresh cool cloth. The water is effectively pulling out the inflammation as the cloths are alternated. This may take 15 minutes or more but is very effective in reducing the inflammation in the area.

- **ALTERNATING HOT AND COLD WATER:** increases the blood supply dramatically to the area and increases waste elimination, thus reducing inflammation. This was explored in more detail in the Hydrotherapy chapter, page 291.

Depending on the injury, the age, and mental state of the person, the water treatments can be adjusted. The body's response is always the best guide.

- **POULTICES AND COMPRESSES** can bring relief, depending on the cause, injury and area of the pain. This is explained in the chapter Healthy Healers, page 305.

## STEP TWO: LONG TERM MAINTENANCE

The SUSTAIN ME principles outlined in this book will not only bring healing to many health issues, but more importantly can assist in preventing many of these diseases and the pain they cause. These principles furnish the body with everything it needs to function optimally.

Other treatments and lifestyle changes you can make to assist with long term maintenance of pain include the following:

- **CHIROPRACTIC OR OSTEOPATHIC TREATMENTS** can help to realign the basic skeletal structure.

- **OSTEOPATHS, PHYSIOTHERAPISTS, AND MASSAGE THERAPISTS** can help to soften tight muscles. These professionals can also advise on daily stretches and moves to strengthen the muscles, tendons, and ligaments that are able to compensate and support when there has been a skeletal injury.

- **HYDROTHERAPY AND POULTICE THERAPY** can also play a part in bringing relief and boosting healing to an area.

Trying these various natural remedies and observing the results will be your guide. If it works, do it.

We live in an amazing living organism that is constantly adapting and adjusting to heal itself, including compensating when there has been a major injury or loss of some part of the body. We can access that inbuilt force to bring about relief and healing.

## WHAT ABOUT PAINKILLERS?

There may be a place in a crisis for painkilling drugs, but these are addictive and can damage kidney and liver function. Painkillers and fever reducers that contain acetaminophen are a common cause of liver injury.[1] Ideally, if they are used, it is for as brief a time as possible.

There are some very cost effective alternative herbs that can have a painkilling effect without the risk of dangerous side effects or addiction.

# NATURAL PAINKILLERS

Some herbs can reduce pain by reducing inflammation.

▸ **TURMERIC** is well known for its anti-inflammatory action in the body. The main active ingredient that has this effect is curcumin. A study comparing the effectiveness of curcumin to Diclofenac, a standard anti-inflammatory drug, found curcumin relieved arthritis pain a similar degree to the drug, but without any of the side effects encountered by using Diclofenac.[2] When combined with cayenne pepper, it is even more powerful.

The plant chemical piperine, contained in the cayenne, enhances the absorption of the curcumin. Turmeric can be taken in quite high doses, even up to 6,000mg a day.

▸ **CAYENNE PEPPER** has an analgesic effect and can be use internally and externally. When cayenne pepper is applied topically to skin, it can help with pain by reducing the amount of a chemical messenger known as substance P, which travels to your brain to signal discomfort. With less substance P, you feel less pain.[3]

One man, whose hand was crushed in a roller, found that taking half a

1. A.D.A.M. Medical Encyclopedia [Internet]. Johns Creek (GA): Ebix, Inc., A.D.A.M.; c1997-2024. *Drug-induced Liver Injury*; Reviewed 2021 Oct 31; cited 2024 March 12. Available from: <https://medlineplus.gov/ency/article/000226.htm>.

2. Shep D, Khanwelkar C, Gade P. et al. (2019) "Safety and efficacy of curcumin versus Diclofenac in knee osteoarthritis." *Trials* 20, 214. <https://doi.org/10.1186/s13063-019-3327-2>.

3. Graefe SB, Rahimi N, Mohiuddin SS. "Biochemistry, Substance P." [Updated 2023 Jul 30]. *In: StatPearls* [Internet]. StatPearls Publishing. <https://www.ncbi.nlm.nih.gov/books/NBK554583>.

teaspoon of cayenne pepper internally had an effect equal to that of the painkiller Tylenol. When it was severe, he would take the cayenne pepper hourly, he told me this brought him more relief than the drug.

A friend with a recent serious injury to her toes, found taking two capsules three times a day brought the most relief. As the wound healed she found she could reduce the amount of cayenne pepper she was taking.

## PAINKILLER HERB MIX

- Four parts Jamaican dogwood
- Two parts devil's claw
- Two parts red clover
- Two parts turmeric
- One part licorice
- One part cayenne

These herbs may be purchased as a glycerin tincture.

Twenty drops can be taken in a little water every two hours if required.

### LISTEN

Part of being your own doctor is to listen.

Part of managing pain is to listen.

Listen and respond to the first whisper. If you don't and you ignore that whisper, the body will start screaming, and when the screaming commences, damage is being done.

Many silence the whisper with painkillers. The body continues to speak, but you can't hear the voice. So, there is no response, and the damage increases.

Have you ever been to a health professional who will not listen to you? Don't be that person. If the body speaks, we must respond—it is speaking for a reason.

This principle is often termed mindfulness.

Mindfulness is listening when the body speaks, no matter what it says and where it says it.

It speaks for a reason, and our best response is "I hear you!"

The body is so faithful, it will speak when any part needs help. It will speak and let you know what will bring relief.

Our role is to listen.

CONCLUSION

# THE SELF-HEALING BODY

Considering the information and experiences cited in this book, it is not hard to come to the conclusion that we each live in a self-cleansing, self-healing organism. A body that has been designed to heal itself, but so many are sick. The body will heal itself when given the correct environment or conditions. Many are ignorant to these basic conditions.

These basic conditions are often bypassed as being of no account: too small or insignificant to have an effect. However, just as dripping water on a stone will eventually form a dent, or groove, so these conditions have an effect. It is not the first drip, or tenth, or even hundredth, that causes the dent. It is the consistent, regular dripping over a period of time.

Many bodies deteriorate under that same process. The first or even tenth cigarette doesn't cause lung cancer. Just so, the body heals. When consistent daily, weekly, and monthly implementation of the basic requirements for healing are adhered to, the body will respond and recover, and regeneration can be seen.

This living organism is very faithful, it knows what to do. How quickly it will begin to respond when the owner decides to work with the inherent healing powers placed in the body by the Creator.

**This living organism is very faithful, it knows what to do. How quickly it will begin to respond when the owner decides to work with the inherent healing powers placed in the body by the Creator.**

In the book *Ministry of Healing*, Ellen G. White advises that those who persevere in obedience to nature's laws, will reap the reward in health of body and of mind.

There is much truth in the advice given by Ellen G. White on page 29 of *Counsels on Diet and Food*:

> *"Every man and every woman is the architect of their own fortune. Right physical habits promote mental superiority. Intellectual power, physical strength, and longevity depend on immutable laws. There is no happen-so, no chance, about this matter. Nature's God will not interfere to preserve men from the consequences of violating nature's laws."*

Ask yourself: how do my lifestyle choices SUSTAIN ME?

# INDEX

## ABOUT THE AUTHOR
# BARBARA O'NEiLL

B arbara O'Neill was born in 1953 in Ingleburn, New South Wales, Australia. Barbara was born into a conventional Australian home and she was the second child with one older brother and three younger sisters. Her father owned and operated a Shell Service Station at Lugarno, NSW, and Barbara had the misfortune to see her mother die at the young age of 51 from rheumatoid arthritis.

Barbara's first work on leaving school was as a hairdresser and some years later trained and worked as a psychiatric nurse at North Ryde Psychiatric Hospital.

Barbara's journey into natural health commenced when her first child Emma contracted whooping cough and spent six weeks in hospital. This became the motivation for Barbara to search out the cause, find a remedy and live a lifestyle that would prevent this from happening again.

With her partner, she embraced an alternative 'hippie' lifestyle and moved from Sydney to a north NSW rainforest area west of Coffs Harbour.

Removed from close proximity to conventional medical facilities, Barbara studied health and home schooled her six children. Her reputation grew as a 'healer' and people brought their sick children to her for advice and assistance, and she became locally known as 'earth mother'.

In addition to her passion for health, Barbara embraced Christianity at 26 years of age. This put her on a new path to look at the human body in the light that it is not a product of random, uncontrolled evolution, but that it was intricately designed with all its inbuilt mechanisms to self-heal. Barbara was particularly inspired by the health writings of Ellen G White, a 19th century female writer.

After 12 years of living in the rainforest, and in a difficult relationship, Barbara left the marriage and moved closer to civilization to allow her older children to obtain work.

Barbara's interest in health knowledge led her to study and obtain a Diploma in Naturopathy in 1994, and later in 2005, certification as a Nutritionist. Barbara's real healing success springs from the knowledge of the body's ability to heal itself, and then working with the body to achieve the healing response.

After her marriage breakdown in 1993, Barbara put her energies into raising her children and in 1996 moved to Queensland where she worked at Living Valley Springs Health Retreat as a Naturopath. It was here she renewed an old friendship with the Retreat Business Manager, Michael O'Neill and they were married in October 1997.

The following year, Barbara and her family of now eight children (Michael had two children), moved to Narbethong, Victoria where they started a health re-treat as a non-profit organization. They continued there for nearly six years, and in 2003 relocated to their new property near Bellbrook, New South Wales, where they started their new venture, Misty Mountain Health Retreat.

Over the years, Barbara has become a highly sought after health lecturer, as people appreciate her common sense approach to health problems. Barbara's lecture series has circulated throughout the world, via the internet, and have touched the lives of millions of people. Her talks have brought relief to many suffering individuals as they embrace the simple and powerful laws of health.

In 2018, Barbara came under an unwarranted attack from media and pharma-ceutical proponents. Despite not a single case of harm to anyone, this resulted in a permanent ban on her giving health advice in Australia. This is covered in the book *The Assassination of Barbara O'Neill*, written by Michael O'Neill.

Currently retired from her role as Health Director of Misty Mountain Lifestyle Retreat, Barbara is now busier than ever, traveling the world speaking at sem-inars, to teach people the health principles to live a longer, healthier, and happier life.